New edition

Integrated Science
for Caribbean Schools

Book 3

Florine Dalgety **Carol Draper** **David Sang**

Heinemann Educational Publishers
Halley Court, Jordan Hill, Oxford OX2 8EJ
A part of Harcourt Education Limited

OXFORD MELBOURNE AUCKLAND
JOHANNESBURG BLANTYRE GABORONE
IBADAN PORTSMOUTH (NH) USA CHICAGO

© Florine Dalgety, Carol Draper, David Sang 2002

All rights reserved.

First published by Heinemann Educational Publishers in 2002

Design and cover by Jackie Hill 320 Design
Illustration by Joe Little and Keith Lemmon
Typeset by Magnet Harlequin, Oxford

ISBN 0 435 57590 2

Printed and bound in Spain by Edelvives

02 03 04 05 06 07 10 9 8 7 6 5 4 3 2 1

Acknowledgements

The publishers are grateful to the following people for reviewing this title during its development.

Sherril Gardner, Science Educator, Jamaica; Joy Gittens, Combermere School, Barbados; Mr Bertrand Harnanan, Standards Consultant, Trinidad; Pamela Hunte, Education Officer (Science), Ministry of Education, Youth Affairs and Sports, Barbados; Laurie O King, Senior Education Officer (Curriculum), Ministry of Education, Youth Affairs and Sports, Barbados; Natasha Lewis dos Santos, Queen's Royal College, Trinidad; Cheryl Remy, Science Education Lecturer, St Lucia; John Stringer, Educational Consultant, UK; R Worley, Advisor in the CLEAPSS School Science Service, UK

Photo acknowledgements

Cover photographs by Eric Soder/NHPA (waterfall), PhotoDisc (satellite dish)
Page 1 SPL; p. 5 D Davis/Trip; p. 6 Bulter/BAVE/REX; p. 12 RHPL; p.18, Bob Trip; p.20 NHPA (slope), OSF (erosion); p. 23 GeoScience Features Picture Library; p. 25 SPL; p.28 RHPL; p. 30 Ron Gilling/Still; p. 31 Paul Brierley; p.33 ACE Photoagency (brickworks), RHPL (cement factory); p. 34 Pilkington plc; p. 36 SPL; p. 37 Jerry Schad/SPL; p. 55 Richard Knights; p. 56 Roger Scruton (colour blindness chart), SPL (microscope); p. 57 Artie Photography; p. 65 FLPA; p. 66 SPL (ultrasound), The Nation (singer); p. 70 Artie Photography; p. 74, 76 SPL; p. 77 The Nation (identical and fraternal twins), Photofusion (baby in incubator); p. 79 Artie Photography; p. 83 The Wellcome Trust; p. 84 Colorsport; p. 85, 89, 95 SPL; p. 99 Colorsport; p. 101 FLPA; p. 106 Corbis (grease), Beken of Cowes (UK) (seacat), P Millereau/Action Plus (cyclist); p. 121 Stone; p. 122 Panos Pictures (rainforest), FLPA (savannah); p. 123 OSF (cactus), FLPA (swamp); p. 126 Trip; p. 127 OSF; p. 128 OSF (iguana), Bruce Coleman (parrot, dolphin); p. 129 Bruce Coleman; p. 130, 131 FLPA; p. 132 FLPA (whistling duck), Trip (Yanomani Indian); p. 133 Ecoscene; p. 134 FLPA; p. 135 NHPA; p. 136 OSF (coral reef), FLPA (mangrove); p. 138 Artie Photography; p. 141 NHPA (mudslide), Still (cracked soil); p. 142 Still; p. 144 FLPA (terraced hillside), Paul Harrison/Still (strip cropping); p. 145 Corbis; p. 147 Andy Hibbert/Ecoscene; p. 148 Bruce Coleman (port), SPL (oil spill); p. 149 OSF (seabird), SPL (pollution); p. 150 Trip; p. 153 OSF; p. 155, 156, 159 SPL; corner images by PhotoDisc.

FLPA Frank Lane Picture Agency; OSF, Oxford Scientific Films; SPL Science Photo Library; RHPL Robert Harding Picture Library

Contents

Safety in the laboratory ... v

Unit 14: The Earth
14.1 The violent Earth ... 1
14.2 Earthquakes ... 6
14.3 Wind and waves ... 12
14.4 Rocks and weathering ... 20
14.5 New rocks from old ... 22
14.6 Metals from minerals ... 26
14.7 Minerals for construction ... 33

Unit 15: Light and sound
15.1 What is light? ... 36
15.2 The eye ... 52
15.3 Sound ... 58
15.4 The human ear ... 69

Unit 16: Systems in humans
16.1 The human reproductive system, growth and development ... 72
16.2 What are hormones? ... 82
16.3 Birth control ... 87
16.4 Coordination: the human nervous system ... 94

Unit 17: Forces
17.1 Understanding forces ... 99
17.2 Forces and motion ... 105
17.3 Machines – forces at work ... 111

Unit 18: The environment and its maintenance
18.1 What is ecology? ... 121
18.2 Ecosystems in the Caribbean ... 126
18.3 Soil erosion and conservation ... 141
18.4 Water pollution and its control ... 146
18.5 Air pollution ... 153

Questions ... 161

Science words ... 166

Index ... 169

Safety in the laboratory

The laboratory (often called simply the 'lab') is a place of discovery and excitement. The following guidelines are given so that you can enjoy your lab sessions safely, without getting hurt.

Read this page very carefully. Ask your teacher to explain anything that you do not understand. These rules apply to all lab work, now and in the future.

Basic safety rules

- Do not enter the lab unless there is a qualified supervisor present.
- Always walk in the lab. Do not run or play around.
- Keep coats, bags and other belongings tidied away.
- Tie back long hair. Keep your hair well away from flames and hot objects.
- Nails should be neatly trimmed, and jewellery kept to the minimum – earrings should be small and not dangling.
- The teacher, laboratory attendant and laboratory technicians are responsible for the equipment in the lab. Do not touch any piece of equipment, unless instructed to do so by one of these adults. Sometimes a senior student may be given the responsibility of guiding you and your classmates through an experiment. Obey all instructions given.
- Do not interfere with fittings such as gas taps and electrical sockets. Seek adult help if something goes wrong with any of these things.
- Do not touch electrical sockets or switches with wet hands. Never allow any electrical appliance to come into contact with water, unless it is designed to do so. You might get a shock.
- Do not open gas taps before you are ready to light the gas. A build-up of gas in the immediate area can lead to an explosion, and you can be seriously hurt.

What you should know

- Locate the nearest staircase or fire escape that should be used in an emergency. Your teacher will explain the safety procedure and how to leave the lab if there is an emergency.

Safety in the laboratory

When conducting experiments

✓ Check all bottle labels carefully. Chemicals can be dangerous if not handled correctly. Never remove anything from the lab without permission.

✓ Wear eye protection (goggles), gloves, or other protective gear when told to do so, and do not take these items off until told to do so. The symbol on the left shows you when eye protection is needed.

✓ Use the amounts of materials stated in the instructions.

✓ When pouring liquids from a labelled bottle, ensure that the label is held towards the palm of the hand so that you can see the contents, and the chemical does not pour over the label.

✓ When heating material in a test tube, always point the mouth of the test tube away from yourself and others.

✓ If a piece of apparatus gets chipped or broken, tell a supervisor immediately.

✓ Surfaces should be kept clean. Immediately wipe away any spills. There should be special cleaning cloths for this purpose.

✓ Wash your hands thoroughly after handling chemicals, or after handling plant or animal material.

✓ Allow Bunsen burners, tripods, beakers, etc. to cool down before handling them, or wear protective gloves. Do not rest hot apparatus directly on the desk top. Use a heat-proof mat.

✗ Do not hold hot apparatus with your bare hands.

✗ Do not eat or drink in the lab.

✗ Do NOT mix chemicals unless told to do so. Ask for advice if instructions are not clear to you.

✗ Do NOT taste or drink ANY chemical in the lab unless told to do so by a RESPONSIBLE adult. If you accidentally get something in your mouth, spit it out and wash your mouth out with lots of water. Tell your teacher or supervisor. You will be taught the correct way to smell a chemical.

Safety icons

The following symbols, or icons, are used to warn of any possible hazards associated with activities. Make sure you know what they mean, and take notice of them.

Corrosive   Toxic   Harmful or irritant   Highly flammable   Oxidizing   Danger! Care needed!

The Earth

14.1 The violent Earth

▶ Objectives

After studying this topic you should be able to:

- outline the structure of the Earth
- describe how volcanoes occur and what happens during an eruption
- describe the damage that volcanoes can cause, and some of the benefits that may come from them.

Each morning, when you wake up, do you expect the world outside to look much the same as yesterday? It usually does. But nature can be very powerful, and from time to time an earthquake or volcano can cause great destruction to part of the world, leaving it very different from before.

Mexico City was struck by a violent earthquake in 1985. Before the disaster, the city centre was adorned with tall, impressive buildings. After the tremor the city became a mangled, twisted wreck of concrete, steel and glass.

Fig. 14.1 Much of the island of Montserrat came to look like the surface of the Moon after the Soufrière Hills volcano erupted during 1995–98.

Montserrat was severely affected by the Soufrière Hills volcano during 1995–98 (Fig. 14.1). Many residents were evacuated from their homes and farms during the early stages of the eruption; a huge eruption in June 1997 then engulfed much of the evacuated area, and resulted in the deaths of 19 people. The lava flow almost reached the airport. Further eruptions have continued to occur, and much of the island is now barren, looking like the surface of the Moon.

Inside the Earth

Volcanoes remind us that the inside of the Earth is hot – as hot as 4000°C at its centre. Figure 14.2 shows the different layers that make up the Earth. The Earth is a little like a soft-boiled egg – hard on the outside but melted in the middle.

- We live on the **crust**, a layer of solid rock up to 70 km thick. That may sound very thick, but in places the crust is only 6 km thick.

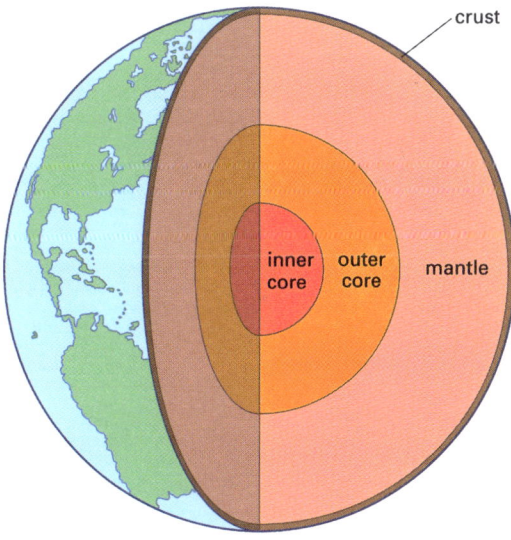

Fig. 14.2 A cutaway view of the Earth showing the various layers beneath its surface.

14.1 The Earth

> **Did you know?**
>
> Over the last 500 years, earthquakes have claimed over three million lives; volcanoes have been responsible for 300 000 deaths.

- A much thicker layer, the mantle, lies below the crust. This is made of hot rock; in some places it is so hot that the rock is partially melted into a liquid (in other words, it is molten). The mantle makes up 80% of the Earth's volume.
- The Earth's core is metallic – it is made of iron and nickel. These are magnetic metals, which explains why the Earth has a magnetic field (see Book 2, Topic 13.7).

What is a volcano?

In places where the Earth's crust is thin, the hot rocks of the mantle may push upwards. If they break through the crust, a volcano is the result. Hot molten rock called **magma** pushes its way upwards and bursts through the Earth's surface. Any water that is underground starts to boil, and pressure builds up. Steam comes belching out, and rocks fly through the air. **Lava** (molten rock) flows down the sides of the volcano. Some or all of these events are called an eruption. An idea of what happens inside a volcano is given in Figure 14.3.

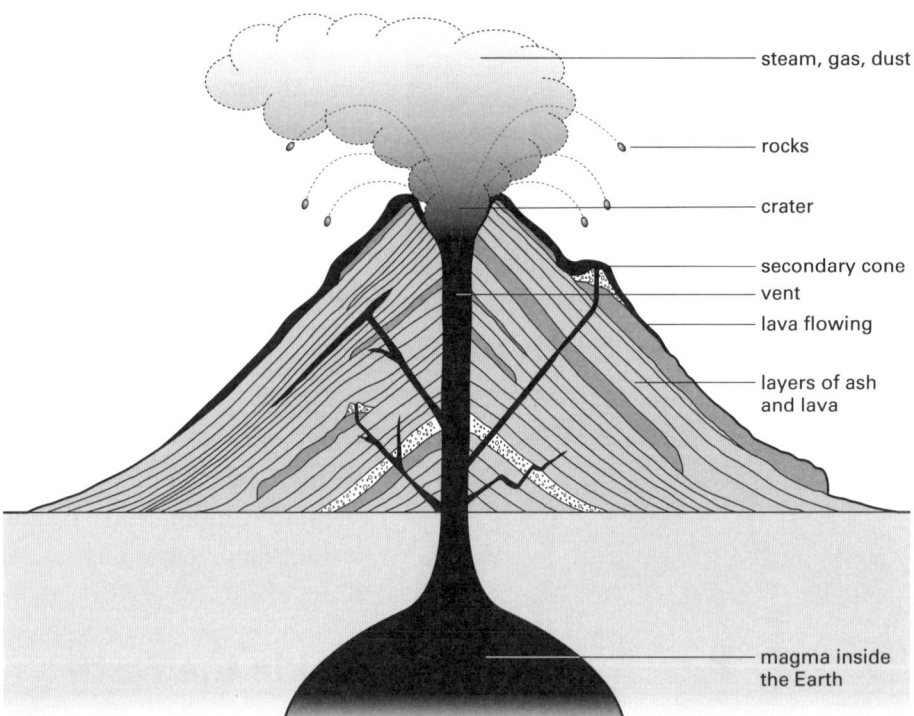

Fig. 14.3 Inside a volcano.

Volcanoes can be described in one of three ways:

- active – one that is erupting or is very likely to erupt (about 500 volcanoes have erupted in living memory);
- dormant – one that is in a resting state;
- extinct – one that is unlikely to erupt ever again.

The violent Earth 14.1

Volcanoes around the world

> **Did you know?**
>
> Why do so many volcanoes have the word 'soufrière' in their names? Soufrière is the French word for a pit from which sulphur is extracted; these are usually on the sides of volcanoes, where lava has escaped through a vent in the side of the cone.

In the eighteenth century, scientists were busy studying rocks in the parts of Europe where they lived. They weren't sure if the rocks they saw had always been there, or whether they might have gradually changed over long periods of time. If they had lived in an area where there were active volcanoes, they would have known for sure that rocks can change very suddenly and violently!

There are active volcanoes in the Caribbean region. Following the huge eruption of the Soufrière Hills volcano on Montserrat in 1997, this volcano is being studied by Caribbean and other international scientists. Some activity was recorded in December 2001. St Lucia boasts of the only 'drive in' volcano crater – the Soufrière volcano there has been dormant for a long time. Steam vents are very active, however, and are a major tourist attraction. Deposits of sulphur can be seen on the rocks around these vents. There are also sulphur springs on the island of Dominica.

There is a seismic research station located in Trinidad. The scientists, seismologists and geologists are paying very close attention to an underwater volcano off the island of Grenada, called 'Kick 'em Jenny'. This volcano showed signs of increased activity in the latter part of 2001. The scientists at the research station also keep a close watch on earthquakes and tremors that occur in the region.

The map in Figure 14.4 shows how volcanoes are distributed across the Earth's surface. You can see that they tend to form lines, marking out areas where the Earth is active.

Fig. 14.4 The triangles show where there is volcanic activity.

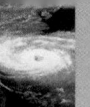

14.1 The Earth

→ Activity On the map

Look at Figure 14.4, showing the regions where active volcanoes are found. Compare this map with an atlas.

Discuss

1 Name the regions where active volcanoes are concentrated.
2 Draw a detailed map showing volcanoes of the Caribbean. For each volcano, indicate:

   a whether the volcano is active, dormant or extinct;
   b when it last erupted.

Making the most of volcanoes

The volcano of La Soufrière, St Vincent, erupted in May 1902. After a series of small eruptions, there was a big bang that sent steam clouds 9 km into the sky. Trees were flattened and large areas were covered in ash. Over 1500 people were killed.

La Soufrière erupted again in 1979, sending ash as far as Guadeloupe, Barbados and Trinidad. However, this time no one was killed. The volcano had been carefully watched by scientists, who could warn everyone that an eruption was likely to happen. Because of this scientific monitoring, the local people were able to leave their homes in safety before the eruption occurred. Today, tourists regularly visit the rim of the crater to enjoy the sight.

Tourism is just one way in which we can make the most of living among active volcanoes. Other ways are listed below.

- We can grow crops on the slopes of volcanoes, because the lava helps to produce a rich soil.
- Volcanoes are valuable sources of minerals. Pumice, a form of solidified lava, can be used for making bricks and concrete; other materials are collected for road surfacing.
- Some dormant volcanoes are surrounded by hot springs (Fig. 14.5). Steam from these can be used to generate electricity. This is an important source of energy in Iceland and New Zealand.

○ What you should know

- The Earth is made of three main layers: the crust, mantle and core.
- Volcanoes erupt when molten rock from the Earth's mantle pushes upwards through the crust.

The violent Earth 14.1

- Although a volcanic eruption can be devastating, volcanoes can also benefit the local economy – for example as tourist attractions, or as sources of useful minerals.

Fig. 14.5 These sulphur springs on St Lucia are on the site of an ancient volcano, which once had seven active cones. They are a popular place for tourists to visit.

Questions

1. Explain the difference between 'lava' and 'magma'.

2. Name two active volcanoes in the Caribbean. In which territories are they found?

3. In each of the following sentences, fill the blank spaces with the correct word(s) chosen from the following list:

    core; crust; extinct; mantle, metals.

    a The Earth's _____ is the surface layer. It lies on top of the _____.

    b Magnetic _____ in the Earth's _____ produce the Earth's magnetic field.

    c An _____ volcano is one that scientists believe will not erupt again.

4. Adopt a volcano. Choose one volcano from around the world. Find out more about it, and write its profile. The future eruption of some volcanoes can be predicted; why do people choose to build and live so close to them?

The Earth

14.2 Earthquakes

▶ Objectives

After studying this topic you should be able to:

- explain why earthquakes occur
- describe how they are recorded
- describe some of the effects of earthquakes.

Fig. 14.6 Earthquakes can cause devastating destruction – as happened in Los Angeles in the USA in 1994.

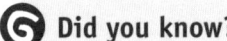

Did you know?

Eleven Caribbean governments support the Seismic Research Unit of the University of the West Indies. The unit is based at St Augustine, Trinidad. It monitors earthquakes across the Caribbean region, as well as some volcanoes.

Are you ready for an earthquake? An earthquake can be very damaging (Fig. 14.6). Buildings fall down, telephone wires are cut, and roads and railways destroyed. There can also be tidal waves, which bring flooding and further misery. The water supply is often hit, and clean drinking water becomes scarce. Disease and food shortages can follow.

Most countries of the Caribbean have plans to make sure that their citizens are well prepared for an earthquake. When an earthquake strikes, you won't have time to think and react sensibly unless you have thought carefully about the situation beforehand. Some typical safety rules, telling people what to do in case of an earthquake, are shown in Table 14.1.

- Earthquakes are terrifying. They occur without warning. When an earthquake strikes any area, the 'solid' earth moves like the deck of a ship in motion.
- Although the tremor lasts for seconds, it seems longer.
- What you do during and immediately after the tremor may make life-and-death differences for you, your family and your neighbours.

Earthquakes 14.2

Table 14.1 Earthquake safety rules.

During the tremor	After the tremor
1 Don't panic. The motion is frightening, but unless it shakes something down on top of you, you will not be hurt. The Earth does not yawn open, gulp down a neighbourhood, and slam shut. Keep calm and ride it out.	1 Check your utilities. Earth movements may have cracked gas, electrical and water conduits.
2 If it catches you indoors, stay indoors. Take cover under a bed, table, bench, in a doorway or against an inside wall. Stay away from glass.	2 If you smell gas, shut off the valve on your cylinder. Open doors and windows and stay out of the house until fresh air has blown through.
3 If the earthquake catches you outside, move away from buildings, overhead electric wires and tall trees. Stay there until the shaking stops.	3 If electrical wiring is shorting out, close the switch at the main meter box.
4 Don't run through or near buildings. The greatest danger from falling debris is just outside doorways and close to outer walls.	4 Turn on your radio or television (if conditions permit) to get the latest emergency bulletins.
	5 Do not use telephones except to report an emergency.
	6 Don't go sight-seeing.
	7 Stay out of severely damaged buildings; aftershock can shake them down.
5 If you are in a moving car, stop as quickly as safety permits, but stay inside the vehicle. A car is an excellent instrument for measuring the vibrations of the Earth; it will bounce fearsomely on its springs.	8 Beware especially of fallen electric power lines.
	9 If you are obliged to drive around, do so with extreme caution. Road surfaces, and especially bridges, may have been seriously damaged.

➲ Activity Figures of destruction

Study Table 14.2, which shows information about six major earthquakes that have struck the region in the past.

Display the figures for 'death toll' as a bar chart, in order of the year in which the earthquake occurred.

Discuss

1. Look for a pattern in the numbers of people killed.
2. Suggest why the death toll from a strong earthquake is bigger now compared with earlier centuries.

14.2 The Earth

Table 14.2 Six large earthquakes of the Caribbean and Latin American regions.

Year	Location	Death toll	Other comments
1692	Port Royal, Jamaica	2000	Houses fell into the sea
1842	Haiti and Dominican Republic	5500	Tidal wave damaged property
1843	Leeward Islands	5000	Severe effects in Antigua and Guadeloupe
1972	Managua, Nicaragua	5000	City badly damaged
1976	Guatemala City, Guatemala	23 000	More than 1 million were made homeless
1985	Mexico City	10 000	City centre destroyed

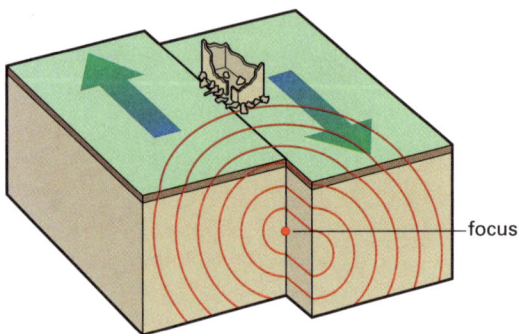

Fig. 14.7 As rocks push past one another, strong vibrations spread out from the focus of the earthquake. It is these shock waves that cause damage on the surface of the Earth.

Underground forces

The rocks that make up the Earth's crust are on the move. They move only very slowly – perhaps just a few centimetres per year – so that we don't generally notice it. However, as one mass of rock slides slowly past another, great forces can build up (Fig. 14.7). The force of friction between rocks can slow down their movement, and this leads to a build-up of energy (known as strain energy) deep underground. When the rocks suddenly become free and push past one another, the surface of the Earth above is jolted. This is an earthquake. It may last for only a few

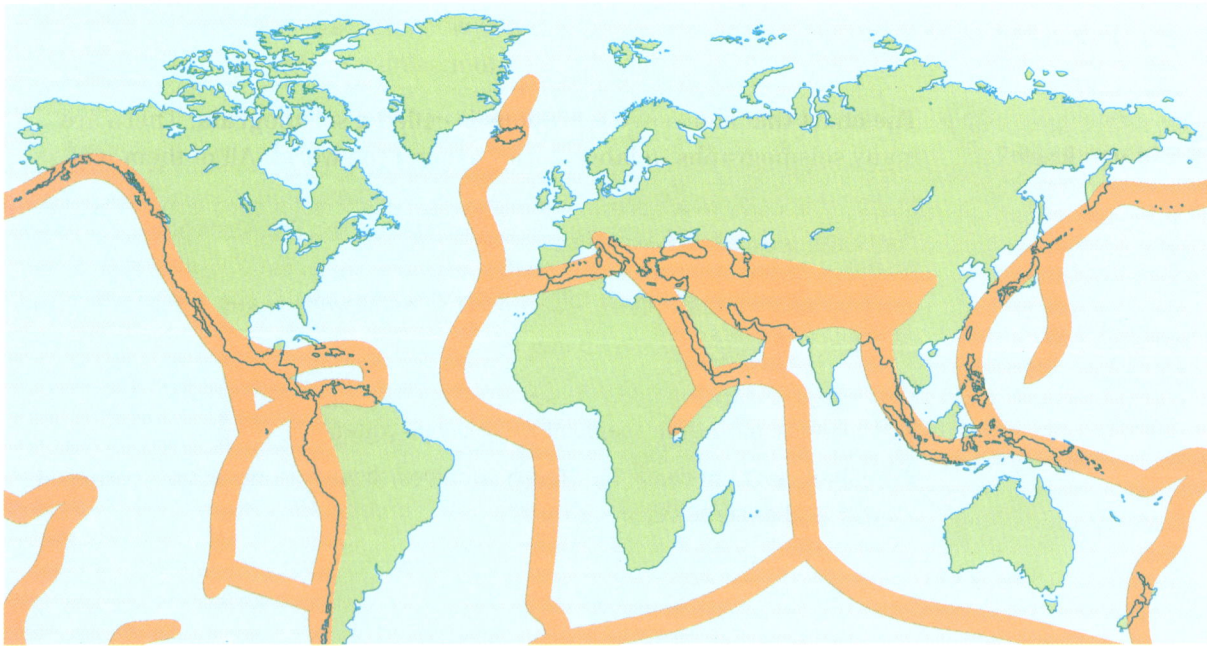

Fig. 14.8 This map shows where there is earthquake activity around the world.

seconds or a minute or two, but a lot of energy is released very quickly and the effects can be dramatic. Figure 14.8 is a map showing the main regions of earthquake activity around the world.

Detecting earthquakes

If an earthquake strikes where you are, you will not need a scientific instrument to tell you! However, earthquakes can be detected all round the world using very sensitive instruments called **seismographs**. Figure 14.9 shows how these work.

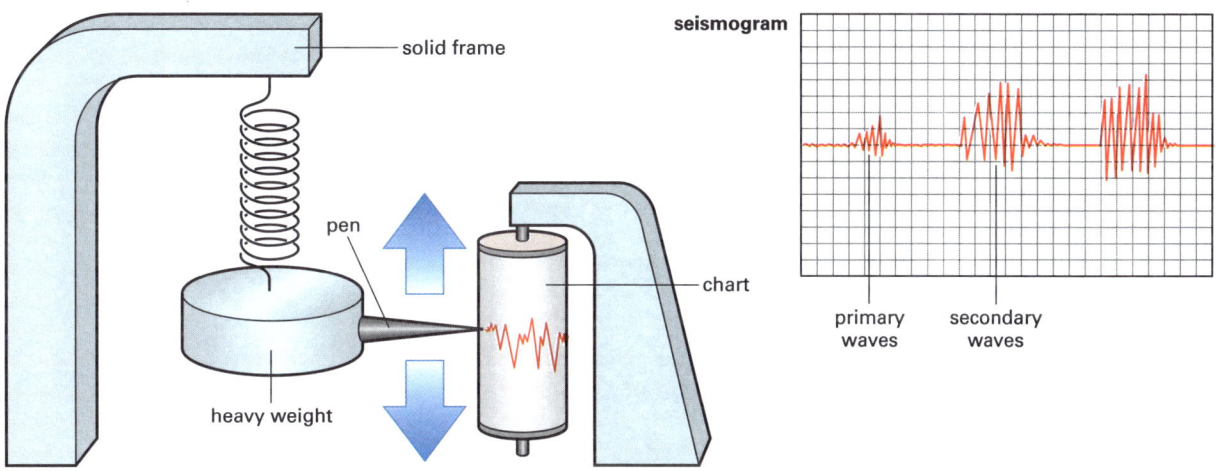

Fig. 14.9 A seismograph for detecting earthquakes. As the chart moves it records movements of the seismograph's needle; the chart is called a seismogram.

- During an earthquake, the heavy weight is caused to vibrate.
- These vibrations cause the pen to move up and down on the chart.

The chart that shows the vibrations is called a **seismogram**. There are many seismographs in laboratories around the world. All of them will detect an earthquake, and the scientists compare their charts. The one that detects the quake first must be nearest to the focus of the quake, and by measuring the chart it is possible to work out exactly where the focus is. The stronger the quake, the more the pen moves up and down, so it is possible to work out how strong the quake is.

Unfortunately, it has proved very difficult to predict when an earthquake will occur. Sometimes, underground strains build up for much longer than expected; sometimes, the strain is released gradually over a period of time, so that no quake occurs. Scientists monitor the situation in earthquake zones, but so far they have not been able to predict accurately when an earthquake will occur.

To avoid the worst damage, tall buildings in earthquake zones can now be built with foundations that absorb the energy of quake vibrations. It is

> **Did you know?**
>
> The centre or **focus** of an earthquake may be several kilometres underground. Its effect is strongest at the surface directly above; this point is called the **epicentre**.

14.2 The Earth

hoped that this will help to prevent the collapse of buildings in future major earthquakes, so that fewer people are killed.

The Richter scale: The strength or magnitude of an earthquake is measured on a scale devised by Charles Richter in 1930. The weakest quake that can be recorded using seismographs has magnitude 1 on the Richter scale; the strongest ever recorded (Chile, 1960) reached magnitude 8.9.

Table 14.3 Earthquake magnitudes on the Richter scale. Note that, on this scale, a quake of magnitude 7 is ten times as strong as one of magnitude 6; magnitude 8 is ten times as strong as magnitude 7, and so on.

Magnitude	Effects
9	Total destruction; river courses altered; vision distorted
7	Most buildings destroyed; general panic
5	Doors swing open; drinks spill from glasses
3	Hanging objects swing; people are woken
1	Detected by sensitive instruments

> **Did you know?**
>
> More than 10 000 earthquakes are recorded in seismograph laboratories every year, including at least one of magnitude 8 or higher, but only a few are strong enough to cause serious damage.

Activity A model seismograph

You will need
- a piece of springy metal
- a heavy weight
- paper and a pen
- other everyday materials

Method
Your task is to make a device that will record vibrations. Stand it on the bench; thump the bench hard, and record the vibrations.

Try to make a sensitive seismograph that can stand on the ground and detect vibrations when you jump up and down.

Activity Warning! Earthquake ahead!

We hope an earthquake never strikes, but it's better to be ready than to be taken by surprise. Make an earthquake safety plan for your family. Here are some points to think about:

- Where are the safe places, indoors and outdoors?
- How should you react to a quake if you are indoors, outdoors or in a car?

- What supplies should you have, ready to use after the quake?
- What action should you take once the quake is over?

Discuss

Compare your plan with a partner's. What improvements can you make?
Be ready to present your plan to the class.

What you should know

- Earthquakes happen when underground rocks try to slide past one another. The point from which the vibrations spread is called the focus.
- Earthquakes are recorded using seismographs.
- The strength, or magnitude, of an earthquake is measured by the Richter scale.

Questions

1 Compare the map that shows where earthquakes occur (Fig. 14.8) with the map of volcanic activity (Fig. 14.4). What similarities can you see? Can you see any major differences?

2 a Explain what is meant by the magnitude of an earthquake.
  b What scale is used to measure magnitude?
  c What instrument is used to record an earthquake?

3 Research an earthquake or series of earthquakes using the internet. Explore the reasons for high or low death tolls. Discover whether there are predictions of future earthquakes, and what is being done to minimize their effect.

The Earth

14.3 Wind and waves

▶ Objectives

After studying this topic you should be able to:

- say what is meant by air pressure, and explain what causes it
- describe how atmospheric pressure is measured
- describe how wind and waves are formed
- discuss hurricanes, how they form and their effects.

Fig. 14.10 Storms bring high winds, which can be very destructive.

The Earth is surrounded by a thin layer of air – the **atmosphere**. This is essential for us, because we breathe air. As you walk around, you might not notice the presence of the air, because it is so thin. But on a windy day, you may feel it pushing hard against you so that it can be difficult to walk. And if there is a **hurricane** – run for safety (Fig. 14.10)!

Air seems very thin so it is surprising to find that, when air starts to move, it can produce large and destructive forces.

→ Activity The pressure of air

Fig. 14.11 Air pressure can have surprising force.

You will need
- a strip of thin plywood (approx. 60 cm × 10 cm)
- a sheet of newspaper

Method
1. Place the strip of plywood on a table with about 25 cm overhanging the edge.
2. Lay the sheet of newspaper so that it covers the part of the plywood on the table (Fig. 14.11).
3. Smack down suddenly on the free end of the plywood.

Discuss
1. Why does the newspaper remain on the table? What force stops it from rising upwards?

2 Measure the length and width of the newspaper, and calculate its area in square centimetres (cm²). Multiply by 10 to find the force that the atmosphere exerts on the paper, in newtons (N). One newton (1 N) is roughly the weight of an orange or apple. How many oranges are pressing down on the paper?

Atmospheric pressure

The Earth's atmosphere is held in place by the pull of the Earth's gravity. The atmosphere is pulled downwards, and it presses on everything on the Earth's surface. It exerts a force of about 10 N on every square centimetre, or 100 000 N on every square metre. This is known as **atmospheric pressure**, and it means that everything is slightly squashed by the atmosphere. If you went to the Moon, you would find there only a very thin atmosphere because the Moon's gravity is much weaker than the Earth's. What would happen if you did the newspaper and plywood experiment on the Moon?

You can do a simple experiment to show the effects of atmospheric pressure. Close your mouth and puff up your cheeks. You have pushed air into your cheeks so that the pressure inside is greater than the pressure outside, and your cheeks swell outwards. Now, suck the air out of your mouth; your cheeks collapse inwards. Atmospheric pressure outside is greater than the pressure inside, and your cheeks are pushed inwards.

Activity The effects of air pressure

Look at the three experiments shown in Figures 14.12–14.14 below and overleaf. (You may have the chance to try them out.) Make sure you understand what is happening in each experiment.

Discuss

Now, try to explain what is happening in each experiment. You need to think about differences in pressure:

- Where is the pressure higher?
- Where is the pressure lower?
- Air pushes from high pressure to low pressure.

Fig. 14.12 The paper moves as you blow air steadily towards it.

14.3 The Earth

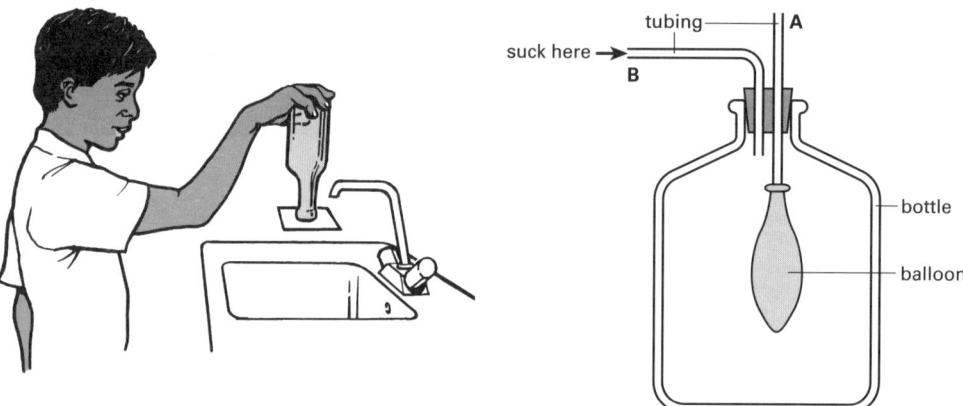

Fig. 14.13 When the bottle of water is turned upside down, the card stays in place.

Fig. 14.14 Air is sucked out of the jar through tube B. The balloon inflates.

Explaining air pressure

Air consists of particles called molecules. These are far too small for the eye to see, even with a powerful microscope. The molecules rush around, bumping into everything around them. It is these collisions that cause the pressure of air on everything it touches.

- Pressure is lower when the air particles are farther apart (lower density), and when they are moving more slowly (when the air is colder).
- Pressure is higher when the particles are closer together (more compressed, higher density), and when they are moving more quickly (when the air is hotter).

If you blow into a balloon, you are pushing more air into the space inside the balloon. This increases the pressure inside and the balloon inflates.

If you submerge an empty bottle in hot water, the air inside will warm up. As its pressure increases, bubbles of air will be pushed out of the open neck of the bottle.

⇒ Activity Compressing air

You will need
- a small plastic syringe

Method
1. Pull the plunger of the syringe out almost as far as it will go.
2. Put your finger quite firmly over the nozzle (Fig. 14.15). How far can you push the plunger in?

Wind and waves 14.3

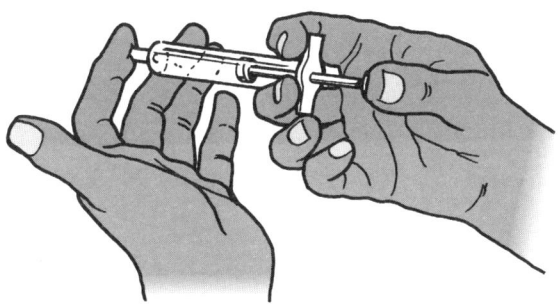

Fig. 14.15 Trying to compress air with a plastic syringe.

Discuss

1 Can you compress the air in the syringe? Can you squash it to half its original volume, or even less than that?

2 Air is 0.1% molecules and 99.9% empty space. Use this information to explain why it is easier to compress air than a liquid or solid.

Measuring air pressure

In the laboratory, **pressure gauges** are used to measure air pressure. One type is called a Bourdon pressure gauge. This works rather like the 'blozoom' shown in Figure 14.16. When you blow into the paper tube, it stretches out. The harder you blow, the more it uncurls. When you stop blowing, a springy wire causes it to curl up again.

Fig. 14.16 Blowing into a 'blozoom' causes the paper tube to uncurl. You should get a funny noise as well!

Inside a Bourdon gauge is a curled-up length of brass tubing. When air pushes into the tube, it straightens out slightly and this causes the needle to move around the scale. Bourdon gauges are sometimes used to measure the pressure of car tyres.

Barometers are used to measure atmospheric pressure. Some people have one on the wall at home. You have to tap the glass so that the needle will move; then you can see if the pressure is rising or falling.

Inside an aneroid barometer is a sealed can containing air. The can is made of thin, springy metal. If the atmospheric pressure outside the can increases, it squashes the can a little. If the atmospheric pressure decreases, the can pushes back and expands a little. These movements make the needle move up and down the scale.

As you go upwards through the atmosphere, the air gets thinner and thinner. Modern passenger aircraft tend to fly at a height of about 10 000 m, where atmospheric pressure is about one-third of its value at sea level. This is why the cabin of an aircraft has to be pressurized, so that the passengers and crew can breathe comfortably. Because pressure decreases as you get higher, aircraft are fitted with barometers. By measuring the pressure, the crew can find out how high they are. A barometer like this is known as an **altimeter**.

Did you know?

Mexico City is at a high altitude, about 2350 m above sea level, and the atmospheric pressure is low. When the Olympic Games were held there in 1968, the athletes had to spend several weeks living at high altitude before the competition in order to get used to the shortage of oxygen.

Activity Using a Bourdon gauge

Fig. 14.17 Blowing into a Bourdon gauge.

You will need
- a Bourdon pressure gauge
- a bicycle pump

Method
1. Blow down the tube attached to the gauge (Fig. 14.17). Note the greatest pressure you can reach on the scale.
2. Connect the bicycle pump to the tube. Note the pressure produced by a *single* stroke of the pump.

Discuss
1. The pressure of your lungs is greater than atmospheric pressure – otherwise you would not be able to breathe out. How much greater is it?
2. Which is greater, the pressure from your lungs or the pressure from the pump?

Activity Make your own barometer

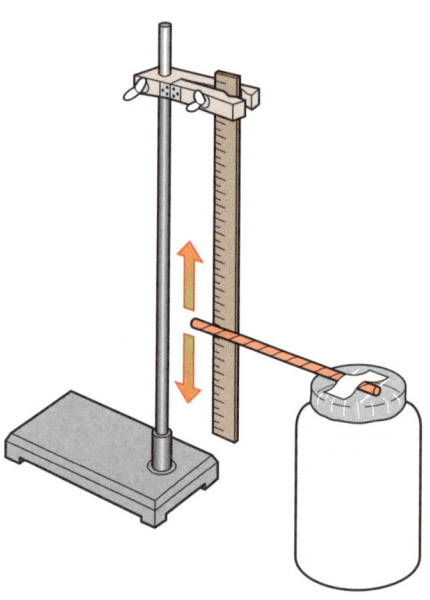

Fig. 14.18 A simple jar barometer.

You will need
- a small glass jar
- plastic wrap (cling film)
- a drinking straw
- a ruler

Method
1. Wrap a piece of plastic film tightly over the open end of the jar, making sure that no air can escape from the jar.
2. Fix one end of the straw to the middle of the wrap (Fig. 14.18). Place the ruler so it is held vertically in a clamp, next to the free end of the straw.
3. Place your jar in a warm place, so that the air inside warms up and expands. What happens to the wrap? How does the straw move?
4. What will happen if you place your barometer in a cold place, such as a fridge?

Discuss
1. Why does the straw move as the pressure inside the jar changes?
2. How could you adapt your model to show changes in atmospheric pressure?
3. In what way is your model barometer similar to an aneroid barometer?

Differences in pressure

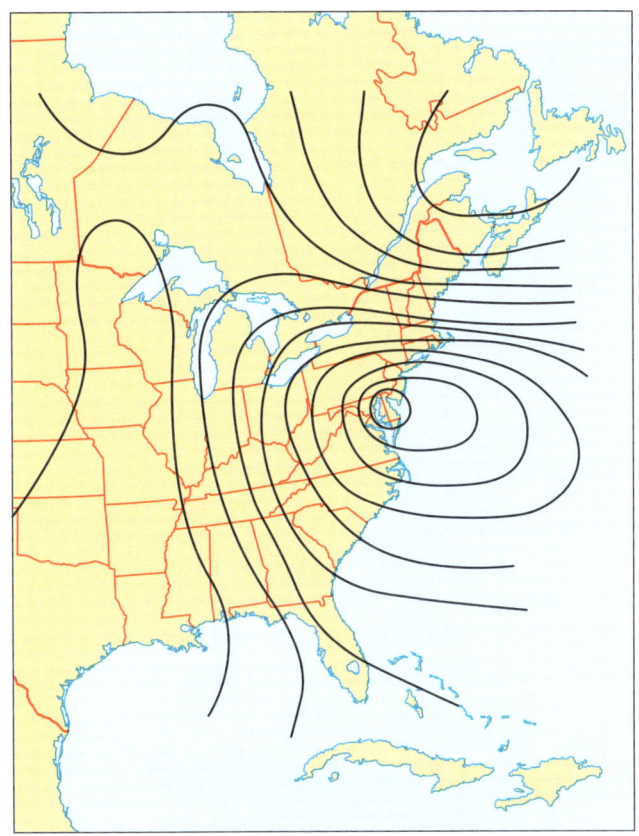

Atmospheric pressure is measured by **meteorologists** (people who study the weather). This helps them to draw their weather maps and to predict how the wind will blow, and how strong it will be.

- If there are big differences in pressure, strong winds will blow.
- If there is little variation in pressure, winds will be light.

On a weather map (Fig. 14.19), the **isobars** show how the pressure varies from place to place. Isobars are lines that join places with the same air pressure. Winds blow from regions of high pressure to regions of low pressure. In fact, the wind tends to spiral around regions of high and low pressure, rather like water swirling down a plughole.

Fig. 14.19 The black lines on this map are isobars. They are rather like the contour lines that show hills and valleys. Winds tend to spiral down from regions of high pressure into regions of low pressure.

Making waves

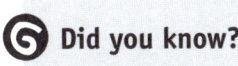 **Did you know?**

If you drive up a mountain or go up in an aircraft, your ears may 'pop'. This is because the higher pressure inside your ears is adjusting to match the lower pressure outside.

The wind blows across the sea, and this creates waves. It is the force of friction that whips up the surface of the water. Energy from the wind is being transferred to the water. When the wind dies down, it can take some time before the waves settle down and the sea becomes calm again.

You rarely see big waves on a pond or lake. This is because the wind does not have a big enough distance to whip up large waves. On the open sea, the wind may blow across several hundreds of kilometres and so big waves can be produced.

High winds

Hurricanes are the biggest, most powerful of storms. Winds may reach speeds of 200 kph (kilometres per hour) or more. Hurricanes form over warm tropical waters when the temperature rises above 27°C. Warm, moist air rises upwards, leaving behind a region of low pressure. The ocean and atmosphere start to spin around this centre of low pressure, the eye of the hurricane. The sea is pushed up in the region of the eye, because of the low pressure. The spinning is caused by the Earth's rotation, which throws air away from the Equator.

14.3 The Earth

We can think of a hurricane as having a life cycle which lasts about 10 days. The main features of this life cycle are shown in Table 14.4.

Table 14.4 The life cycle of a hurricane.

Day 1	Wind speed about 50 kph. Thunderstorm grows, and begins to swirl or spin. A depression has formed
Day 3	Wind speed approaching 70 kph. Storms concentrate near the eye. A tropical storm is born
Day 5	Wind speed reaches 120 kph – hurricane force. The eye begins to form
Day 10	The hurricane moves across the sea, eventually reaching land. Friction with the land causes it to lose energy, and it gradually dies down

 Did you know?

Hurricanes form in the Atlantic Ocean. In the Indian Ocean they are known as cyclones; in the Pacific Ocean they are known as typhoons.

Hurricanes can cause terrible damage (Fig. 14.20). The high winds can wreck islands in their path. The high sea in the region of the eye, which is up to 10 m above normal levels, can also swamp low-lying land, especially at high tide.

Fig. 14.20 High winds and flooding brought about by a hurricane can cause vast amounts of damage, as happened here at Pinney's Beach, Nevis St Kitts.

Wind and waves 14.3

❓ Finding out

Hurricane alert!

Weather forecasters now follow closely the development of hurricanes, and watch their movements. They even give them names. Find out the names of some recent hurricanes in the Caribbean, and which islands they affected.

The forecasters can say when and where a particular hurricane is likely to reach land, and what level of damage it will cause. Get a recent hurricane bulletin for your island, and discuss what precautions are needed for hurricane safety.

⭘ What you should know

- Air has pressure, because its particles are moving about and colliding with everything around them.
- Air can be compressed by increasing the pressure on it.
- The pressure of air is measured with a pressure gauge; barometers are used for measuring atmospheric pressure.
- Atmospheric pressure decreases as you go upwards to higher altitudes.
- Winds are caused by differences in atmospheric pressure.
- Waves are caused by friction as the wind blows across the sea.

@ Questions

1. Which of the following is the correct answer?

   A barometer is used to measure:

   a wind speed;

   b air pressure;

   c air temperature;

   d the height of the atmosphere.

2. A blown-up balloon is carried up a high mountain. Will it get bigger or smaller? Explain why its volume changes.

3. Imagine drinking a drink through a straw. You suck to reduce the pressure inside the straw. Explain how this causes the drink to move up the straw. (You will have to think about the air pressing on the surface of the drink.)

4. People with asthma use a special instrument to measure the speed that they can blow air. This is a measure of how strong their lungs are. You can also measure strength of blow and lung capacity (how much air your lungs can hold). Design your own instruments for making measurements like these. (You should never completely empty your lungs, as you may pass out.)

The Earth

14.4 Rocks and weathering

Fig. 14.21 Changes in temperature cause repeated expansion and contraction of the rock face, leading to its break-up and resulting in a build-up of rock fragments at the foot of the slope.

Fig. 14.22 Erosion can be caused by the action of the sea. Here softer rock has been worn by the waves much more than the harder rock.

▶ Objective

After studying this topic you should be able to:

- describe the ways in which rocks are broken up or worn away.

Rocks are all around us. If you climb to the top of a rocky mountain, or scramble over the rocks on the seashore, you might think that rocks are a permanent, unchanging feature of the Earth. But if you live near a volcano, you will know that this is not so.

Rocks are generally hard and difficult to break. For a long time, people thought that the rocks around us must have been here since the start of time. However, geologists – the people who study rocks – noticed that rocks can wear away. Rain and river water cause rocks to break up. Frost makes them crack. Around the mouths of rivers there is a build-up of material that has been washed downstream from higher up the river. This build-up is called a river delta. Sandy beaches form along the coast in a similar way. All these things show that rocks are being constantly broken down.

The process by which rocks are worn away is called **weathering**; this may be caused by reactions with rainwater (which is slightly acidic) or other chemicals, or by freezing and thawing of water in the rocks. Just the repeated daytime heating, followed by cooling at night, can cause rock surfaces to break up (Fig. 14.21).

Erosion is when rocks are worn down and carried away by ice, streams, rivers or the sea (Fig. 14.22). Rocks are broken down into tiny particles called sediments. You are likely to find muddy **sediments** on the bed of any stream or river.

Rocks and weathering 14.4

→ Activity Looking at rocks

You will need
- stones collected from different places, e.g. a quarry, a volcano, by the sea
- a hand lens
- a hammer
- a Bunsen burner
- tongs
- a plastic beaker of cold water
- a test tube
- dilute hydrochloric acid
- an old cloth

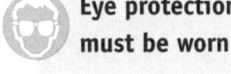
Eye protection must be worn

Method
1 Examine each stone with the hand lens.
2 Wrap each stone in an old cloth and hit it with a hammer.
3 Heat each stone strongly for 5–10 minutes, then plunge it into cold water.
4 Drop a piece of each stone into a test tube of dilute hydrochloric acid.

Record
Note down your observations in a table.

Discuss
1 Are there any crystals in any of the stones? Are there any fossils?
2 Do the stones appear to be pure substances, or mixtures?
3 Are some stones easier to crush than others?
4 Did the acid affect the stones in any way?

◘ What you should know

- Erosion is when rocks are broken up or worn away by natural forces.
- Weathering is any form of erosion that depends on the weather, especially rainwater, wind, frost and heating.
- Erosion can also be caused by ice, streams, rivers or the sea.

@ Questions

1 Suppose there is a large slab of rock standing in the sea. It is made up of three horizontal rock layers, rather like a sandwich. For each of the arrangements described below, draw the shape that you might expect to find after the 'sandwich' of rock has been pounded by the waves for a few thousand years.

   a A 'soft-rock sandwich': two layers of hard rock with soft rock in between.

   b A 'hard-rock sandwich': two layers of soft rock with hard rock in between.

2 What do we call someone who studies rocks?

3 Look for different rock formations in your area. Collect information about them. Use a digital camera to record them. Do a presentation on 'your' rocks – what they are and how they are changing.

14.5 New rocks from old

▶ Objectives

After studying this topic you should be able to:

- describe the formation of three types of rocks: sedimentary, metamorphic and igneous
- outline the rock cycle
- give some examples of important minerals and their uses.

Fortunately for us, new rocks form as quickly as old rocks are worn away. Otherwise all of the land we live on would long ago have eroded away into the sea. The processes of rock formation and erosion tend to be slow, taking place over thousands or millions of years, which is why we don't notice them in everyday life. However, they are important to us, for the erosion of rocks is the first step in producing the fertile soils that we need for farming. How do new rocks form?

We can divide rocks into three types, according to how they form.

Sedimentary rocks: Rivers bring sediments down to the sea. Mud and sand sink to the bottom of the sea, where they come under pressure from the water above. The particles of the sediments gradually stick together. Mud and silt (fine particles) become mudstone, and sand (coarser particles) becomes sandstone. The chalky skeletons and shells of sea animals become chalk and limestone. Sedimentary rocks often show horizontal layers of the materials from which they were formed.

Metamorphic rocks: Sedimentary rocks may be pressed more and more as new rocks form on top of them. As they are pushed further into the Earth they get hotter. Eventually, the rock becomes harder and denser ('metamorphic' means 'changing shape or form').

Table 14.5 lists the various types of sedimentary and metamorphic rocks that are formed from different types of sediment.

Table 14.5 Types of sedimentary and metamorphic rocks formed from different sediments.

Type of sediment	Sedimentary rock	Metamorphic rock
Mud and silt	Mudstone	Slate
Sand	Sandstone	Quartzite
Shells	Chalk and limestone	Marble

14.5 New rocks from old

Fig. 14.23 A piece of granite, polished so that you can see the crystals that formed as the molten rock cooled and became solid.

Igneous rocks: New rocks form around volcanoes. Hot magma from inside the Earth pushes upwards. It may pour out of a volcano, or it may cool while it is still underground. ('Igneous' means 'made by fire'.) This is how basalt and granite are made (Fig. 14.23).

Some Caribbean islands, such as Barbados, are made almost entirely of coral, which is a form of limestone (sedimentary rock). Others, such as St Lucia and Montserrat, are made of old volcanic (igneous) rocks.

The rock cycle

By now, you should be getting a picture of how rocks form, how they weather away to make sediments, and how these then form new sedimentary and metamorphic rocks. The whole process goes round and round, and is known as the **rock cycle**. This is shown in Figure 14.24.

It is surprising to discover that whole mountains can gradually weather away, while new ones form. The Andes mountains of South America are thousands of metres in height, but the rock they are made of was

Fig. 14.24 The rock cycle.

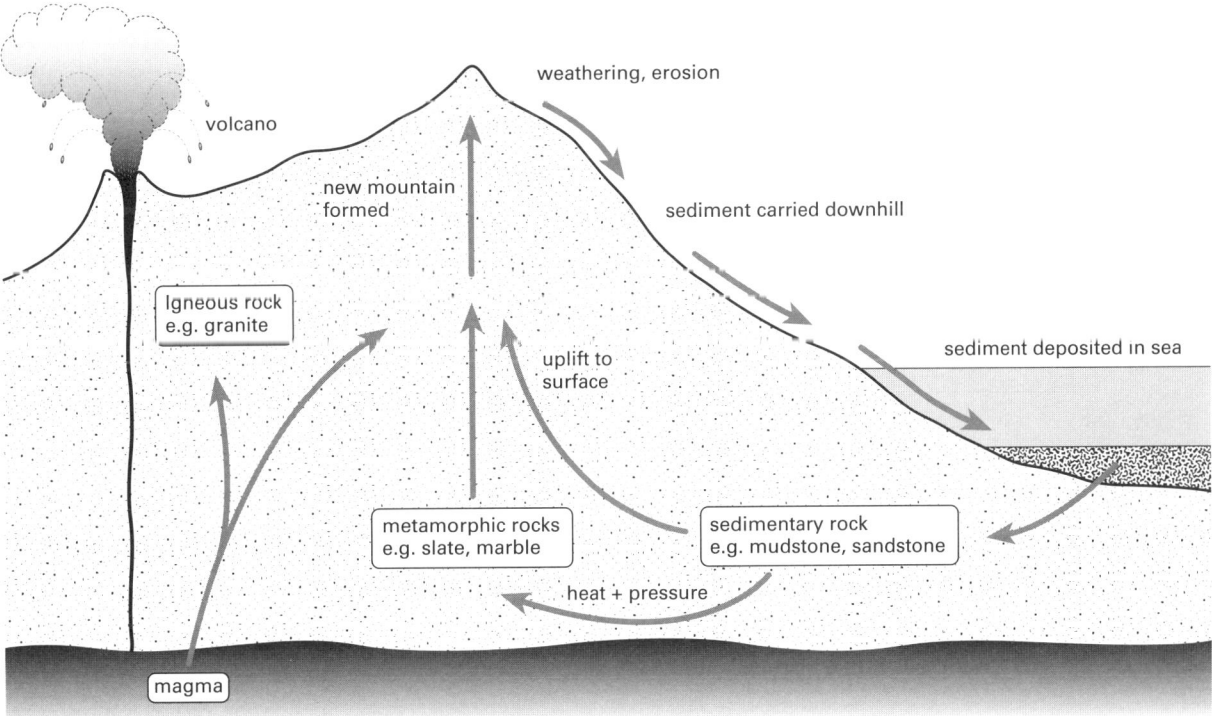

14.5 The Earth

originally formed at the bottom of the sea. We know this because fossils of sea animals are found in the rocks of the highest summits.

Minerals

Some rocks are made of just one substance. For example, limestone may be calcium carbonate or calcium silicate. Bauxite is aluminium hydroxide. Other rocks are made up of tiny crystals of several different substances (you can see this in the photograph of granite shown in Figure 14.23). The substances from which rocks are made are known as **minerals**. Most minerals are oxides, silicates, carbonates or sulphates.

Minerals can be very important for us. For example, if you live in Jamaica or Guyana, you will know that bauxite is mined there in large quantities. It is a reddish-brown rock that is fairly easily powdered. It is important because all the world's new aluminium, millions of tonnes each year, is extracted from bauxite. (Much of aluminium is recycled, of course.)

The Earth is made of minerals, and many of them are useful to us. Each mineral is made of two or more elements. Table 14.6 and Figure 14.25 show the percentages of the commonest elements in the Earth's crust. You can see that three-quarters of the Earth's crust is made up of just two elements: oxygen and silicon. Together these make silica (silicon dioxide); sand is often almost pure silica (Fig. 14.26).

Table 14.6 The most common elements in the Earth's crust.

Element	Approximate percentage by mass
Oxygen	50
Silicon	26
Aluminium	7
Iron	4
Calcium	3
Sodium	2
Potassium	2
Magnesium	2
Hydrogen	1
Others	3

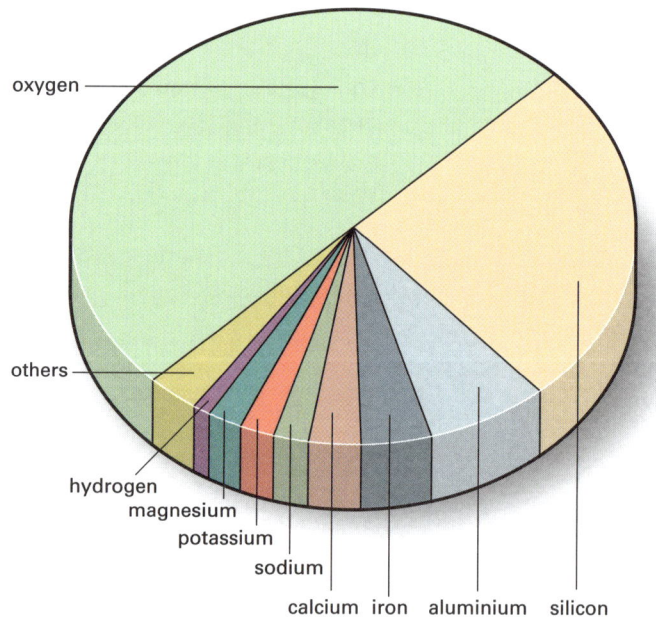

Fig. 14.25 Pie chart showing how the Earth's crust is made up.

New rocks from old 14.5

❓ Finding out

The rocks around us

Some of the islands of the Caribbean are made of volcanic rocks, while others are made of rock that has been built up as reefs in the sea. The rocks of the Andes range extend through Guyana and into Trinidad.

Find out about the different rocks of the Caribbean. You could look in encyclopedias, geography books and travel books.

Which islands are volcanic, and which are made of sedimentary rocks? How old are these rocks?

Suppose you are visiting different Caribbean countries. What features of the landscape can tell you about the local rocks?

Illustrate your answers with a map.

Fig. 14.26 Crystals of quartz, which is a form of pure silica. If these crystals were crushed, they would become sand.

◯ What you should know

- As existing rocks are eroded, new rocks are slowly being formed all the time.
- We can divide rocks into three types, according to how they are formed: sedimentary, metamorphic and igneous.
- Rocks are made of minerals, which are chemical compounds.

@ Questions

1. Basalt is formed when hot magma rises up from deep inside the Earth and then cools. Chalk is formed from the remains of dead sea animals that sink to the bottom of the sea. Slate forms when mudstone is heated under pressure. Classify each of the rocks described above as sedimentary, metamorphic or igneous.

2. Answer the following questions about minerals:
    a. Sand is made largely of which two elements?
    b. What are the main chemical compounds found in limestone?
    c. Aluminium hydroxide is the main chemical compound in which mineral?

3. Research aluminium extraction on the Alucan site. Why is it so expensive? Why is it so important to recycle aluminium cans? How can you help?

The Earth

14.6 Metals from minerals

▶ Objectives

After studying this topic you should be able to:

- describe how metals can be extracted from their ores by smelting and by electrolysis
- describe the basic features of electrolysis.

We use many different metals in our lives, for a wide range of things. Metals are useful because:

- they are usually stiff and strong and can be shaped into useful items (e.g. saucepans, screwdrivers, parts of cars);
- they conduct electricity (e.g. copper wires);
- they conduct heat (e.g. aluminium cooking foil);
- they look shiny and attractive (e.g. gold and silver jewellery).

However, we rarely find pure metals in nature. Pure gold may be found as flakes in a river bed, or as a seam in other rocks. It shines brightly in the light, and causes great excitement when it is found. However, most metals are found as compounds – in chemical substances where they are combined with other elements. We have to extract the metal we want from these compounds.

A mineral that is a source of a useful metal is called an **ore**. Table 14.7 shows some important ores, and the metals that are extracted from them. We have already mentioned one of these – bauxite, from which aluminium is extracted. Ores are usually oxides, sulphides, carbonates or silicates. When you look at an ore such as bauxite, it looks like any rock. It is hard to imagine that a shiny metal can be extracted from such a dull material. No one is really sure how Stone Age people, living thousands of years ago, first discovered that copper, tin and iron could be extracted from rocks.

We don't find pure metals in nature because they tend to corrode. This means that they react with the other substances around them. You will know that iron rusts when it is in contact with oxygen and water vapour in the air – a corrugated iron roof doesn't last forever in a humid climate. Copper corrodes to become copper carbonate, and so on. These reactions may be quite slow, but they have been going on in the Earth for millions of years, so few unreacted metals remain. Gold and silver react very very slowly, which is why they are used for jewellery. You wouldn't want to wake up in the morning and find that your rings and bangles had suddenly turned to rust!

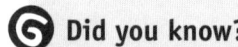

Did you know?

The steel pan is one of the few really new musical instruments invented in the twentieth century, if not the only one. Caribbean people were very innovative in finding this novel use for dustbins! Now people in many parts of the world are playing 'pan,' incorporating its distinct sound into their musical ensembles. How did this technology arise and how is it improving? Find out all you can about this important part of our heritage.

14.6 Metals from minerals

Table 14.7 Some important ores, and the metals that are extracted from them.

Ore	Composition	Metal extracted
Bauxite	Aluminium oxide	Aluminium
Haematite	Iron oxide	Iron
Chalcopyrite	Copper sulphide	Copper
Galena	Lead sulphide	Lead
Cinnabar	Mercury sulphide	Mercury
Chalk, limestone, marble	Calcium carbonate	Calcium

> **Did you know?**
>
> Jamaica is the world's second-biggest producer of bauxite, the ore from which aluminium is extracted.

Extracting metals

Separating metals from their ores is not the same as separating mixtures. Mixtures can be separated using techniques such as evaporation and distillation, which you saw when you studied the separation of sugar and of crude oil in Book 2, Unit 9.

Ores are compounds in which the metal elements are chemically combined with other elements. Compounds must be separated by other means, each of which involves a chemical reaction.

Metal oxides (such as iron oxide) are heated with coal or coke (which is mostly carbon). The oxygen breaks away from the metal and combines with the carbon. We can write this as a simple word equation:

metal oxide + carbon → metal + carbon dioxide

So, in the case of iron oxide, the equation is:

iron oxide + carbon → iron + carbon dioxide

Because carbon dioxide is a gas, it escapes, and the metal is left behind. This process is known as **smelting**.

Other ores must first be converted to oxides before the metal can be extracted. For example, metal carbonates can be heated strongly so that they split into the metal oxide and carbon dioxide:

metal carbonate → metal oxide + carbon dioxide

Metal sulphides are heated in air so that the sulphur can react with oxygen:

metal sulphide + oxygen → metal oxide + sulphur dioxide

Both of these reactions produce metal oxides, which can then be heated with carbon (Fig. 14.27).

14.6 The Earth

Fig. 14.27 Hot iron is poured from a blast furnace at a steel works. Inside the blast furnace, iron oxide and carbon are heated together. The iron oxide is converted to iron, and carbon dioxide escapes from the top.

Activity Metals from ores

You will need
- crucible
- Bunsen burner
- tripod
- claypipe triangle
- galena (lead sulphide [toxic])
- iron pyrites (iron sulphide)
- lead(II) oxide
- powdered coal, coke or carbon

Danger!

Care needed!

Method
1. Heat 0.5–1.0 g powdered iron sulphide in a crucible (Fig. 14.28).
2. Observe, and carefully smell any gas given off.
3. Repeat with lead sulphide.

Eye protection must be worn

Discuss
1. The residue is the solid material that is left behind. What does it look like? How does it compare with the starting material?
2. Now heat a mixture of lead(II) oxide and carbon over a very hot flame. Do you observe any metallic lead in the residue?

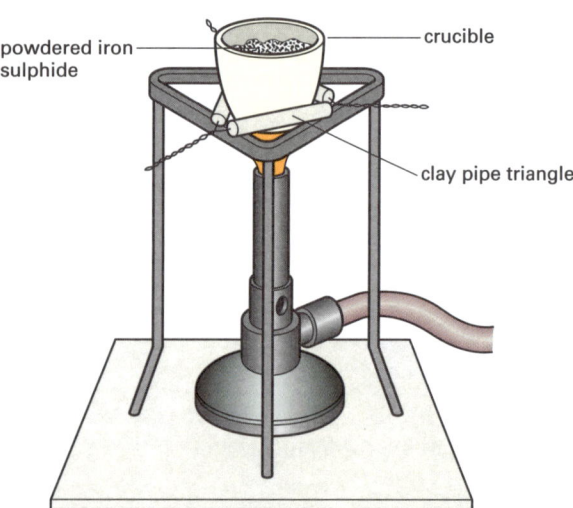

Fig. 14.28 Heating metal sulphides produces a strong-smelling gas. What is it?

Extracting metals by electrolysis

Some metals have to be separated from their ores using electricity – one example is aluminium; other examples are sodium, potassium, calcium and magnesium. Oxides of these metals cannot be separated using carbon because the metal has a stronger attraction for the oxygen than carbon does. The process of splitting a chemical compound using electricity is known as **electrolysis**.

Metals from minerals 14.6

Activity Splitting up copper(II) chloride

You will need
- copper(II) chloride (toxic) – about 10 g
- beaker containing 50 cm³ water
- two carbon rods
- 6 V battery or power pack
- connecting wires
- press switch

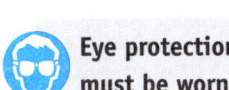

Method

1. Dissolve 10 g of copper(II) chloride in the water.
2. Set up the circuit as shown in Fig. 14.29. Make sure that the two carbon rods are not touching.

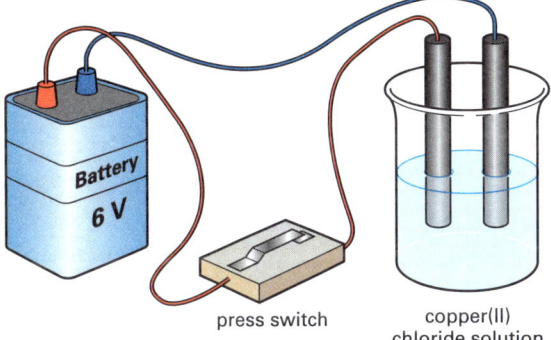

Fig. 14.29 Make a prediction: what will happen if you swap over the leads on the battery?

Discuss

1. When you close the switch to complete the circuit, what do you see happening at the two carbon rods?
2. What metal do you think is being produced?
3. What gas can you smell? (Hint: think about the name 'copper chloride'.)

Electrolysis

In the activity above, the two carbon rods carry the electric current into and out of the solution. They are known as **electrodes**. The one connected to the negative terminal of the supply is the **cathode**, the one connected to the positive electrode is the **anode**.

In the activity above, copper chloride was split into two substances, copper and chlorine. Copper appeared at the cathode – it is a reddish-looking metal, although it may not have looked very shiny. The gas given off at the anode was chlorine, which smells like bleach (because bleach contains chlorine).

You can split water into two gases in a similar way. If you know the chemical formula for water, H_2O, you will not be surprised to learn that these gases are hydrogen and oxygen. Perhaps we should call water 'hydrogen oxide'.

Aluminium from bauxite

Fig. 14.30 Huge machinery is used to mine bauxite in Surinam.

Bauxite is the ore from which aluminium is extracted. It is a very important raw material for Jamaica and Guyana, and it is exported around the world (Fig. 14.30). At one time aluminium was a rare and expensive metal. This was before the method for extracting it from bauxite by electrolysis was discovered. Now aluminium is produced in large quantities and it has many uses. Aluminium is a very light metal (its density is low), and we could not build modern aircraft without it. It is also used for making cooking pots, some electrical appliances, in packaging and other household items.

Bauxite is not a pure ore. It is a mixture of alumina (aluminium oxide), which we want, with iron oxide and silica, which we don't want. When the aluminium oxide has been purified, it is a clean white powder. This is shipped to other countries where aluminium is extracted from it. There is no point in transporting the impurities around the world.

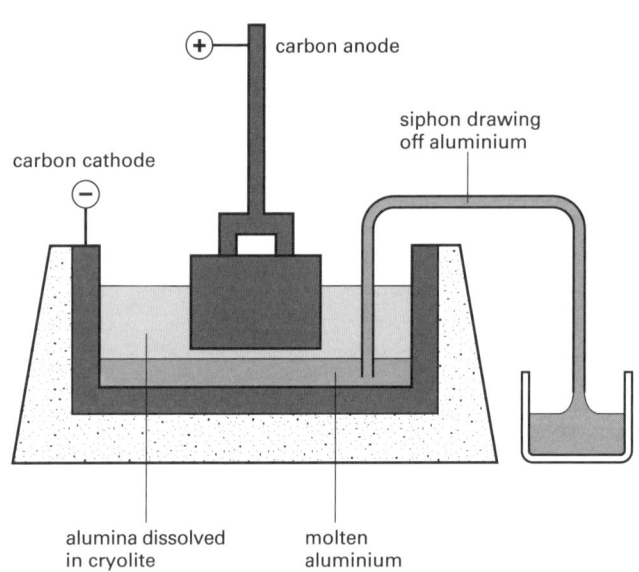

Fig. 14.31 Electrolysis is used to separate aluminium from alumina (aluminium oxide).

The problem now is to turn the alumina into a liquid. It cannot be dissolved in water, and it melts at a very high temperature. So how can it be electrolysed? This problem was solved by adding another mineral called **cryolite**. When alumina and cryolite are mixed together, they melt at a temperature of about 900°C. Figure 14.31 shows how the mixture is electrolysed using carbon electrodes.

The cathode is the carbon-lined tank in which the mixture is melted. Aluminium is released at the cathode. The anode is a carbon block. Oxygen is released here; the carbon burns vigorously with the oxygen, so that carbon dioxide is produced.

14.6 Metals from minerals

Because the anode burns away, it has to be replaced regularly. Fortunately, the cryolite is not used up in the process, so it can be reused over and over again.

The large-scale separation of aluminium takes place in a smelter. This is an industrial site that houses lots of electrolytic cells, and can purify thousands of tonnes of alumina each year (Fig. 14.32).

The bauxite industry is very important to Jamaica. It earns a lot of money each year and the government gains millions of dollars from taxes. The industry employs thousands of people. However, environmentalists are concerned about the effect that the industry has on the environment. Here are some of the problems they worry about:

Fig. 14.32 The electrolytic reduction cells can be seen inside this aluminium smelter.

Denudation and deforestation: To mine the bauxite, all the vegetation and topsoil is removed; to get to the mines many acres of forest are cleared. This opens up the way for other people who cut down the trees for lumber, making charcoal and getting sticks to support yam plants.

Contamination of underground water: When bauxite is processed, the waste is alkaline since it contains caustic soda. This often filters into the local underground water supply and can cause health problems.

Dust pollution: The raw bauxite and alumina form a fine dust that may affect the respiratory system of residents living close by. It also settles on their property.

The bauxite companies often put measures into place to reduce or prevent these problems.

Activity Bauxite mining and the environment

Find out

a What are the effects of deforestation and the removal of top soil?

b How can sodium affect your health?

c What respiratory diseases can be caused by dust? What can happen if the dust is continually settling on objects in your house?

d What are some of the things that bauxite companies do to reduce or prevent these problems?

Role play

After you have done your research your teacher will put you in groups to act out this scenario:

a group of environmentalists are demanding that the government shut down a bauxite company in a rural area.

Each group will be one of the following: environmentalists, residents of the area, a member of the government, the manager of the bauxite company.

What will your group say? Prepare your arguments. Remember to base it on scientific information, not on your own personal opinions. Select those who will represent the group. Take turns to state your case.

What you should know

- Most metals are extracted from mineral ores.
- Metal oxides are heated with carbon (e.g. coal) to release their oxygen in the form of carbon dioxide. This is called smelting.
- Sulphides and other types of ores are first converted to the oxide.
- Some metals, such as aluminium, have to be released from their oxides by electrolysis.
- Electrolysis requires an electrical circuit containing two electrodes: a cathode (negative terminal) and an anode (positive terminal).

Questions

1. Iron is extracted from its ore, iron oxide, by smelting. Copy and complete the word equation for this process.

   Iron oxide + _____ → iron + _____

2. Bauxite is a mixture of several different chemical compounds, including alumina, iron oxide and silica.

   a What metal can be extracted from bauxite?

   b Bauxite must be purified before this metal can be extracted. Which compound do we want to purify?

   c What process is used to extract the metal from this compound?

   d List four uses of the metal.

3. Research bauxite mining in your area. Where does it take place? How much ore is extracted? What is done to repair any environmental damage?

The Earth

14.7 Minerals for construction

▶ Objective

After studying this topic you should be able to:

- name some construction materials that are obtained from minerals, and describe their uses.

Fig. 14.33 Inside a brickworks.

Stone and bricks: Some buildings are made from stone, which is quarried and cut into shape. Where stone is not available, bricks are often made instead (Fig. 14.33). Bricks are made from clay, which is shaped into blocks and then heated in a furnace called a kiln. The clay particles are partly melted so that, when they cool down, they stick together. There are clay brick factories in Guyana.

Cement and concrete: These are building materials that are made from minerals. To make cement, clay and limestone are heated together to very high temperatures. This is done in a kiln that rotates so that the materials are mixed together well. Cement is manufactured in Barbados, Jamaica and Trinidad (Fig. 14.34).

To make concrete, sand and gravel (known as aggregate) are added to cement. When the cement or concrete is about to be used, water is added and mixed in. A chemical reaction occurs, and when the material dries out, it is solid. Cement is used to hold bricks together; concrete is much harder and can be used for building houses, bridges and roadways.

Fig. 14.34 A cement mill in Barbados.

Pottery: You probably know that clay is also used for making pottery, including domestic items such as plates, cups and toilets. This is because clay can be shaped before it is fired in a kiln. After firing, it is hard and rigid, but it is also porous. To prevent water penetrating it, it must be

14.7 The Earth

glazed with a thin coating of glass. It can also be painted before being glazed and fired.

Glass: Glass is another important material that is made from minerals. It is useful for bottles and windows, of course, but also for many other applications; important examples include spectacle lenses and the optical fibres that are used nowadays instead of metal wires to carry telephone messages and cable television signals. Glass is made by heating together sand, limestone and soda (Fig. 14.35). Pure sand (silica) and pure limestone (calcium carbonate) are valuable raw materials.

? Finding out

Useful stuff

Each Caribbean country has some minerals that can be dug up and used. Find out about these. Look in encyclopedias and geography books. Search the internet for 'mining companies'. Make a table listing the important minerals that are mined in each country.

Fig. 14.35 Flat glass is made in a continuous ribbon.

➔ Activity Building detective!

Look out for a major building project in your locality. It might be a new block of housing, a hotel, or a new roadway or bridge. A lot of materials are needed for big buildings, and they must all come from somewhere. But where?

The main materials might be:
- brick
- stone
- concrete
- steel
- glass
- bitumen

The search

1 When you have chosen your building project, identify the main building materials. Then find out the name of the company responsible for the building. Contact the project engineer, or someone else in charge who can help you track down where the materials come from.

2 Find out the names of the companies supplying the main materials. Then find out if the materials are made in your country, or imported. Are there any quarries in your country? What do they produce? Is there a cement works, or a steel works?

Minerals for construction 14.7

3 Arrange a visit to a quarry. What type of rock is being quarried? Alternatively, visit a cement works, a brickworks or a similar manufacturing site. Where do their raw materials come from?

4 Explain the origins of bitumen. What is its link to your earlier studies of oil and distillation (Book 2, Topic 9)?

The findings
Draw a diagram to show the main construction materials, and what they are used for. Draw a map to show where the raw materials come from, where they are processed into building materials, and how they get to the construction site.

What you should know

- Minerals provide us with many useful materials.
- Clay is used to make bricks and pottery.
- Cement is made from clay and limestone.
- Sand and gravel are added to cement to make concrete.
- Glass is made from silica (sand) and other raw materials.

Questions

1 The following are all stages in making an earthenware teapot but they have been jumbled up. Put them in the right order.

  a glazing;
  b painting;
  c mining the clay;
  d firing in a kiln;
  e shaping the pot on a potter's wheel.

2 Suppose you are an engineer, and are given the following five materials:

  iron, glass, concrete, brick and aluminium.

  Say which material(s) you will use to make each of the following, and why you will use them:

  a an aeroplane wing;
  b a highway;
  c a road bridge;
  d a house;
  e a sports stadium.

3 Adopt a mineral and research its origins, uses, value and history. Who first used it? What is the most unusual use of it?

Light and sound

15.1 What is light?

> ### Objectives
>
> After studying this topic you should be able to:
>
> - understand the difference between luminous and non-luminous sources of light
> - explain why light travels in straight lines
> - explain what happens when light hits an object
> - understand how mirrors form images
> - explain refraction of light
> - know how lenses bend beams of light.

Most of what we know about the world around us comes from our sight. The eye is our most sensitive and precious **sense organ**. It responds to light from our surroundings and without light we cannot see.

Fig. 15.1 A laser produces a very intense beam of light. This infrared laser is being used to cut a steel plate.

Imagine being in a totally enclosed room without windows or any other source of light. You would not be able to see your hand in front of your face! So it is the light that enters our eyes that enables us to see things. But what is light? We now know that it is a form of energy that travels through space. We also know that light travels very quickly. When you switch the light on in a room there seems to be no delay at all between pushing the switch and the light reaching your eye. Light travels through space at a speed of 300 million metres per second. In fact, the physicist Albert Einstein proposed the idea that nothing can travel faster than light (Fig. 15.1).

Sources of light

The most obvious source of light on Earth is the Sun, which gives out light because it is an extremely hot ball of gas. Other artificial sources exist. A candle flame, for example, also gives out light because of hot gas in the flame. An electric light bulb is another source of light. This gives out light from a very hot wire inside the bulb. Sources like the Sun, candles, electric light bulbs, etc. are called **luminous sources** – they *produce* light.

Most objects are not luminous. They do not produce light but we can see them because light from another source bounces off them into our eyes.

15.1 What is light?

Fig. 15.2 The Moon is not luminous; the stars are luminous sources.

We say that the light is reflected by the object. Sources of this type are non-luminous. Most of the things that we see in the world are non-luminous and we only see them because there is an external luminous source.

Examples of luminous and non-luminous sources are seen in the sky. The stars are luminous (they are in fact other suns very far away). The Moon, on the other hand, is not luminous. Even though it may seem to give out 'moonlight' this light is sunlight that is reflected from the Moon (Fig. 15.2). At different times of the month different parts of the Moon's surface are lit up by the Sun.

How does light travel?

We see things because light travels from the object to our eyes just as we hear things because sound travels to our ears. But there is a very important difference. If a person is in another room and calls to you, you can still hear him, even if you cannot see him. Why is it that we can hear round corners but we cannot see round corners?

Did you know?

In 1962 American scientists produced a laser beam so powerful that it could be reflected off the Moon. It produced a spot of light on the Moon's surface about four miles in diameter.

Activity Light travels in straight lines

You will need
- a flashlight
- three pieces of card (one should be dark)
- books or laboratory stands to prop up the cards

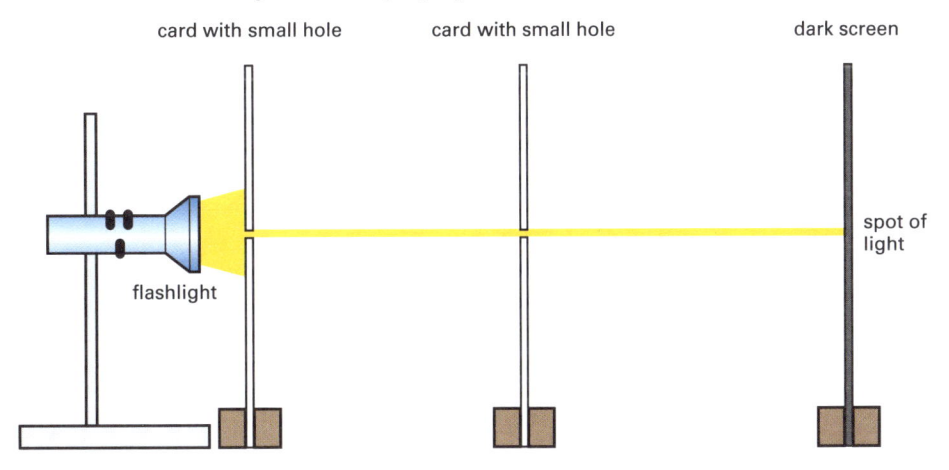

Fig. 15.3

15.1 Light and sound

Method

1 Make small holes in two of the cards and arrange them as shown in Figure 15.3. You should see a spot of light on the dark card (it is easier to see if you do this in dim light).
2 Now move the middle card up and down or from side to side. The spot of light should move.

Discuss

Think of the positions of the two holes and the spot. What can you say about how moving the holes affects the spot?

....

The experiment with the cards shows that the two holes and the spot of light are always in a straight line. Light always travels in straight lines (unless it is diverted in some way). It is usual to think of light as lines, called rays, with arrows showing the direction of travel away from the source. A number of rays of light make up a **beam** of light. Now look at Figure 15.4. Usually a beam of light spreads out as it moves away from the source. This is called a **divergent beam**. A beam that has the same thickness is a **parallel beam**. It is possible to make a beam of light become narrower as it travels. This is called a **convergent beam**.

A parallel beam of light   A divergent beam of light   A convergent beam of light

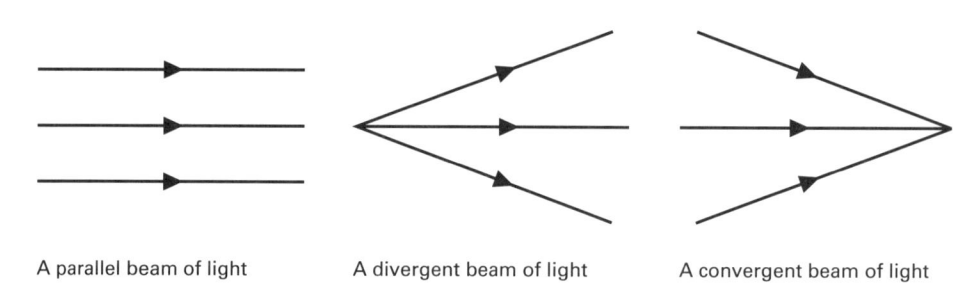

Fig. 15.4 Different types of light beam.

➔ Activity To see a beam of light

You will need
- a flashlight
- a large cardboard box
- plastic wrap (cling film)

Method

1 Look at Figure 15.5. Make a hole in one end of the box and another hole in the side.
2 Place plastic wrap over the top of the box.
3 Arrange the flashlight so that it is shining through the end of the box.

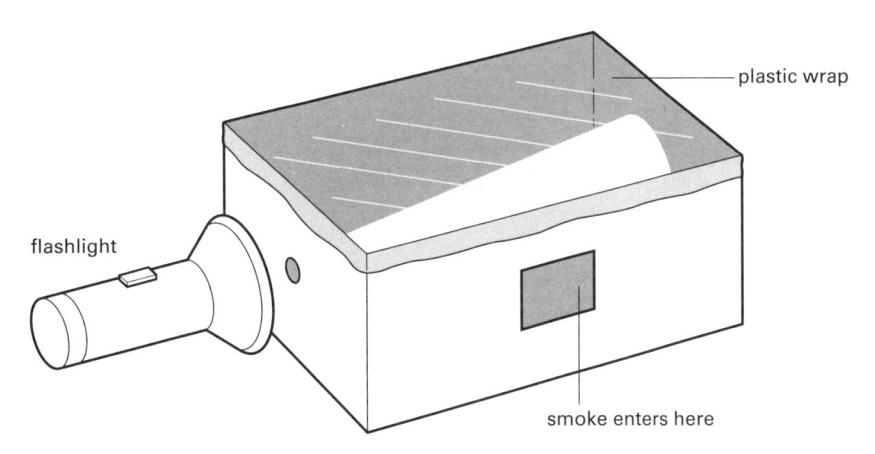

Fig. 15.5 A smoke box lets you see a beam of light.

⚠️ **Danger!**

Care needed!

4. Now fill the box with smoke. The simplest way of doing this is to screw up a length of paper, light one end, and blow it out quickly. Take care not to burn your fingers or anything else!
5. While it is still smoking, hold the paper in the hole in the side of the box. If you look down through the plastic wrap, and the smoke is not too dense, you should see the beam of the flashlight.

Discuss
1. Why can you see the light in the flashlight beam if smoke is present?
2. What happens as the smoke clears?

The activity with the smoke box is rather messy and there are other ways to see a beam of light. In a cinema it is often possible to see the projector beam, especially if the air is dusty. Also, in bright sunlight, you can often see a beam of sunlight in a room, coming through a chink in the curtains or blinds. You can see the beam because of small particles of dust or smoke in the air. These reflect some of the light sideways into your eye.

What happens when light falls on an object?

Different objects behave towards light in different ways, depending on what they are made of (Fig. 15.6). A sheet of glass or clear plastic, for example, lets most of the light through without being affected. This is why you can see through a window. Materials that can let light through in this way are said to be **transparent**.

Some materials let some of the light through but things on the other side cannot be seen clearly. Examples are greaseproof paper, cloudy plastic, and frosted glass. Materials like these are described as **translucent**. In translucent materials some of the light is absorbed inside the object. Also some of the light is scattered in different directions inside the object. This scattering is called **diffusion**. Coverings for fluorescent light tubes are called diffusers and are good examples of translucent objects.

15.1 Light and sound

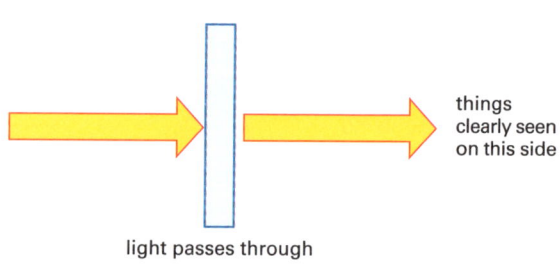

A transparent object — light passes through — things clearly seen on this side

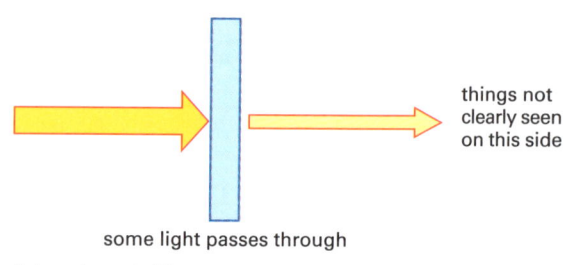

A translucent object — some light passes through — things not clearly seen on this side

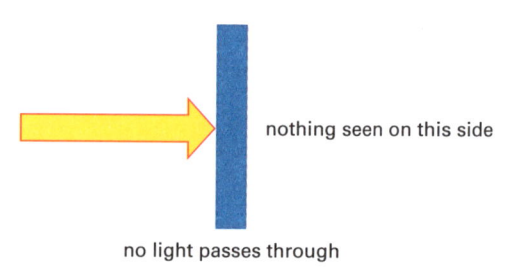

An opaque object — no light passes through — nothing seen on this side

Fig. 15.6 Different objects behave towards light in different ways.

Other things do not let light through at all. A piece of cardboard or a brick wall, for example, stop the light completely. These things are described as **opaque**. In the case of opaque objects two things happen to the light. Some is absorbed within the object and some is reflected (bounces off the surface). A mirror is an example of an object in which most of the light is reflected. A piece of black cardboard is one in which a large amount of light is absorbed. In this case some light is also reflected (this is what allows us to see the piece of cardboard).

Shadows

We are all familiar with shadows formed when light falling on a surface is blocked by an opaque object. The shadow is the dark area where no light reaches the surface.

➔ Activity Investigating shadows

You will need
- a lamp with a large frosted bulb
- an opaque object, such as a ball
- a light-coloured screen
- piece of cardboard with a small hole in it

Method

1. Look at Figure 15.7. Arrange the lamp and screen about 50 cm apart and place the card close to the lamp. Light from the hole falls on the screen.
2. Now hold the opaque object between the card and the screen.

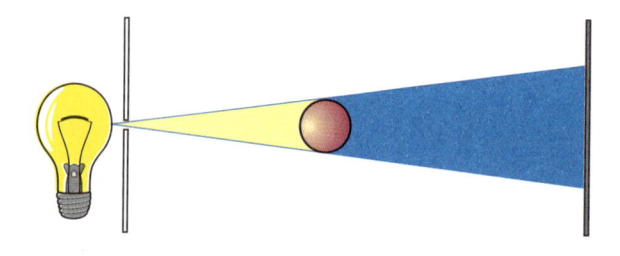

A shadow formed using a small light source. In this case we get total shadow

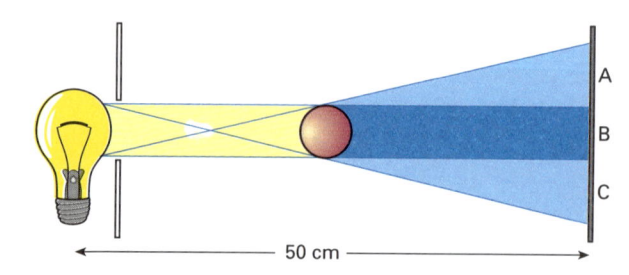

A shadow formed using a large light source. The region B is in total shadow. Region A and C are in partial shadow

Fig. 15.7 Shadows can change in various ways.

3 Move the object closer to the light and further away. Observe what happens to the size of the shadow.

4 Remove the card and observe what the shadow now looks like.

Discuss
How does the size of the shadow change as you move the object? What happens to the shadow when you remove the card?

When the card with the hole is close to the light bulb the source of light is very small, so that rays of light are coming from a small point. This means that the shadow has a sharp outline on the screen. As the position of the ball changes, the size of the shadow also changes. If the object is close to the lamp, it blocks out more light and the shadow is large. As the object moves further away, less light is blocked and the shadow becomes smaller.

When the card with the hole is removed from in front of the bulb you will see that the shadow has two parts: a dark centre part and a less dark outer part. This happens because the source of light is now large. Some parts of the screen are in full shadow and some are in partial shadow. The inner dark full shadow is called the **umbra**; the outer less-dark partial shadow is the **penumbra**.

You will notice that your own shadow in the Sun does not have a penumbra. Why is this when the Sun is so large? It is because the Sun is so far away that the light reaching Earth appears to come from a single point in the sky.

One of the most spectacular examples of a shadow is an eclipse of the Moon. This happens when the Earth moves between the Moon and the Sun. During the eclipse the Earth's shadow moves across the face of the Moon. An eclipse of the Sun is more spectacular but much less common. In this case the Moon moves between the Earth and the Sun, and the Moon's shadow is thrown onto the Earth (Book 1, Topic 8.2).

➔ Activity Making a pinhole camera

You will need
- a light-proof box (e.g. a shoe box)
- a piece of black paper
- a piece of translucent paper (e.g. tracing or greaseproof paper) to serve as a screen
- a pin
- rubber bands
- candle

15.1 Light and sound

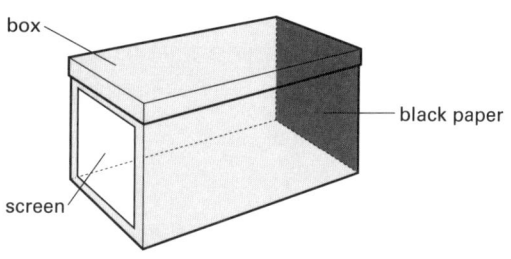

1 Set up the box as shown in the diagram

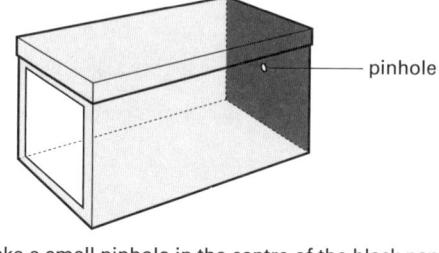

2 Make a small pinhole in the centre of the black paper

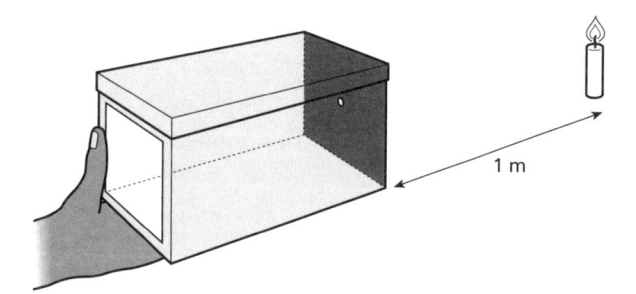

3 Hold the camera at arm's length, pointing it to a bright object such as a lighted candle

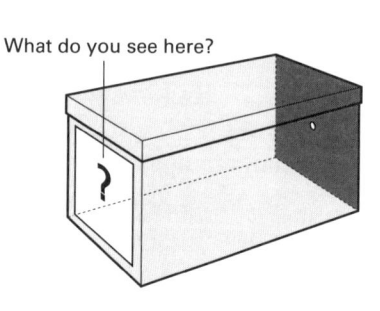

4 Look carefully at the translucent screen and describe in detail the image formed. Is the image on the screen bright? Is it clear? Is it erect or upside-down (inverted)?

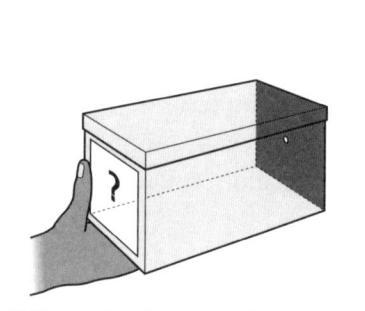

5 Try moving the camera closer to the object. How does the image change? How would the image change if a longer box were used?

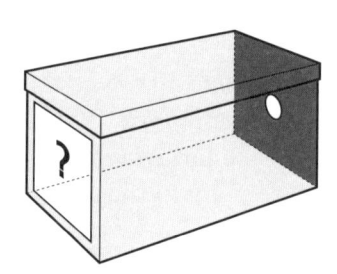

6 Make one large hole in the black paper. Comment on the image formed, if any

Fig. 15.8 Making and using a pinhole camera.

Method

1. Set up the box as shown in Figure 15.8.
2. Make a small pinhole in the centre of the piece of black paper.
3. Hold the camera at arm's length, pointing it to a bright object such as a lighted candle.
4. Look carefully at the translucent screen. Describe in detail the image formed. Is the image on the screen bright? Is it clear? Is it the correct way up (erect) or upside-down (inverted)?
5. Move the camera closer to the object. How does the image change? How would the image change if a longer box were used?
6. Make a large hole in the black paper. What happens to the image? Is it still there?

The pinhole camera works because light travels in straight lines. You should find that a clear picture is obtained only if:

(a) the pinhole is small, and
(b) the object is a bright one.

Note also that the image formed on the screen of a pinhole camera is always upside-down (inverted). This happens because a ray of light from the top of the object reaches the bottom of the screen and a ray of light from the bottom of the object reaches the top of the screen. This means that the image is inverted. A bright object forms a bright image and a dim object forms a dim image. If the pinhole is too large the image is blurred. In order to give a clear image the pinhole must be small.

Reflection of light

Diffuse reflection

Regular reflection

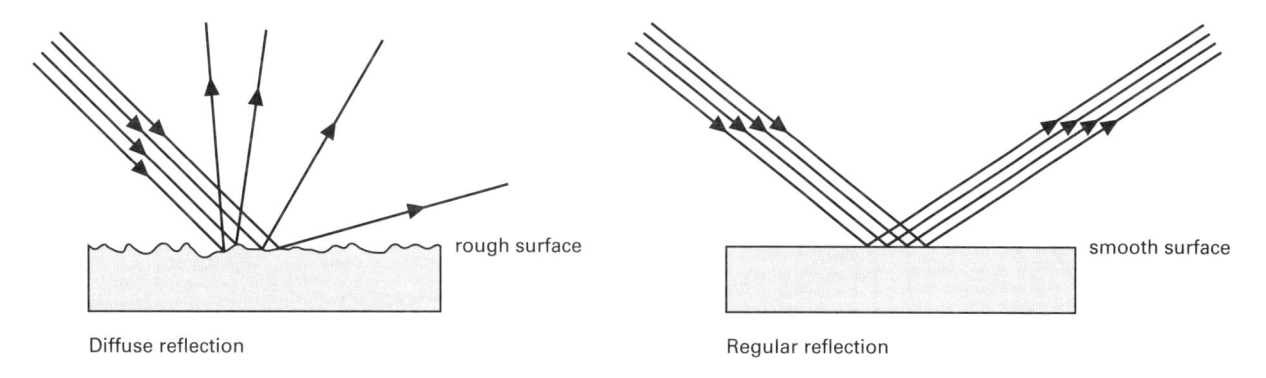

Fig. 15.9 Different surfaces reflect light in different ways.

We learnt earlier that non-luminous sources of light reflect light into our eyes. Reflection takes place when light bounces off objects (Fig. 15.9). If the surface of the object is rough the light bounces off in many directions. This is called **diffuse reflection**. If the surface of the object is very smooth, as in a piece of polished metal, the reflection is in a definite direction. This is called **regular reflection**. Metals are good reflectors of light. A glass mirror is a sheet of glass coated with silver to reflect the light. To be a reflector, an object does not have to be opaque. Transparent objects can also reflect light if they have a smooth surface. Just think of the number of times you have admired your reflection in a shop window!

In regular reflection we see an **image** formed in the mirror. If the mirror is flat it is called a **plane mirror**. Images in plane mirrors look to be the same size as the object. There are certain rules obeyed in regular reflection (Fig. 15.10). A ray of light hitting the mirror is an **incident ray**. The ray bouncing off the mirror is the **reflected ray**. If a line is drawn at right angles to the mirror then the angle the incident ray makes with this line is the **angle of incidence**. The angle the reflected ray makes is the **angle of reflection**. It is one of the laws of reflection that these two angles

15.1 Light and sound

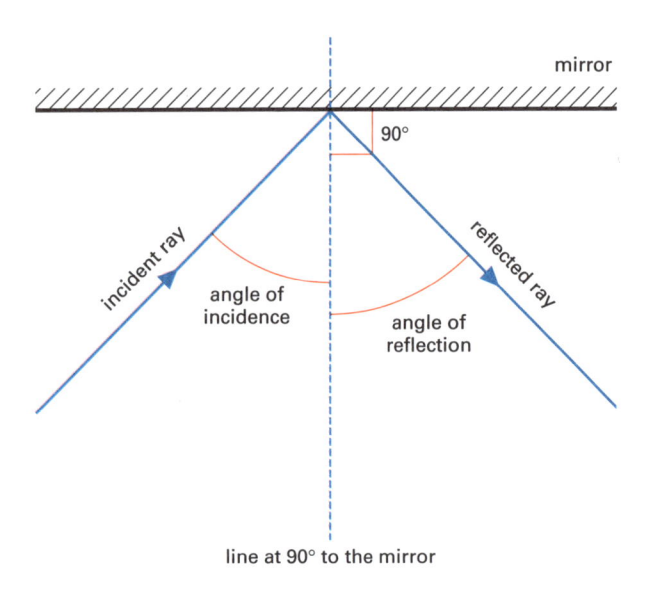

Fig. 15.10 Light reflected from a mirror.

are equal. In other words, the light bounces off the mirror in the same way that a cricket ball bounces off a pitch if the ball bounces regularly (without spin or roughness in the pitch). Cricket balls, of course, do not behave perfectly, but light does!

What is a mirror image?

When you look in a mirror you see an image of yourself. You are the object and your reflection is the image. Stand in front of a large mirror and look at your image. Now take a few steps backwards. You will notice that your image steps back too. The image in a plane mirror is as far behind the mirror as the object is in front of it. Images have another property. Raise your left hand. You will notice that your image raises its right hand. In fact, when we see ourselves in a mirror, we do not see ourselves as we really are. The image is reversed from left to right, so that a left hand looks like a right hand and vice versa (Fig. 15.11). This is known as lateral inversion. To get a good impression of lateral inversion try holding a newspaper up in front of a mirror. Can you read the headline in the mirror? You may have noticed that ambulances often have the word AMBULANCE in mirror writing on the front of the bonnet. This is so that a driver in front sees the correct form of the word in the rear-view mirror.

Fig. 15.11 A mirror image is reversed from left to right.

→ Activity Inversion in a mirror

You will need
- a large mirror
- a piece of paper and a pencil

Method
Make four dots on the paper at the corners of a square. Now stand in front of the mirror. Look at the paper in the mirror and try to join the dots on the paper together without looking directly at the paper.

15.1 What is light?

Discuss
1. Did you think it would be easy?
2. Why is it so difficult?

Activity Making a periscope

You will need
- a long box, such as a large, clean, empty milk carton
- a pair of scissors
- two pocket-sized mirrors
- sticky tape

Danger!
Take care using scissors!

Method
1. Look at Figure 15.12. Cut a hole in one side of the carton, near the top, and another in the opposite side, the same distance from the bottom.
2. Tape the mirrors inside the box, facing each other as shown in the diagram. Make sure that they are parallel to each other and slant across the box at 45°.
3. Tape the top of the carton shut.
4. Place the periscope at a suitable location (a corner, for example), holding it so that only one hole is sticking out.
5. By looking through the other hole you will be able to see around the corner.

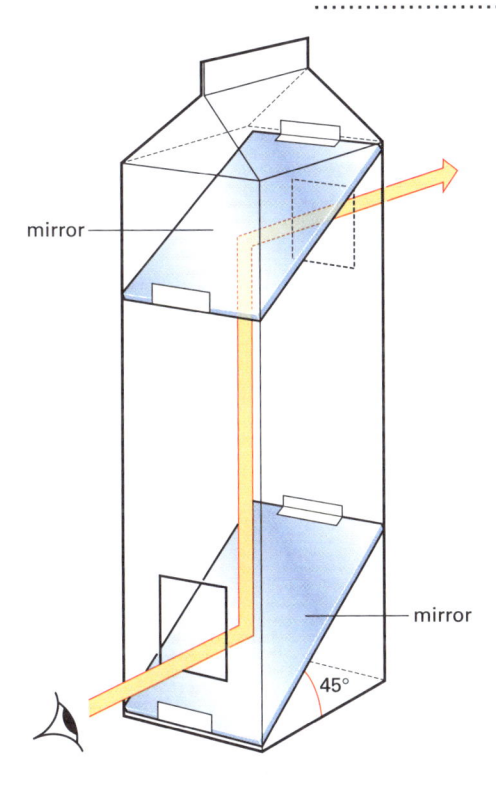

Fig. 15.12 A home-made periscope.

Discuss
What happens to the light inside the periscope? Draw a diagram of the path of light. Use the periscope to look at some printing or writing. Does the image have lateral inversion?

We know that light always bounces off a mirror at the same angle at which it hits it. If light hits the mirror at 45°, it is reflected at 45°. This means that the light is turned through an angle of 45° + 45° = 90°. This enables the light to turn corners. This is the principle on which the periscope works. You should also see that the image does not have lateral inversion (i.e. writing is readable in a periscope). This is because there are two reflections. One mirror inverts the image and the other inverts it again to produce the correct view.

15.1 Light and sound

Did you know?

Concave mirrors are used in large astronomical telescopes for looking at objects deep in space. Today's largest astronomical telescopes use mirrors 8 metres in diameter. Astronomers are planning to build a telescope with a 100 metre mirror. This will allow them to see planets orbiting distant stars.

Curved mirrors

So far we have learned about plane mirrors, which have a flat surface. Curved mirrors can also be used. An example of a curved reflecting surface is a large polished metal spoon. You have probably looked at the reflection of your face in a spoon at some time. One thing that you will notice is that the image is distorted. Also that the appearance of your face is different in the bowl of the spoon, which is curved inwards (concave), to the image in the back of the spoon, which is curved outwards (convex). Curved mirrors are used for a number of things in which it is necessary to change the size of the image. Convex mirrors are used at road junctions or in stores to give a wide view of the scene (Fig. 15.13). Rear-view mirrors in cars (Fig. 15.14) are also convex. Concave mirrors can be used to expand a narrow view, magnifying it. Some make-up mirrors are concave. Concave mirrors are also used to produce a parallel beam of light. If you unscrew the front of a flashlight you will see that the bulb is held at the centre of a curved reflector. Similar reflectors are used in high-power spotlights and searchlights.

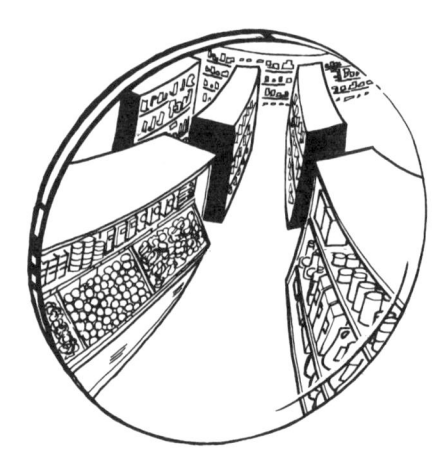

Fig. 15.13 A convex mirror allows a security guard to monitor a whole shop.

Fig. 15.14 A rear-view mirror in a car is convex, allowing the driver to see behind and to the sides.

Refraction of light

At the beginning of this section we said that light travels in straight lines. However, there are circumstances in which light can be made to change its direction. The case of reflection at a mirror is one of these. Light can also change direction when it passes from one substance to another. For example, if light travelling through water comes out through the surface into the air at an angle, it changes direction. This change of direction only happens for light passing from one substance to another at an angle. It happens because the speed of light in water is different from the speed of light in air. This effect of refraction has some consequences (Fig. 15.15).

What is light? 15.1

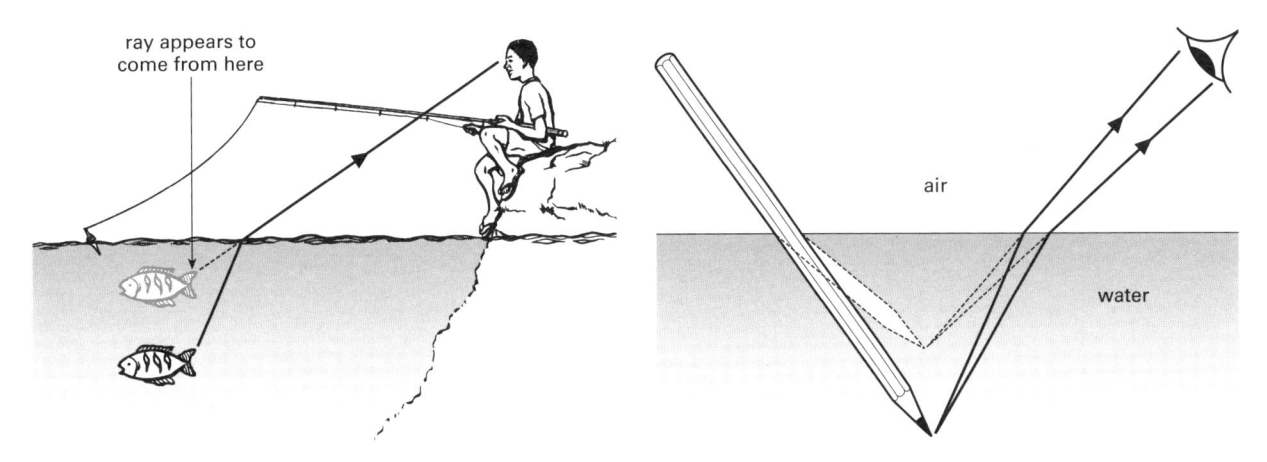

Fig. 15.15 Refraction makes the fish appear closer to the float than it actually is.

Fig. 15.16 Refraction makes the pencil appear bent.

For example, the water in a pool or swimming bath may look more shallow than it actually is. A stick held partly under water can appear to be bent (Fig. 15.16).

Lenses

Refraction also occurs between glass and air, and is made use of in lenses for bending rays of light. There are two main types of lens (Fig. 15.17). **Convex lenses** bulge outwards – they are thicker at their centre than at their edges. **Concave lenses** are the opposite. They are thinner at their centre than at their edges.

The two kinds of lens have different effects on a beam of light passing through them. Convex lenses cause the beam to converge (become narrower). Concave lenses cause the beam to diverge (spread out).

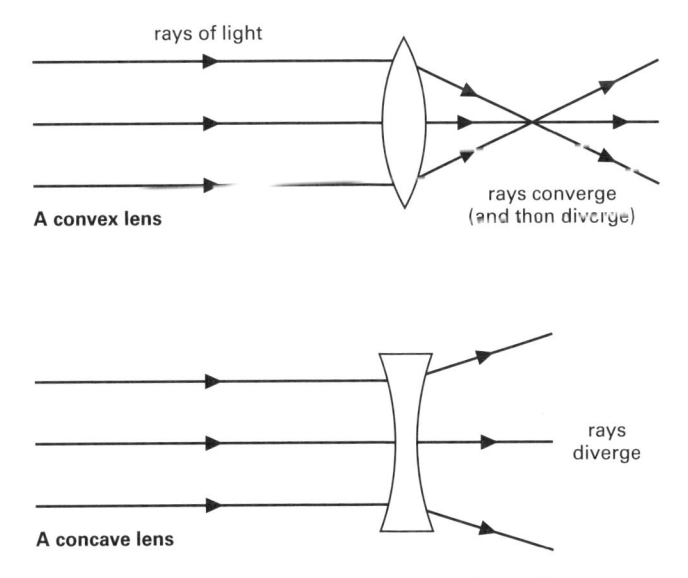

Fig. 15.17 The two main types of lens refract light differently.

15.1 Light and sound

➔ Activity Investigating refraction

You will need
- a lamp
- a thick slab of clear glass
- a concave lens
- two pieces of cardboard
- a convex lens

Method

1. Look at Figure 15.18. Make a small hole (about 0.5 cm diameter) in one of the pieces of card and support the card close to the lamp. Place the other piece of card about 50 cm away, so that you see a spot of light on the card.

2. Hold the slab of glass between the pieces of card so that it is in the path of the light beam. Observe the spot. Tilt the slab at an angle.

3. Now hold the convex lens in the light beam and observe the spot. Move the lens closer to the light and then further away.

4. Now hold the concave lens in the beam and observe the spot. Move the lens backwards and forwards.

Discuss

1. What happens when you place the glass in the beam?
2. How does this change when you tilt the glass slab at an angle?
3. How does the convex lens affect the beam?
4. How does the concave lens affect the beam?

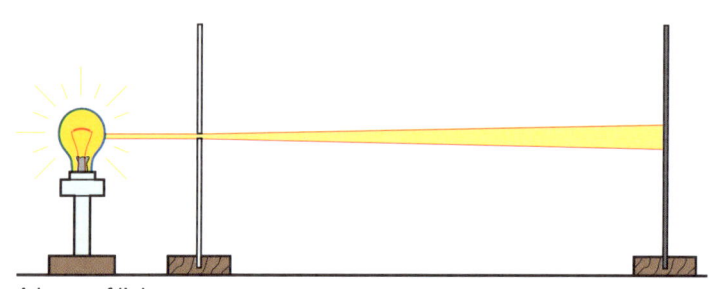

A beam of light

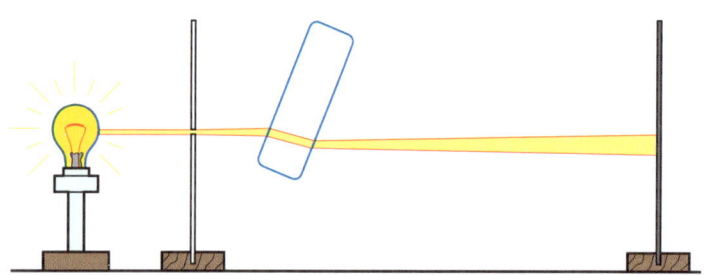

A slab of glass displaces the beam

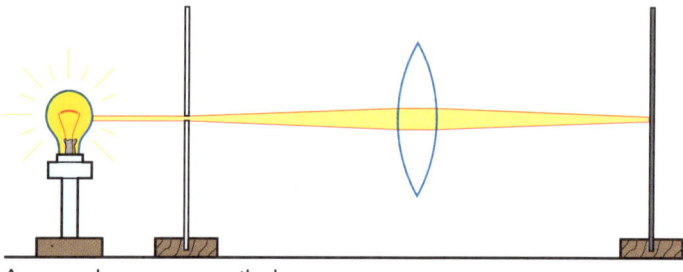

A convex lens converges the beam

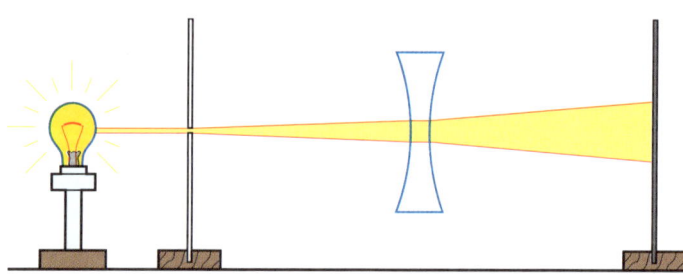

A concave lens diverges the beam

Fig. 15.18

The effects of transparent objects on a beam of light are explained by refraction. You should find that the slab of glass displaces the spot. The convex lens converges the light and the concave lens diverges it.

Activity Using a burning glass

You will need
- convex lenses
- a piece of paper
- a sunny day

Method
1. Look at Figure 15.19. Hold the lens so that a spot of light appears on the paper.
2. Move the lens away from and towards the paper, and observe the size of the spot. If you can form a really small spot on the paper, the paper gets hot and may start to smoulder and burst into flames.

Discuss
What happens to the size of the spot as you move the lens?

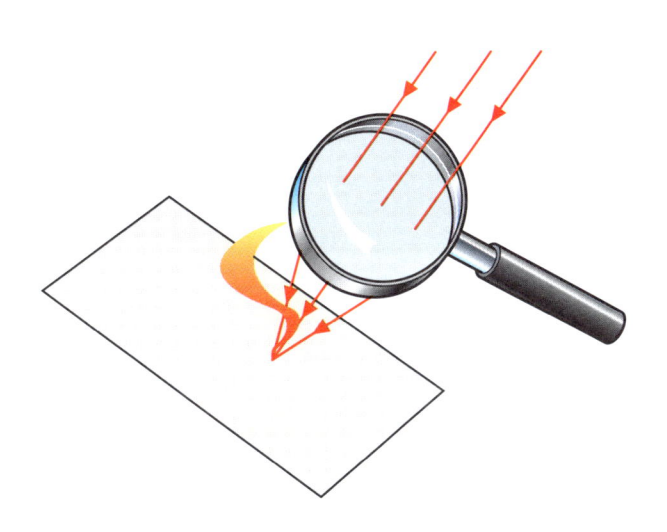

Fig. 15.19 A burning glass can set paper alight.

> **Did you know?**
>
> You should never look directly at the Sun. It will damage your eyes.

You should see that the spot of light becomes smaller as you move the lens towards the paper. The spot gets to its smallest diameter and then gets larger as the lens moves even closer. The reason this happens is that the convex lens makes the rays of light converge to a point, which is called the **focus**. After passing through this point the rays diverge again. At the focus the sunlight is so intense that it heats up the paper (remember that light is a form of energy). Fires have been caused by accident as a result of sunlight being focused through broken pieces of curved glass.

Activity Forming an image with a lens

You will need
- a piece of cardboard
- a number of convex lenses
- a measuring tape

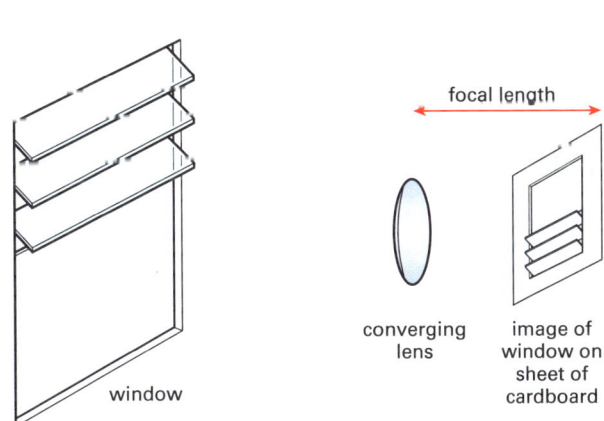

Fig. 15.20 Forming an image.

Method

1. Look at Fig. 15.20. Stand in a room with a window, holding the cardboard in one hand and a lens in the other. Move the lens backwards and forwards to try to produce a picture of the window on the cardboard.
2. When the image of the window is sharp, get your friend to measure the distance from the lens to the image. This distance is known as the focal length of the lens.
3. Repeat the experiment with different convex lenses.

Discuss

1. Is the image the right way up or upside down? Is it changed left to right?
2. Lenses of different thicknesses have different focal lengths. Do thick lenses have a shorter or longer focal length than thin lenses?

Optical instruments

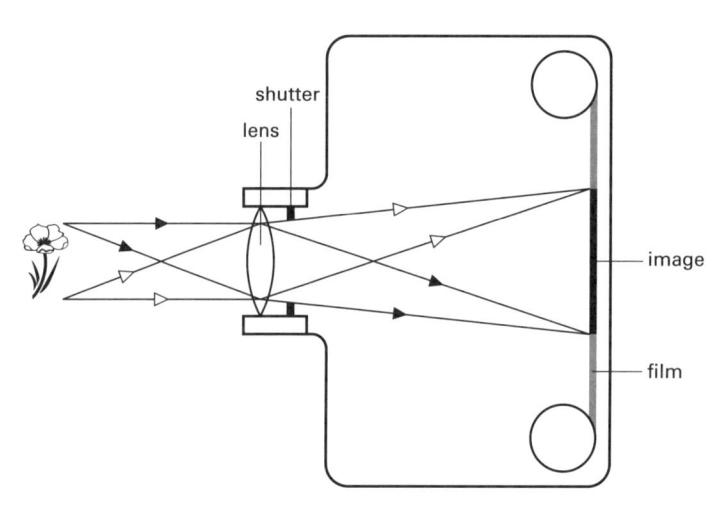

Fig. 15.21 The basic parts of an optical camera.

Lenses (and mirrors) are used in a number of different devices. The simplest optical instrument is probably the magnifying glass, which is simply a convex lens used to make things appear larger. A microscope uses a number of lenses to give much greater magnification. Binoculars and telescopes also use two or more lenses to make distant objects appear closer. Another common optical instrument is the camera (Fig. 15.21). In a camera a convex lens focuses an image onto the back of the camera, where a piece of light-sensitive film is held. The shutter opens for a very short time to allow light in and the image forms on the film.

15.1 What is light?

What you should know

- Light is a form of energy that travels in straight lines.
- Luminous sources produce light; non-luminous sources reflect light.
- Transparent objects let light through clearly; translucent objects let some light through; opaque objects block light.
- Images in mirrors are formed by reflection.
- Refraction is the bending of light when it moves from one substance to another.
- Convex lenses are wider at their centre than at their edges; concave lenses are narrower at their centre than at their edges.
- Convex lenses converge light beams; concave lenses diverge light beams.

Questions

1. Which of the following is a non-luminous source of light?
   - a The Moon
   - b A candle
   - c A television screen
   - d A fluorescent tube

2. Fill in the missing words.

   A beam of light that spreads out d_____.

   A beam that becomes narrower c_____.

   A beam that always has the same width is a p_____ beam.

3. Make a list of all the ways you can think of in which mirrors are useful.

4. Fill in the blanks:

   A c_____ lens causes light to converge; a c_____ lens causes light to diverge.

5. Research stage lighting. How do theatres use different lamps – floods, spots, proscenium arch and footlights – to light up a stage show?

6. Research the use of specialized lights and lasers in pop concerts and festivals. How are acts lit? How are special effects achieved?

Light and sound

15.2 The eye

▶ Objectives

After studying this topic you should be able to:
- describe the structure of the human eye
- understand how the eye forms an image
- describe how the eye focuses near and far objects
- understand why two eyes are better than one
- understand persistence of vision.

The eye is probably the most important way in which humans obtain information about their environment. One way of thinking of the eye is that it acts like a camera. Light entering the eye is focused by a lens (and the cornea) to form an image on a light-sensitive area at the back of the eye (just as in a camera the lens focuses an image on light-sensitive film).

Parts of the eye

A section through the human eye is shown in Figure 15.22. At the front of the eye there is a curved clear layer called the **cornea**. Behind this is a clear **lens**, which is held in place by muscles known as **ciliary muscles**. Light passes through the cornea and then an opening in front of it, known as the **pupil**. This is the black circle in the centre of your eye. The size of the pupil adjusts automatically to regulate the amount of light entering the eye. In bright light the pupil is small; in dim light it is wide to let in more light. The back of the eye has a layer of light-sensitive cells. This layer is the **retina**. When the light falls on the retina the cells produce small electrical impulses, which are carried to the brain by the **optic nerve**. The brain makes sense of these signals. Both front and back parts of the eye are filled with clear liquids.

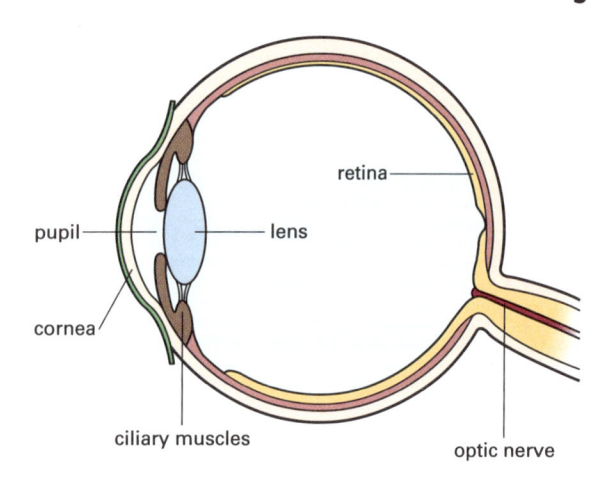

Fig. 15.22 This is a cross-section of the human eye.

How the eye focuses

The eye forms an image by refraction. The light that comes into the eye is refracted in two main stages.
- the curved cornea converges the light;
- the lens converges the rays of light to produce the final image.

The eye 15.2

The eye can focus on objects that are close and on objects that are far away. This is done in two ways: the lens changes its shape (Fig. 15.23), and it also moves slightly backwards or forwards inside the eye. The shape of the lens is changed by the ciliary muscles. When we look at near objects the muscles relax, allowing the lens to bulge so that it is thicker and more able to converge light. When we look at objects that are far away the muscles contract and pull on the lens so that it becomes thinner. This process in which the eye adjusts to focus different objects is called **accommodation**. It happens very quickly and without thinking. Just look at how quickly a cricketer or tennis player has to react to follow the flight of a very fast ball. You can try focusing by holding your finger up in front of you between you and the blackboard. Look at your finger and then switch to looking at the blackboard. You cannot focus on both at the same time.

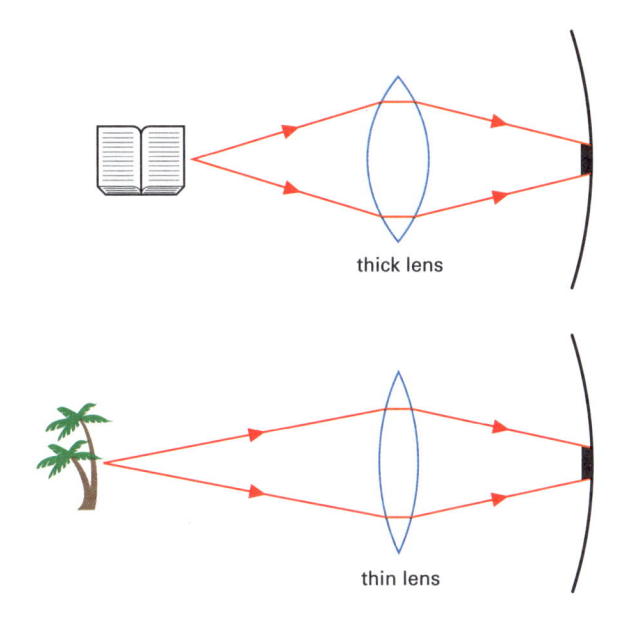

Fig. 15.23 A thick lens focuses near objects onto the retina while a thin lens focuses far objects onto the retina.

Spectacles

Spectacles contain lenses that help people to see better (i.e. they correct defects of vision). One common thing that happens is that as people get older it becomes more difficult for the muscles in the eye to make the lens change shape. Many older people find it difficult to focus on objects that are close. In particular, they find it difficult to read small print. In this case they use reading glasses, which contain convex lenses to help focus the image on the retina. Many people, including young people, have problems with their sight and can be helped by spectacles (or contact lenses). Often, one eye is different from the other and the lenses in the spectacles are also different.

➲ Activity Spectacles or contact lenses?

Find out as much as you can about contact lenses and the latest technologies in spectacles. You can visit an optical shop, and talk to the sales people. You can also read about them or talk to people who wear them.

Imagine that you are working and earning a good salary. You discover you are short sighted. Which would you buy – glasses or contact lenses? Why? In making your choice, what did you have to give up in order to get the properties you really wanted? Is the one you chose better in every way?

15.2 Light and sound

Two eyes are better than one

Have you ever wondered why we have two eyes and not one? Two eyes help us to judge depth and distances better than one eye. The activity below is a simple experiment to demonstrate this.

→ Activity One eye or two?

You will need
- a plastic cup
- a coin

Method
1. Look at Figure 15.24. Place the cup on a table or bench and move to stand about 3 metres away from it.
2. Cover one eye. Ask your partner to hold the coin at arm's length above the cup, but slightly in front of it.
3. Watching only the cup and the coin, tell your partner in which direction to move his or her arm so that the coin will fall into the cup when he or she releases it.
4. Tell your partner to drop the coin.
5. Repeat the activity with both eyes open.

Discuss
Why is it more difficult to get the coin in the cup with only one eye open than with two?

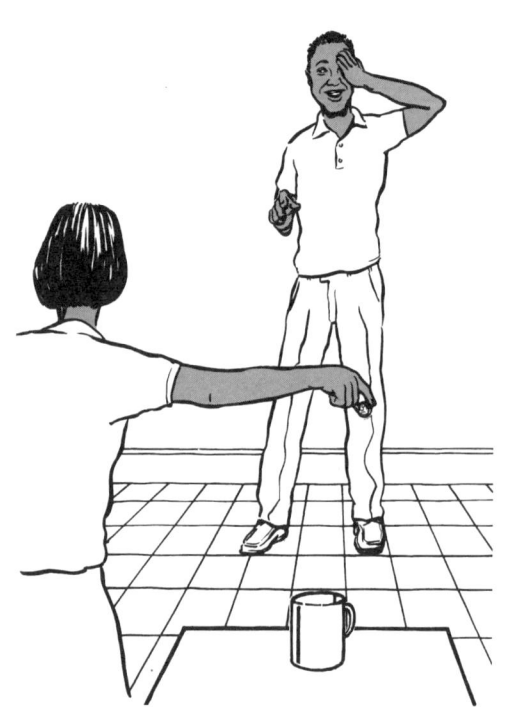

Fig. 15.24 Which is better: one eye or two?

Our eyes are set apart so they see things from different angles. The image the brain gets from each eye is slightly different. By comparing these images our brain forms three-dimensional pictures which help us to judge distances. We are able to judge distances because we have **binocular vision**. Binocular comes from Latin ('bi' = two, and 'oculus' = eye). When we have one eye covered we no longer have binocular vision and we see in only two dimensions. Photographs, for example, are two-dimensional, which is why it is so difficult to judge distances in photographs.

15.2 The eye

Fig. 15.25 When shown in rapid sequence, these frames will show movement.

Persistence of vision

If you look at a lamp while it is switched off it is common to 'see' the lamp for a short time afterwards. This is called an afterimage. It happens because the cells in the retina are still affected for a short time after the actual image has gone.

The cinema depends on this 'persistence of vision'. In a film a sequence of 'still' pictures (called 'frames') are focused on the screen one after the other very quickly (Fig. 15.25). In fact 24 pictures appear on the screen every second. Each picture shows the object in a slightly different position from the one before it. For instance, it might be a series of pictures of a man walking. One picture shows him with his leg a little way off the ground; in the next one it is just a bit higher up; in the next one it is a little higher up still, and so on. If the pictures are flashed on the screen quickly, one after the other, the image of one picture does not fade from the retina before the next one appears. It looks as though the man is walking along.

➲ Activity A bird in a cage

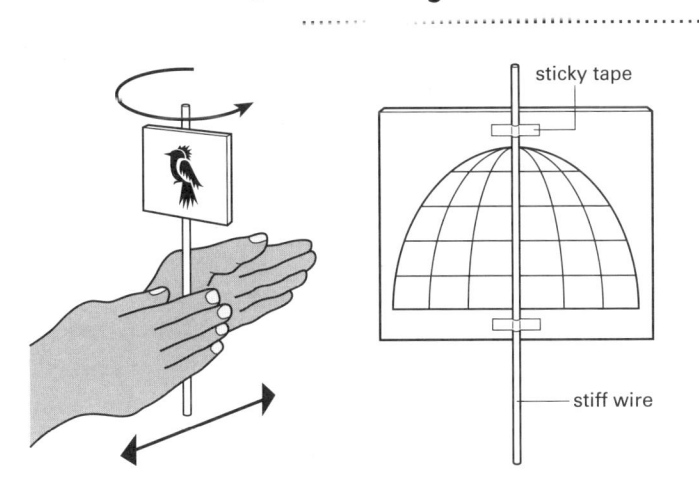

You will need
- thin cardboard or stiff drawing paper about 15 cm square
- a piece of stiff wire
- sticky tape

Method
1 Look at Figure 15.26.

Fig. 15.26

15.2 Light and sound

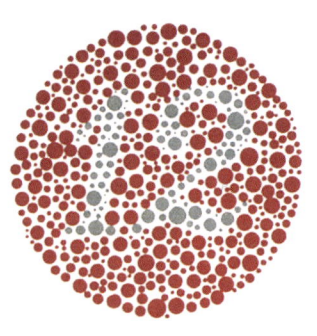

2. On one side of the card draw a bird, and on the other side draw a fairly large cage (big enough for the bird to fit into) with not too many bars.
3. Take a fairly stiff piece of wire and stick this down the centre of one side of the paper, fixing it in place with sticky tape.
4. Now spin the wire very quickly between your hands.

Discuss

How does the bird appear to get into the cage?

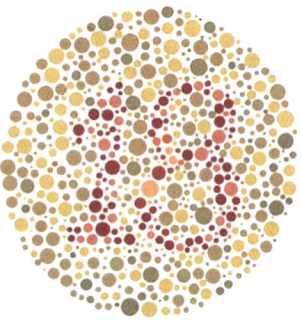

Seeing colours

Do we all see the same colours? If I say that something is yellow does that mean the same thing to you as it does to me? We cannot really answer this question, but we do know that some people cannot distinguish certain colours as well as others can.

Persons who cannot see colours properly are said to be colour blind. They are not really blind, of course, and it is nothing to worry about. Millions of people are colour blind but they do not know it, because it makes no difference to them. About 1 in 12 males have difficulty in distinguishing between red and green. It is remarkable that hardly any girls are colour blind, but they can pass on colour blindness to their boy children. Doctors use special charts with coloured dots to test for colour blindness (Fig. 15.27). (Colour blindness is sometimes called colour vision deficiency.)

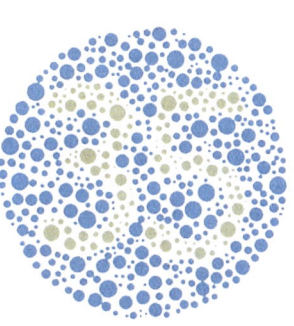

Fig. 15.27 You should be able to see numbers in the patterns. If you can't, you may be colour blind.

Did you know?

Cats, dogs and many other animals do not see colours at all. They see everything in shades of grey, as in a black-and-white film. Some people also suffer from this very rare form of colour blindness.

Extending sight

In science we often help our senses by using instruments. For example, the eye cannot see things which are very small. If we look at trench or pond water we might not be able to see anything in it, although it may contain very many tiny objects or animals. By using a microscope we are able to see these tiny things (Fig. 15.28). The microscope

Fig. 15.28 Using a microscope to see small objects.

The eye 15.2

has extended the range of our vision by helping us to see very small things. In a similar way, if you are standing on the beach and looking out to sea, you might think you can see a small boat. To be quite sure you could use a pair of binoculars (Fig. 15.29) or a telescope, which help you to see things which are a long way off. By using telescopes, astronomers have been able to see some stars which are so far away that they cannot be seen at all with the unaided eye.

Fig. 15.29 Binoculars are used to look at distant objects.

What you should know

- The eye is a sense organ that detects light and forms images of objects.
- The eye focuses by changing the shape of the lens.
- Two eyes give us the ability to judge distance.
- Moving pictures rely on persistence of vision.

Questions

1. In bright light does the pupil of the eye:
   a become wider;
   b become smaller;
   c stay the same size?

2. When looking at a far-away object is the lens in the eye thick or thin?

3. Fill in the blanks:
   The image in the eye is formed by refraction by the c_____ and the l___.

4. How do short-sighted and long-sighted people differ? How can this be corrected? Why can short-sightedness improve with age?

5. What is a cataract? What part of the eye does it affect? How can it be corrected?

15.3 Sound

▶ Objectives

After studying this topic you should be able to:
- explain how sound is produced
- explain how sound travels
- understand the difference between pitch and loudness
- understand how echoes occur.

What is sound?

Just as the eye detects light, the ear is a sense organ that detects sound. Sound is quite different from light in the way that it is produced and the way it travels. The production of sound involves movement. Think of a string of a guitar. When it is plucked it moves backwards and forwards very quickly. This sort of regular to-and-fro movement is called vibration (or oscillation). As the string vibrates it causes waves of pressure in the air. As the string moves forwards it causes an increase in pressure and as it moves back the pressure decreases (and increases in the opposite direction). The sound is carried by these travelling pressure waves in the air. One point about sound is that it needs air (or some other medium) to carry it. There is no sound in outer space because there are not enough molecules to transmit it. Sound is a form of energy.

All sounds are caused by some sort of vibration in the object. When you hit a drum you cause it to vibrate. In a wind instrument the vibrations are set up in a column of air by blowing. We tune musical instruments using a tuning fork (Fig. 15.30).

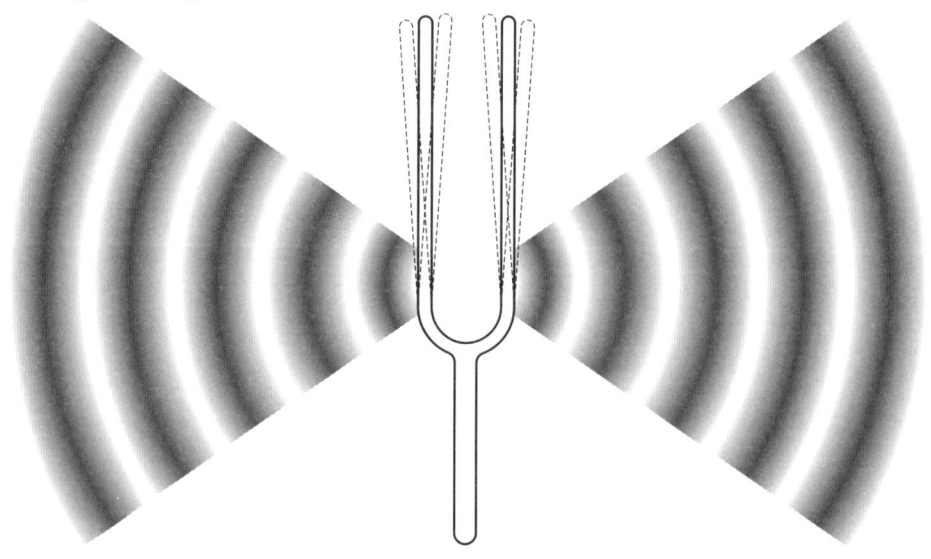

Fig. 15.30 As the tuning fork vibrates, it pushes out waves of pressure in the air.

Sound 15.3

→ Activity Which materials carry sound?

You will need
- a hard table top
- a bucket of water
- a comb
- classmates or friends

Method

1 Look at Figure 15.31. Have a classmate stand at one end of the table while you stand at the other.

2 Get your classmate to tap on the table. Listen to the sound reaching you through the air.

3 Now put your ear to the table while your classmate continues tapping.

4 Put your ear to the side of the bucket of water. Get your classmate to put the comb under the water and pass his finger over its teeth.

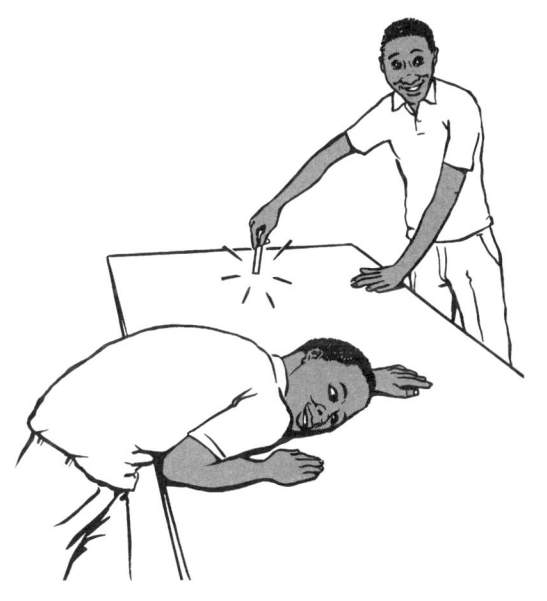

Fig. 15.31

Discuss

1 Does the sound travel through the table top?
2 Does it travel faster than through air?
3 Does it travel through water?
4 Which material transmits sound best? Why do you think this is?

Most sounds come to us as vibration in the air, but sounds also travel through substances such as wood, metal and water. They also travel to us through the bones of our head and through our teeth. Sound travels better through hard materials than through soft materials. Soft materials are often used as sound insulators.

The pitch or frequency of sounds

You are probably able to recognize that some sounds have a higher **pitch** than others. The keys at the right hand end of a piano keyboard give higher pitched sounds than the keys on the left. The pitch is determined by how quickly the object vibrates. If it moves backwards and forwards many times per second then the vibration has a high **frequency** and the sound produced also has high frequency (or pitch). If the object vibrates fewer

15.3 Light and sound

times per second it has a lower frequency and the sound also has lower pitch. If an object vibrates 440 times per second the frequency is 440 hertz (440 Hz). The unit 'hertz' (equal to 1 vibration per second) is named after the German physicist Heinrich Hertz (1857–94).

→ Activity Ruler sounds

You will need
- a metal ruler
- a desk or hard table

Method

1. Look at Figure 15.32. Hold the ruler on the desk with one hand, with part of the ruler protruding over the edge. Now flip the end of the ruler so that it vibrates up and down.
2. Note the pitch of the sound produced.
3. Now change the position of the ruler so that a greater length protrudes. Try again.
4. Investigate how the pitch of the sound depends on the length of the vibrating ruler.
5. Now try varying how far you bend the ruler initially. How does this affect the loudness?

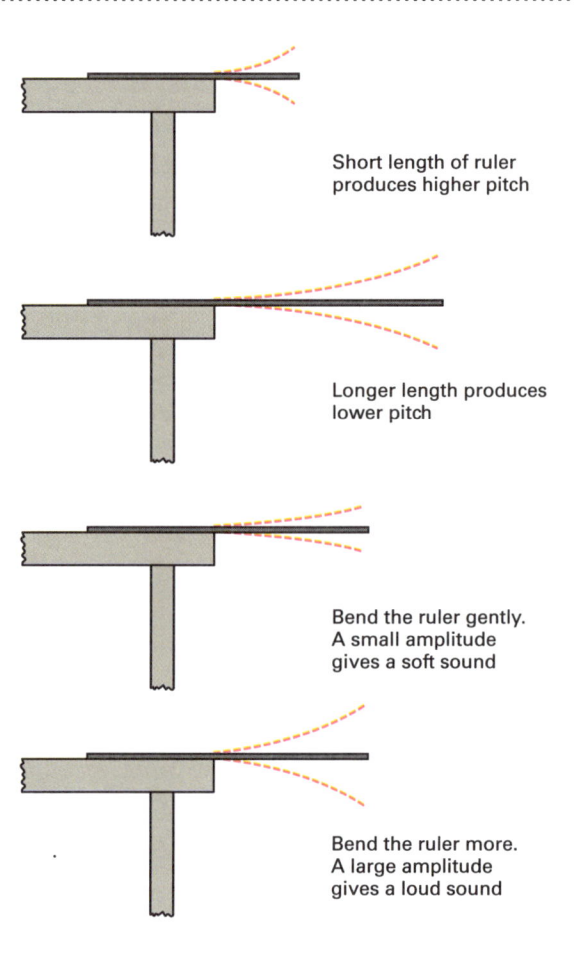

Short length of ruler produces higher pitch

Longer length produces lower pitch

Bend the ruler gently. A small amplitude gives a soft sound

Bend the ruler more. A large amplitude gives a loud sound

Fig. 15.32 Use a ruler to investigate the characteristics of sound.

You should find that a long part of the ruler vibrates more slowly than a short part, and gives a lower pitched sound. This is a fairly general rule in producing sound. Larger objects with slow vibrations produce sounds with lower pitch. We learn more about loudness on page 62.

Activity Making music with rubber bands

You will need
- an empty can with two nails driven into the top edge (Fig. 15.33)
- rubber bands of different lengths

Method
1. Stretch a rubber band between the two nails.
2. Twang the rubber band.
3. Wrap the rubber band around the nails a few times and twang it again.
4. Repeat using a thicker rubber band.
5. Repeat using a thinner rubber band.

Fig. 15.33 Music with rubber bands.

Discuss
1. What effect does stretching the band tighter have?
2. Does it matter whether the band is thick or thin?
3. What general rules can you make about the shape of a rubber band and the sound produced?
4. You would hear a different sound if the nails were in a block of wood. Why?

Many musical instruments make sounds by using vibrating strings. The science of these was first investigated by the Ancient Greeks. If you play with rubber bands or strings, you should find that the note produced depends on two things:

- The length – the shorter the string, the higher the pitch of the sound.
- The tension – the tighter the string or elastic band is stretched, the higher the pitch of the sound.

You can see how this is used in a guitar. You tune the guitar by tightening or loosening the strings. You change the note by placing your finger on the strings between the frets. This changes the length of the vibrating strings. In the activity above, the can acted to make the sound louder (i.e. amplify the sound). The hollow body of a guitar has the same effect.

Wind instruments

In a wind instrument such as a flute, saxophone or trumpet, there is obviously no string. What is vibrating? Different instruments have different forms but in all wind instruments the note is produced by the column of air inside it, which you set vibrating by blowing into it.

15.3 Light and sound

➲ Activity A wind instrument

You will need
- a test-tube rack with eight clean test tubes
- water

Method
1. Look at Figure 15.34. Place a small amount of water in the test tube at one end of the rack.
2. Place a little more water in the second test tube, a little more in the third one, and so on.
3. Blow across the mouths of the test tubes.
4. Adjust the amounts of water in the tubes to make a musical scale.

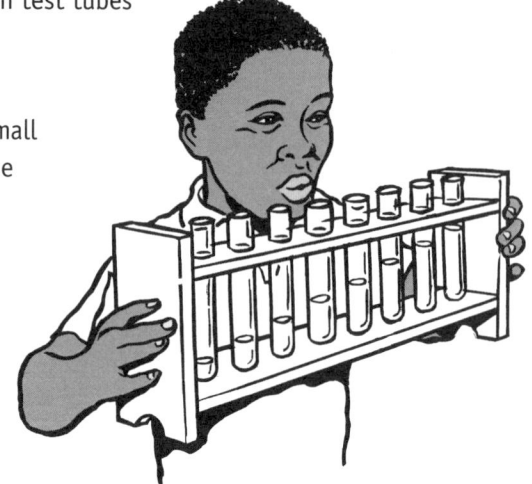

Fig. 15.34 You can 'play' the test tubes.

Discuss
1. Which test tube gives the lowest note?
2. Which test tube has the shortest column of air?
3. Which test tube has the longest column of air?
4. Which test tube gives the highest note?
5. Which is vibrating – the water or the column of air?
6. Write a general rule about making a range of sounds.

You can also do this experiment with glass or plastic bottles.

You should find that the longer columns of air (i.e. less water) produce lower notes than the shorter columns. Wind instruments produce sounds in a similar way. You may notice that the pipes of an organ in church are of different lengths. Which pipes give low notes – the short pipes or the long pipes? Ask the organist to help you investigate this.

Loudness

The pitch is one way in which sounds differ from each other, but there is a more obvious way – the loudness of the sound, which can be described as the intensity. The intensity depends on how far the vibrating object moves from its rest position; this is called the **amplitude**. The larger the amplitude, the louder the sound. You may have noticed in the activity with a vibrating ruler (page 60) that the loudness of the sound produced by the ruler depended on how far you initially bent the ruler. So loudness depends on amplitude. It also depends on how far away the source of sound is.

The loudness of sound is measured in units called **decibels** (dB). Some typical values of sound levels are given in Table 15.1. The decibel scale is logarithmic. This means, for example, that a 20 dB sound is much more than twice as loud as a 10 dB sound.

Table 15.1 Typical values for sound levels.

Type of sound	Measurement in dB
Heartbeat	10
Whisper	20
Ordinary conversation	40–60
Loud radio or TV	80–90
Aircraft engine	100–150

Very loud unwanted sound is called noise. If a person spends large amounts of time in noisy places (factories, discos, etc.) it is possible for their hearing to be damaged. Noise is also unpleasant for people and is regarded as a form of environmental pollution. In some countries there are laws forbidding too much noise in public places.

Another meaning of the term 'noise' is applied to the frequency of the sound rather than to its loudness. A musical note has a regular frequency (pitch). If the sound has a random jumble of frequencies, it is described as 'noise'. You can often hear hissing or crackling noise from a radio when the reception is poor.

Musical sounds

Often what makes sound musical depends on the listener. However, it is recognized that musical notes have a definite frequency and that a scale of notes is used. So the frequency of middle C is 256 Hz. The frequency of upper C is 512 Hz (i.e. twice the frequency of middle C). When the frequency of one note is twice that of another, we say that the notes are one **octave** apart.

Musical notes demonstrate one other property of sound. You have no difficulty telling the difference between the same note played on a guitar, on a piano and on a trumpet. The frequency is the same and the difference has nothing to do with loudness, but they obviously sound different. The reason that these notes sound different is that they are not a single frequency (e.g. 256 Hz). Mixed with this **fundamental frequency** are a number of fainter different frequencies (called **harmonics** or **overtones**). It is the particular mix of fundamental and overtones that gives a sound its unique **quality**.

Wave forms

We said earlier that sound travels through the air as a series of waves, in which the pressure of air increases and decreases. You can draw a graph of the changing pressure to represent different sounds. Some examples are shown in Figure 15.35.

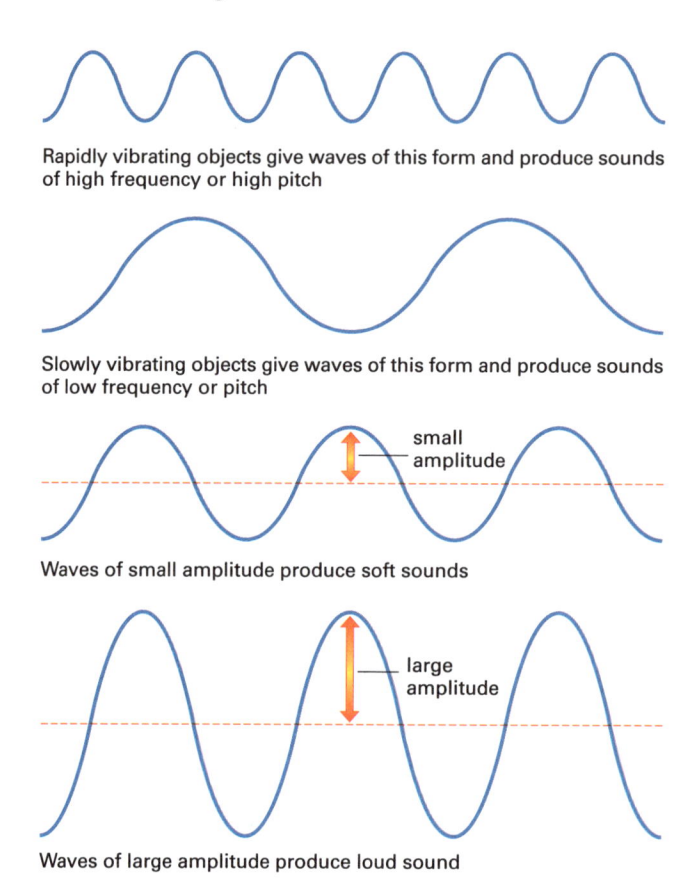

Rapidly vibrating objects give waves of this form and produce sounds of high frequency or high pitch

Slowly vibrating objects give waves of this form and produce sounds of low frequency or pitch

Waves of small amplitude produce soft sounds

Waves of large amplitude produce loud sound

Fig. 15.35 Wave forms.

Echoes

In Topic 15.1 we talked about how light can be reflected from a surface. Sound also can be reflected. You have probably been in a large empty building or in a cave or close to a cliff and shouted your name. You can hear the sound reflected back after a very short delay. The delay happens because it takes time for the sound to reach the barrier and travel back to the listener. One thing that we know from echoes is that sound travels much more slowly than light does. Echoes can be a nuisance. In a hall with wide hard plain walls, sound bounces off the walls and the **reverberation** may make it difficult to hear a speaker clearly or may ruin a musical performance. Concert halls have a special design to reduce this effect. Echoes may also be useful. For example, **echo sounding** is a method of measuring the depth of oceans by sending a short burst of sound downwards and measuring the time taken for it to travel to the sea

Sound 15.3

bed and return to the ship. If we know the speed of sound in water then we can find the depth of the sea.

Activity Echoes

Fig. 15.36 Investigating echoes.

You will need
- two long cardboard tubes
- a smooth wall or similar surface
- clamps to hold the tubes
- a watch or clock that ticks

Method
1. Your teacher will help you to set up the apparatus as shown in Figure 15.36.
2. Clamp one tube near the wall, placing the clock or watch at the end furthest from the wall.
3. Listen to the watch or clock through the second tube.

Discuss
Describe the sounds you hear, if any. Explain how you hear them.

The ticks from the watch or clock travel through the first tube, bounce off the wall and are reflected through the second tube into your ear. You are listening to echoes.

Ultrasound

Most young people can hear sounds between frequencies of 20 Hz and 20 000 Hz but as people get older they are less able to detect high frequencies. Animals such as cats and dogs can detect sounds that have a higher frequency than the highest frequency humans can hear. Bats can detect frequencies as high as 100 000 Hz. They use this for navigating in the dark by emitting high-pitched sounds and detecting the echoes from objects in their path. This is known as **echolocation** (Fig. 15.37).

Did you know?

Bats are not the only ones to use echolocation. In submarines a system called SONAR is used to detect objects underwater.

Fig. 15.37 A bat uses echolocation to find its food.

15.3 Light and sound

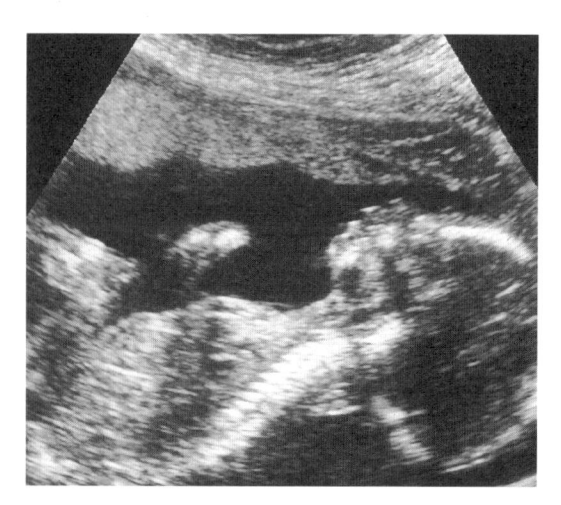

Fig. 15.38 This picture of a 20-week-old fetus developing in the womb was taken using ultrasound.

Electronic devices can be used to generate sounds with frequencies above 20 000 Hz. Such sounds are described as **ultrasonic** (i.e. above the range heard by humans) and the waves themselves are called **ultrasound**. Ultrasonic waves have a number of uses:

- for cleaning objects and materials: the material is placed in a liquid through which ultrasonic waves are passed; the vibrations shake off the dirt;
- to detect weaknesses (flaws) in metals and other materials;
- in medicine to look at the inside of the body (Fig. 15.38); ultrasound is safer than X-rays.

The human voice

When we are speaking or singing we produce sound. We also often have to raise or lower the pitch of our voice. How do we do this? You have already found out that vibrating strings produce sounds and that vibrating air columns also produce sounds. The human voice makes use of both these types of vibrations.

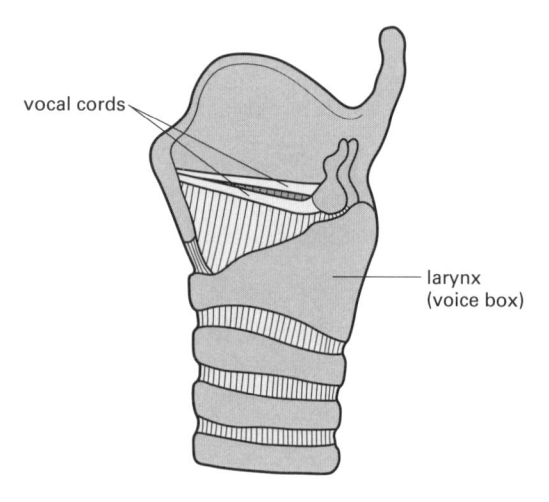

Fig. 15.39 Sounds are produced in the upper throat.

In the upper throat, under the chin, is a slightly bulging portion called the Adam's apple. Inside it is a box-like chamber called the voice box (or **larynx**) (Fig. 15.39). Two tough membranes, called **vocal cords**, are stretched across the voice box. There is an opening between the vocal cords. When we speak or sing, air is forced through the opening, causing the vocal cords to stretch and vibrate. Muscles in the voice box control the extent to which the vocal cords are stretched (i.e. tightened or loosened). If the opening is narrow, high-pitched sounds are produced. If the opening is wide, lower-pitched sounds are produced. Changes in the position of the lips and shape of the mouth also lead to changes in the sound produced. The lips, tongue and teeth affect the quality of the sound (Fig. 15.40).

Fig. 15.40 The sounds we make depend on how we form our lips and on the shape of our mouths.

Sound 15.3

Activity Estimating the range of the human voice

You will need
- a measuring tape
- three or four friends

Method
1. Look at Figure 15.41. Choose a convenient area in the school yard or playground.
2. Stand at a pre-determined spot.
3. Ask three or four friends to stand about 60 metres away from you.
4. Speak to them in a normal voice (no shouting). Can they hear you from this distance? Probably not.
5. Ask them to come forwards by about 10 metres.
6. Try speaking to them again in a normal voice. Can they hear you this time?
7. If not, ask them to come closer and repeat the above procedure until you can just be heard.
8. What happens if you cup your hands to your mouth?
9. What if they cup their hands around their ears?

Fig. 15.41 What is the range of your voice?

Record
Measure the distance between yourself and your friends when they can just hear your voice. That measured distance is the range of your voice under the conditions of the experiment.

15.3 Light and sound

By cupping your mouth you reduce the angle through which the sound spreads, and the volume is increased along the forward direction. The megaphone works on this principle. If you have access to a megaphone find out its range.

You could use a computer with a sound sensor for this activity. How does sound intensity change as you get closer to the sensor? Why is a standard sound – like that from a tape recorder – better than the sound of your voice for this activity?

What you should know

- Sound is a form of energy that travels in waves.
- The frequency of a sound is the number of vibrations per second.
- The loudness of a sound is its intensity.
- The frequency of a vibrating string depends on its tension and its length.
- Echoes are produced when sound reflects off objects.
- Ultrasound is sound with very high frequency.
- The human voice is formed by forcing air through the vocal cords in the larynx.
- The vocal cords stretch and vibrate depending on the type of sound we wish to make.

Questions

1. Fill in the blanks in the sentence below:

   The properties of a sound are its p____ (or f_____), its i_____ and its q_____.

2. Make a list of any unpleasant or loud noises that you have noticed in your local area or in your school.

3. How do popular bands make, record, change and even distort sound? Research electric guitars, amplifiers and distortion pedals.

4. Make a list of different musical instruments. For each one, write down what actually vibrates to make the sound. How are musical instruments classified? What are the differences between stringed, woodwind, brass and percussion instruments? How do they make and adapt sound?

Light and sound

15.4 The human ear

▶ Objectives

After studying this topic you should be able to:
- understand how the human ear works
- explain what deafness is.

The ear is the sense organ that detects sound. It is made up of three main parts: the outer ear, the middle ear, and the inner ear. The structure of the human ear is shown in Figure 15.42.

The outer ear: the outer ear consists essentially of the flap (or pinna) and the ear canal (tube). Sound waves are collected by the ear and funnelled through the ear canal to the ear drum. The ear drum is a thin membrane that is drawn right across the canal leading from the outer to the middle ear, a bit like the 'skin' of a drum.

The middle ear: the middle ear, which is filled with air, contains three tiny bones called the **hammer**, the **anvil** and the **stirrup** (Fig. 15.43). These bones get their names from their shapes. The three bones form a chain connecting the ear drum to the inner ear. Sound waves reaching the ear drum cause it to vibrate. These vibrations are then passed to each of the three bones in turn and then to the inner ear. The middle ear is an amplifying system. It gives the vibrations a greater force as they pass from the ear drum along the tiny bones to the liquid in the inner ear.

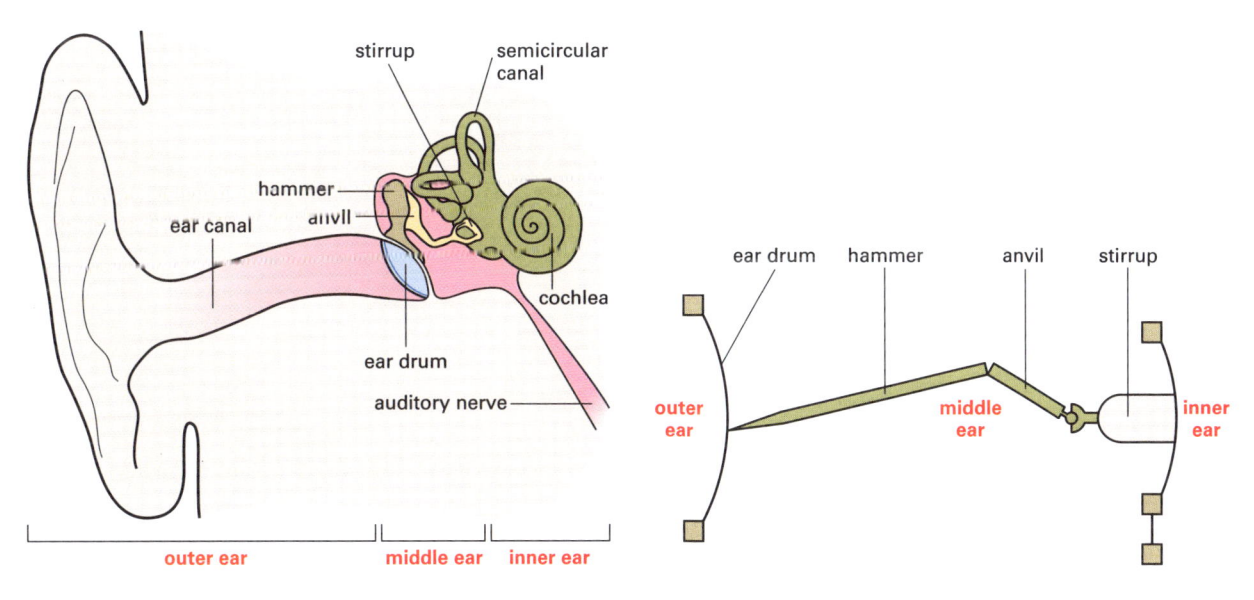

Fig. 15.42 The structure of the ear.

Fig. 15.43 The middle ear.

15.4 Light and sound

The inner ear: the inner ear contains a spiral section (cochlea) with sense cells which vibrate according to the pressure of the liquid reaching them. These sense cells send messages along the **auditory nerve** to the brain. The brain sorts and interprets these messages as different sounds.

The fact that we have two ears helps us to judge the direction of a source of sound.

The ear has another function besides detecting sound. It helps us maintain our balance. The inner ear contains liquid-filled sections called the **semicircular canals**. When you move your head the liquid in these canals also moves. Movement of this liquid causes 'hairs' at the base of each canal to send messages by nerves to the brain. The brain interprets these and helps us to keep our balance.

Deafness

Deafness or partial deafness may result from defects at birth, from disease, from damage to the hearing mechanism, or it might occur because of old age. The hearing of partially deaf people can be improved by the use of hearing aids. Early hearing aids were big and cumbersome. The ear trumpet acted as a funnel to concentrate the sound (Fig. 15.44). You can get a similar effect by cupping your hand to your ear. Nowadays hearing aids are so small that they can be fitted in a way that hardly shows (Fig. 15.45). Modern hearing aids consist of three main parts – a microphone, an **amplifier** and an earphone. The microphone picks up sounds. The amplifier makes the sounds louder and then feeds them to the earphone. When speaking to someone who is wearing a hearing aid it is not necessary to shout. Simply face the person and talk slowly and clearly.

> **Did you know?**
>
> The great German composer Ludwig van Beethoven (1770–1827) began to go deaf at the age of 30. Despite this he carried on composing. Before he died he said, 'I shall hear in Heaven'.

Fig. 15.44 Early hearing aids such as this ear trumpet were large and cumbersome.

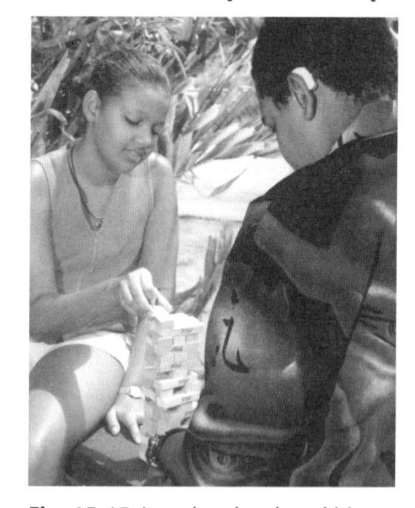

Fig. 15.45 A modern hearing aid is very small and discreet. It makes it much easier for someone who is deaf to hold a normal conversation.

15.4 The human ear

◯ What you should know

- The ear allows us to distinguish the different sounds around us.
- The ear helps us to maintain our balance.
- When we hear sounds our brain, making use of our memory, helps us decide what has made the sound and how we should respond.

◉ Questions

1. Fill in the blanks in the following sentences:

    The ear has three parts: the o_____ ear, the m_____ ear and the i_____ ear.

    The bones in the middle ear are called the h_____, the a____ and the s_____. Why do they have these names?

2. Why is a hearing aid better than an ear trumpet?

3. Animals such as bats that have very good hearing often have large ears. Name some other animals with big ears. (Elephants have big ears for another reason. Find out what it is.)

4. Research the use of ear defenders. Who wears them – and why? How should they be worn? Devise a poster to advise on when to wear ear defenders and the correct way to wear them.

5. Some musicians have caused permanent damage to their ears because of loud music. Research this problem and advise on ways of reducing it.

Systems in humans

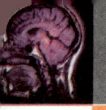

16.1 The human reproductive system, growth and development

▶ Objectives

After studying this topic you should be able to:

- explain the meaning of the term sexual reproduction
- describe the male and female reproductive systems
- explain how sexual intercourse takes place
- describe the development of the baby in the womb
- describe what happens during the birth of a baby
- describe parental care in humans and other animals
- explain the changes that occur during puberty.

What is sexual reproduction?

In Book 1, Topic 2.1, you learned that all living things produce new individual organisms or offspring. In this topic you are going to learn about sexual reproduction in humans.

Sexual reproduction involves special types of cells called **sex cells**. The male sex cells are called **sperms** and the female sex cells are called eggs or **ova** (singular: **ovum**). When a sperm joins up with an egg, the new cell will develop into a new human being. The new cell is called a **zygote**. The joining up of the sex cells is called **fertilization**. The sex cells are made in the sex organs.

The male sex organ is the testis (there are two **testes**) and the female sex organ is the ovary (there are two **ovaries**).

The female reproductive system

The female reproductive system (Fig. 16.1) is in the abdomen. One of the ovaries produces an egg every 28 days. The egg passes into a tube called the **oviduct** and then into the **womb** (**uterus**). The uterus has a thick muscular wall and

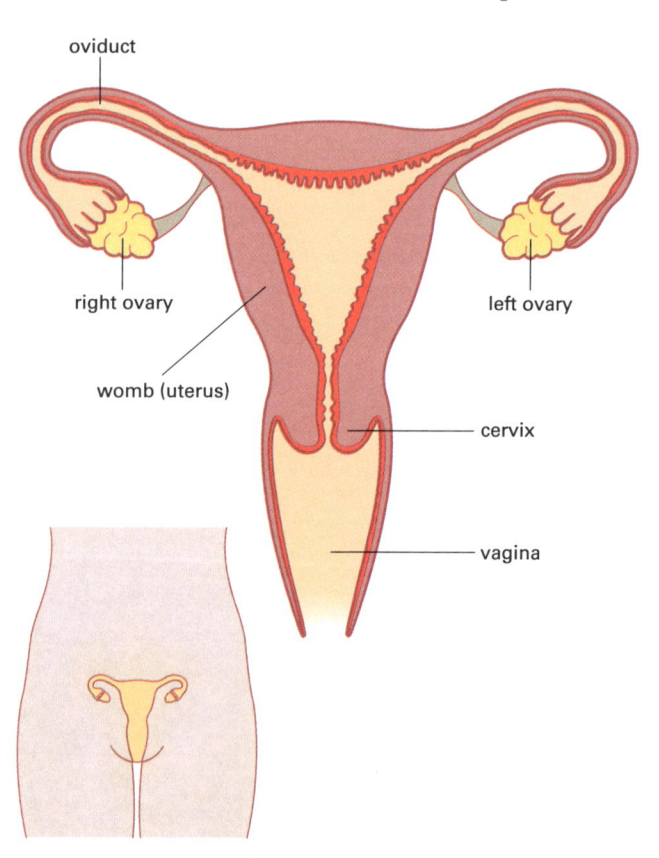

Fig. 16.1 Front view of the human female reproductive system.

The human reproductive system, growth and development 16.1

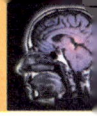

a good blood supply. This is where the egg will develop if it is fertilized. The womb narrows at the lower end to form the **cervix**. The cervix leads into the **vagina**, which opens to the outside.

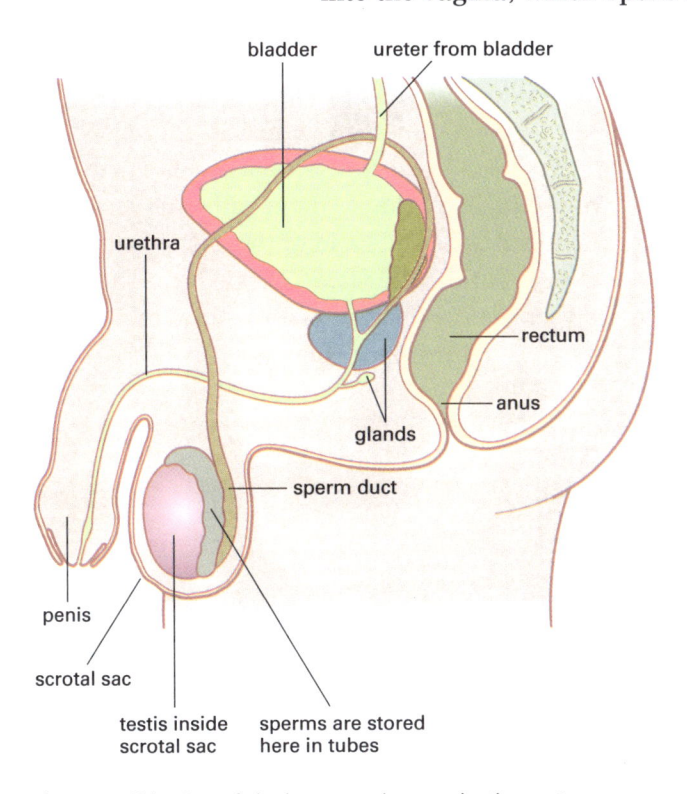

Fig. 16.2 Side view of the human male reproductive system.

The male reproductive system

The male reproductive system is shown in Figure 16.2. The testes (singular: **testis**) are outside the abdomen in a bag of skin called the scrotum. The testes make millions of sperm and the cooler conditions outside the abdomen are more favourable for sperm production. Sperm are made all the time. They are stored in a tube outside each testis. Each tube leads into a **sperm duct**. The sperm ducts lead into the **urethra** and then into the **penis**. There are two types of glands where the sperm ducts lead into the urethra. These glands add a fluid to the sperm, forming semen.

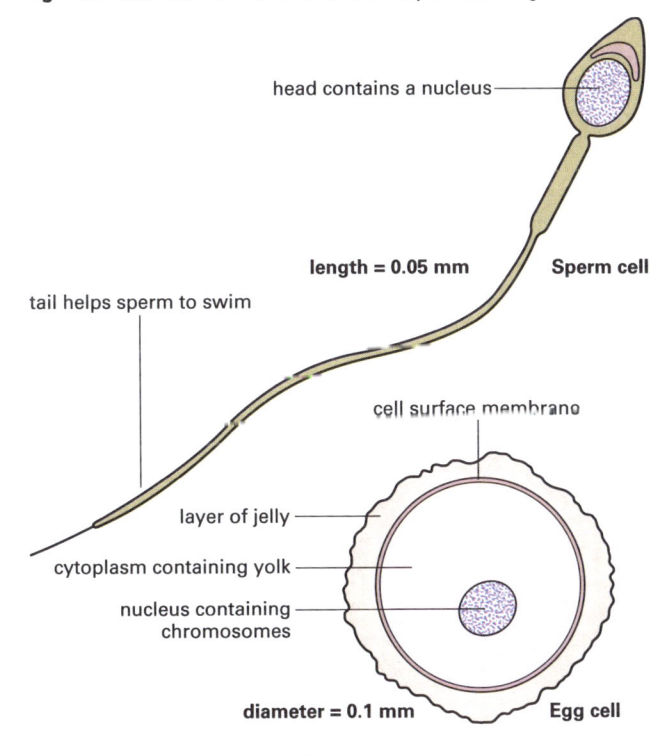

What do the sperms and eggs look like?

An egg is larger than a sperm. Each has a nucleus and cytoplasm. A sperm has a 'head' containing the nucleus, and a tail to enable it to swim (Fig. 16.3).

What happens in sexual intercourse?

In sexual intercourse between a male and a female, the penis becomes stiff. This is known as an **erection**. The penis is then placed in the vagina of the female and moved in and out many times. The stored sperm pass along the sperm ducts, into the urethra and penis and out into the top of the woman's vagina near the cervix to enter the womb.

Fig. 16.3 A human sperm and egg.

73

16.1 Systems in humans

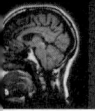

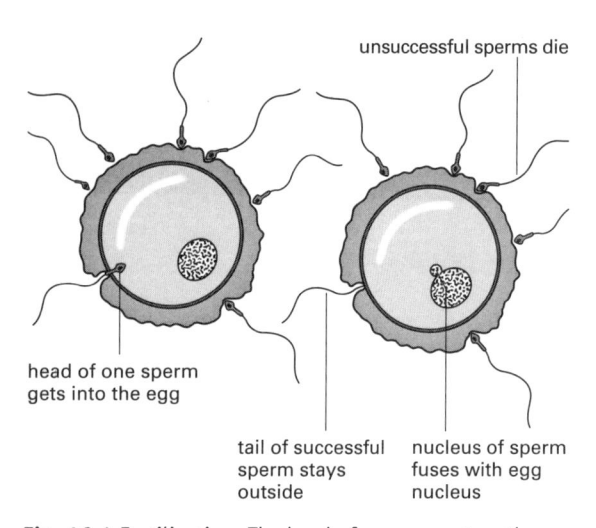

unsuccessful sperms die

head of one sperm gets into the egg

tail of successful sperm stays outside

nucleus of sperm fuses with egg nucleus

Fig. 16.4 Fertilization. The head of a sperm enters the egg and its nucleus fuses with the egg nucleus.

Fertilization

Fertilization takes place in the oviduct. The tiny sperm have a long way to go from the vagina and few will make the whole journey. This is why millions of them are produced in one go. They swim up into the oviducts. If there is an egg in one of the oviducts, the sperm cluster around the egg. One of them will enter the egg and fertilize it. The head of the sperm enters the egg, but the tail stays outside (Fig. 16.4). The sperm live for two or three days and so if an egg is not present when they first arrive, one might arrive in the oviduct during this time. After this period, the sperms die.

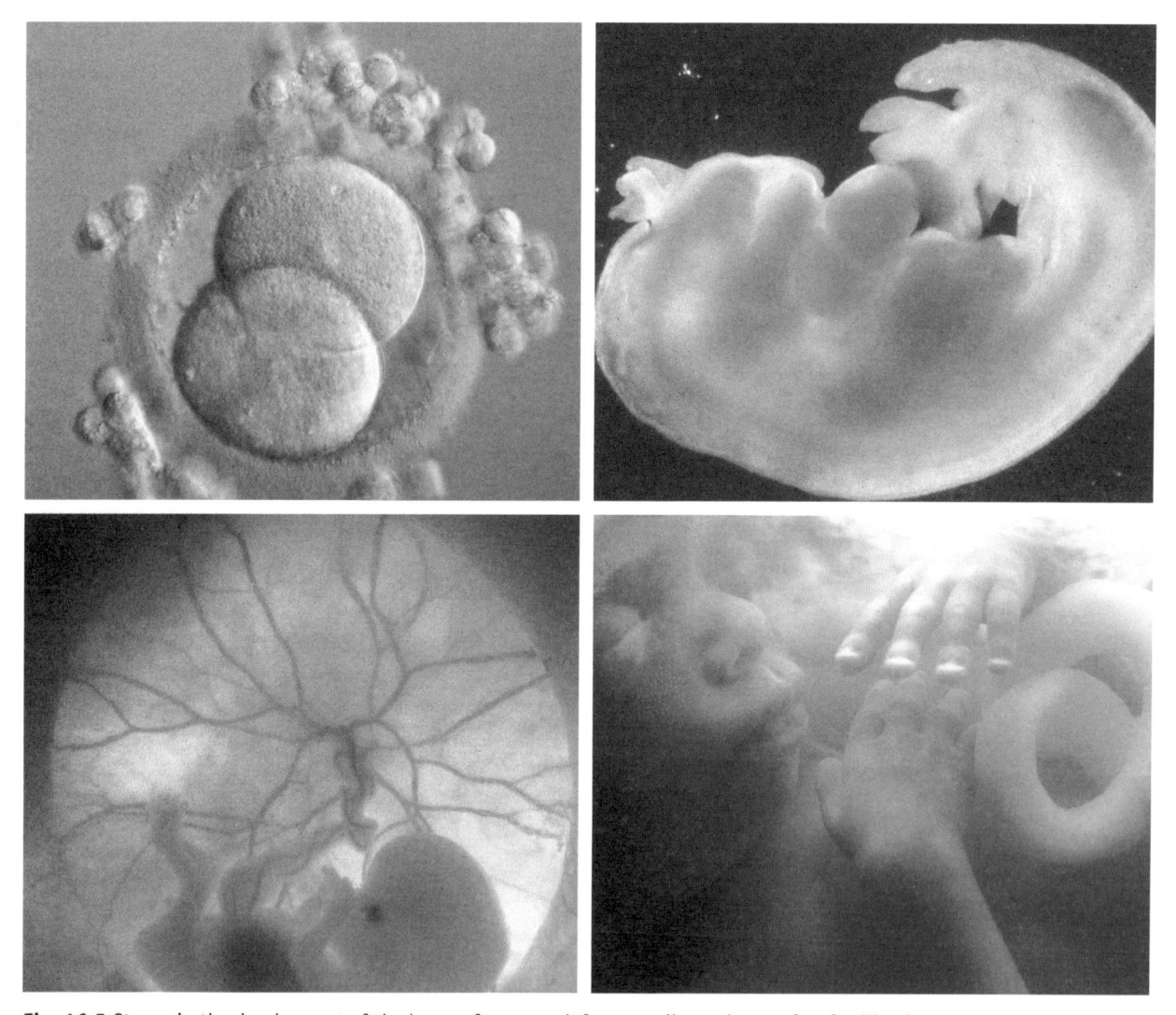

Fig. 16.5 Stages in the development of the human fetus: top left, two cells, 30 hours after fertilization; top right, 28 days; bottom left, 11 weeks; bottom right, 20 weeks.

The human reproductive system, growth and development 16.1

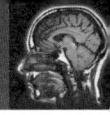

What happens to the fertilized egg?

This is the beginning of pregnancy. The fertilized egg starts to divide many times to form a ball of cells, which is called an embryo. The tiny embryo moves down into the uterus and pushes its way into the uterus wall. This is called implantation. The lining of the womb with its good blood supply nourishes the developing embryo.

Pregnancy

Human pregnancy lasts for about 40 weeks (Fig. 16.5). When the body tissues, organs and limbs start to form, the embryo is called a fetus. The fetus develops inside a bag called the amnion, which contains a watery fluid called amniotic fluid. This allows the fetus to move and float around freely. It also protects the developing fetus from damage, for example, if the mother falls or is accidentally bumped or has to run suddenly for some reason.

Part of the uterus wall develops into the **placenta**, which has a good blood supply. The fetus is joined to the placenta by the **umbilical cord**. The developing baby gets food and oxygen from the mother's blood system through the blood vessels of the placenta and umbilical cord. The baby's waste substances and carbon dioxide pass from the baby into the mother's blood system to be excreted.

Caring for pregnant women (pre-natal care)

When a woman is pregnant, she needs to visit a clinic regularly so that the health of both the mother and her unborn baby can be checked. She will get a lot of help and advice, especially if it is her first baby. She also needs to have a healthy balanced diet. Smoking, drinking alcohol and taking drugs should be avoided as this could affect the baby's development. Certain diseases such as German measles (rubella) could seriously harm the baby, especially in the first two or three months of pregnancy. Anyone with this disease should keep well away from an expectant mother.

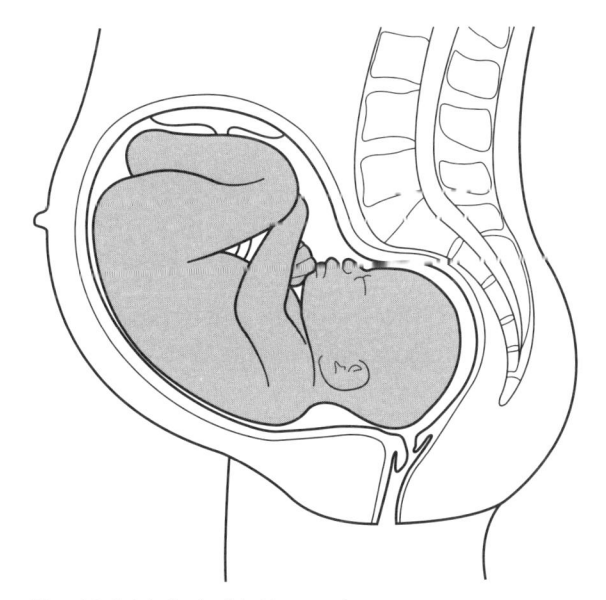

Birth

Just before birth, the baby has usually turned so that its head is just above the cervix. Labour begins when the muscles of the uterus contract and start to push the baby out. The amnion bursts and the watery fluid flows out through the vagina. This known as 'breaking the waters'. The cervix gets wider and the baby passes through, into the vagina and out into the world (Fig. 16.6). It

Fig. 16.6 A baby inside the womb.

16.1 Systems in humans

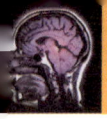

immediately takes its first breath on its own and usually cries. The doctor ties and cuts the umbilical cord and the baby is wrapped up to keep it warm. Your navel is the scar left by the umbilical cord when you were born. The placenta then passes out through the cervix and vagina a short time afterwards.

Parental care

Newborn babies need to be kept warm, even in hot countries like the Caribbean. Their bodies cannot yet cope with temperature changes like an older child or adult. At first, the baby drinks only milk. This is produced in the mammary glands of the mother's breasts (Fig. 16.7). At this stage, the baby has no teeth and cannot eat solid foods. The mother's breasts become larger during pregnancy. The baby sucks on the nipples and this stimulates the breasts to produce more milk. Of course, a baby can be fed on cow's milk from a bottle, but many doctors believe that the mother's milk is best. As well as being a perfect food for babies, it protects them from diseases as it contains antibodies that kill germs. Some babies cannot digest cow's milk. They can be given a special formula made from soya beans.

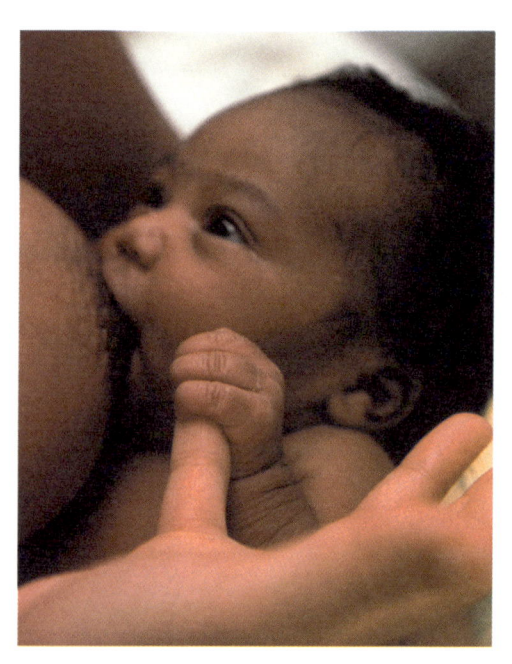

Fig. 16.7 A baby gets all the nutrients it needs, and antibodies, from its mother's milk.

After a few months the baby is fed on semi-solid food and then progresses to solid food.

Post-natal care

Post-natal care involves looking after the mother and baby after the birth. They may visit a clinic to have a health check a few weeks after the birth and/or a health worker may visit them at home. Both mother and baby need love, care and support from their family and friends.

⊙ Activity How are mothers and babies cared for in my local area?

Invite a health worker to talk to you about the care of mothers and babies in your local area. Your teacher may also be able to arrange a visit to a local clinic.

Discuss
1. How good is the system of care in your area?
2. Suggest ways in which it could be improved.
3. Share your own experiences of caring for younger relatives.

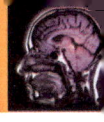

The human reproductive system, growth and development   16.1

→ Activity Bathing and dressing the baby

Ask your teacher to invite someone who has a young baby to come into school to show you how to bath and dress a baby. If you have a new baby in your family, perhaps you could tell the class about how you help with the new baby.

Record
Write down the important points you noticed; for example, care is needed with the temperature of the bath water, supporting the baby's head, etc.

Twins

Fig. 16.8 Identical twins.

Fig. 16.9 Fraternal twins.

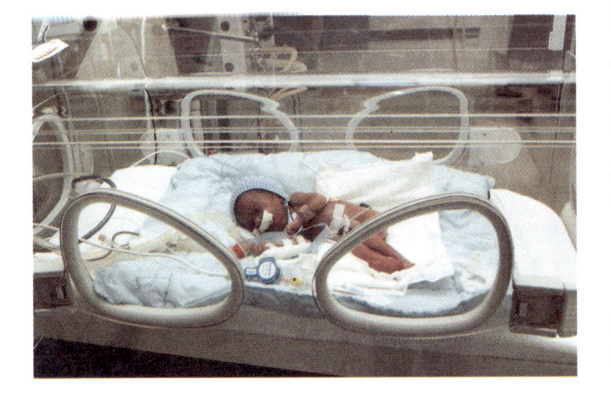

Sometimes, a mother gives birth to twins. There are two types of twins. Identical twins (Fig. 16.8) look very alike and are of the same sex. These twins are the result of a fertilized egg immediately dividing into two and each cell developing into a separate embryo. Fraternal twins (Fig. 16.9) need not be of the same sex. For example, fraternal twins can be a brother and sister. These twins are the result of the ovary producing two eggs. Each egg is fertilized and both babies develop together. The twins may not look any more alike than any other brothers and sisters in a family.

There may also be multiple births, for example: three babies (triplets), four babies (quadruplets), five babies (quintuplets) and six babies (sextuplets). Often these babies are born early (premature) and are very small. They are cared for in hospital in an incubator (Fig. 16.10). An incubator keeps the baby warm, away from disease and supplies the baby with oxygen.

Sometimes people have problems with starting a family and the woman takes fertility drugs to help her to produce eggs. This sometimes results in multiple births. Have you noticed that animals such as cats, dogs and rabbits have multiple births? Why do you think this might be? (Clue: animals do not have the same care and support systems for their young as humans.)

Fig. 16.10 Premature babies are kept warm in an incubator. They are monitored very closely and need a lot of care.

16.1 Systems in humans

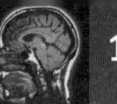

🅖 Did you know?

In asexual reproduction, there is only one parent and each new organism is exactly the same as the parent. In higher animals such as mammals, sexual reproduction is the method of reproduction. It was believed to be impossible to create new individuals from ordinary body cells by asexual reproduction – that is until news of Dolly the sheep astonished the entire world. Dolly was created from a body cell from the udder (mammary gland) of her mother. She has no father! Individuals created in this way are called **clones**.

Many people were delighted and thought that if humans could be cloned, people who could not have babies in the normal way could have a chance to have a family of their own. Other people were horrified. They thought it was unnatural and against God. Some people thought that nasty people might try to create identical people just like themselves! The argument continues today. Some countries have passed laws to stop it happening. What do people in your country think? What do you think?

➡ Activity The young of other mammals

Find out if anyone in your class keeps animals at home, for example, dogs, cats, rabbits, guinea pigs or farm animals. Ask volunteers to describe to the class what happened when any of these animals gave birth to young. Find out, for example, how many young animals were born, their appearance, how the mother cared for them and any other interesting points.

Record

Write down the important things you learned.

❓ Finding out

Do all animals care for their young?

Many animals do not have a period when they care for their young. For example, most fish and frogs lay their eggs in water and fertilization takes place outside the body. The male releases his sperm onto the eggs. This is external fertilization. The young are very vulnerable, and for this reason, these animals lay hundreds or thousands, or even millions of eggs. Not many survive.

Use biology books, encyclopedias and the internet to find out how some other animals, apart from mammals, care for their young; for example, birds, seahorses, crocodiles, bees.

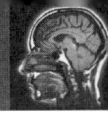

The human reproductive system, growth and development 16.1

Growing up

It takes 15 to 20 years for a baby to develop into an adult. Humans are the most intelligent of all animals, but we have to learn many things about the world before we can lead independent lives as useful members of society. Also, we need time for our bodies to grow and develop fully to become proper adults.

Puberty

Puberty is the stage when the young person begins the journey to sexual maturity. Puberty begins in girls at around 11 years of age, and in boys at about 13.

Internally, the bodies of boys and girls begin to secrete **hormones**. Boys secrete hormones called **androgens**, and girls secrete **oestrogens**. These hormones are responsible for the changes in the body seen at puberty. You will learn more about hormones in Topic 16.2.

During puberty, the reproductive organs develop in size and begin to function. Girls begin to experience a menstrual cycle. Roughly every 28 days an egg is released from one or other of the girl's ovaries. The lining of the womb thickens to receive the egg. Unless the egg is fertilized by a sperm, the lining then breaks down and passes out through the vagina as a bloody discharge, otherwise known as a 'period'. In boys, sperm production and ejaculation begin.

The physical appearance of the body also changes. Boys notice that their voice deepens; they also grow hair on their chins, armpits and around the genital region. Girls also grow hair in the genital region and in their armpits. The breasts begin to develop in girls, and their body shape also changes. These new features that appear at puberty are called **secondary sexual characteristics**. At this age, girls and boys also begin to show more interest in the opposite sex (Fig. 16.11).

The maturing of the reproductive organs can take up to four years. It happens at different times in different people. You mustn't worry if the bodies of some of your friends are maturing, but your body has not yet started to change. Every individual is different. The teenage body, especially the young teen, is not physically or mentally ready for pregnancy and child birth.

Fig. 16.11 Wanting to make friends with people of the opposite sex is part of growing up.

16.1 Systems in humans

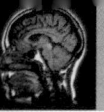

➔ Activity Body changes

List the changes that have taken place in your body over the past year. What differences have they made to your lifestyle?

◯ What you should know

- Fertilization occurs when a male sex cell (sperm) fuses with a female sex cell (egg or ovum) to form a zygote.
- The male and female sex cells are produced in sex organs (testes and ovaries).
- Sexual intercourse takes place when the penis of the male is placed in the vagina of the female.
- Fertilization takes place in the oviduct.
- The fertilized egg divides to form the embryo.
- Pregnancy in humans lasts for about 40 weeks.
- The embryo moves along the oviduct and implants itself in the wall of the womb.
- When the tissues and organs start to develop, the embryo is called a fetus.
- The fetus receives food and oxygen from the mother by way of the placenta and umbilical cord.
- The amnion contains the amniotic fluid, which protects the fetus from injury.
- The baby is born through the cervix and the vagina.
- The baby feeds on milk produced by the mother.
- Both mother and baby need special care before and after the baby is born.
- Humans have a long period of parental care.
- Puberty is the time when many changes take place in the body and the young person becomes an adult.

ⓠ Questions

1 Describe the journey of a sperm from the testis to the penis.

2 What is the difference between an embryo and a fetus?

3 The following statements describe the baby inside the womb. Fill in the missing words. The first letter of each word has been given to help you.

The a_____ is a bag containing a watery fluid that develops around the fetus. It allows the fetus to m___ around freely. It also p_____ the developing fetus from damage. Part of the uterus wall develops into the p_____, which has a good blood supply. The fetus is joined to the placenta by the u_____ c___.

4 Why does every person have a navel?

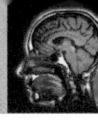

5 Why is mother's milk thought to be best for a baby?

6 At puberty several things happen. Sort out the following list of bodily changes under the headings 'Girls' and 'Boys' (or both).

- secrete oestrogens;
- begin ejaculating;
- develop breasts;
- secrete androgens;
- start periods;
- voice deepens;
- grow genital hair.

7 Advertisements and the media present us with examples of body shapes and sizes that are not always achievable by us all. Compare these stereotypes with your friends and relatives. With friends and older people, discuss the pressures you may feel to conform.

Systems in humans

16.2 What are hormones?

▶ Objectives

After studying this topic you should be able to:
- describe a hormone and its general functions
- describe the role of certain named endocrine glands in the body
- explain that the endocrine system is a coordinating system in the body
- describe what happens when certain endocrine glands are not working properly.

Where are hormones produced?

In Topic 16.1 you learned about two types of hormones that bring about changes in the body at puberty: androgens (in boys) and oestrogens (in girls). But what are hormones? They are chemical 'messengers', which move around the body in the bloodstream and cause changes in different parts of the body.

Hormones are substances that are produced by special glands called the **endocrine glands**. Figure 16.12 shows the positions of some of the endocrine glands in the human body.

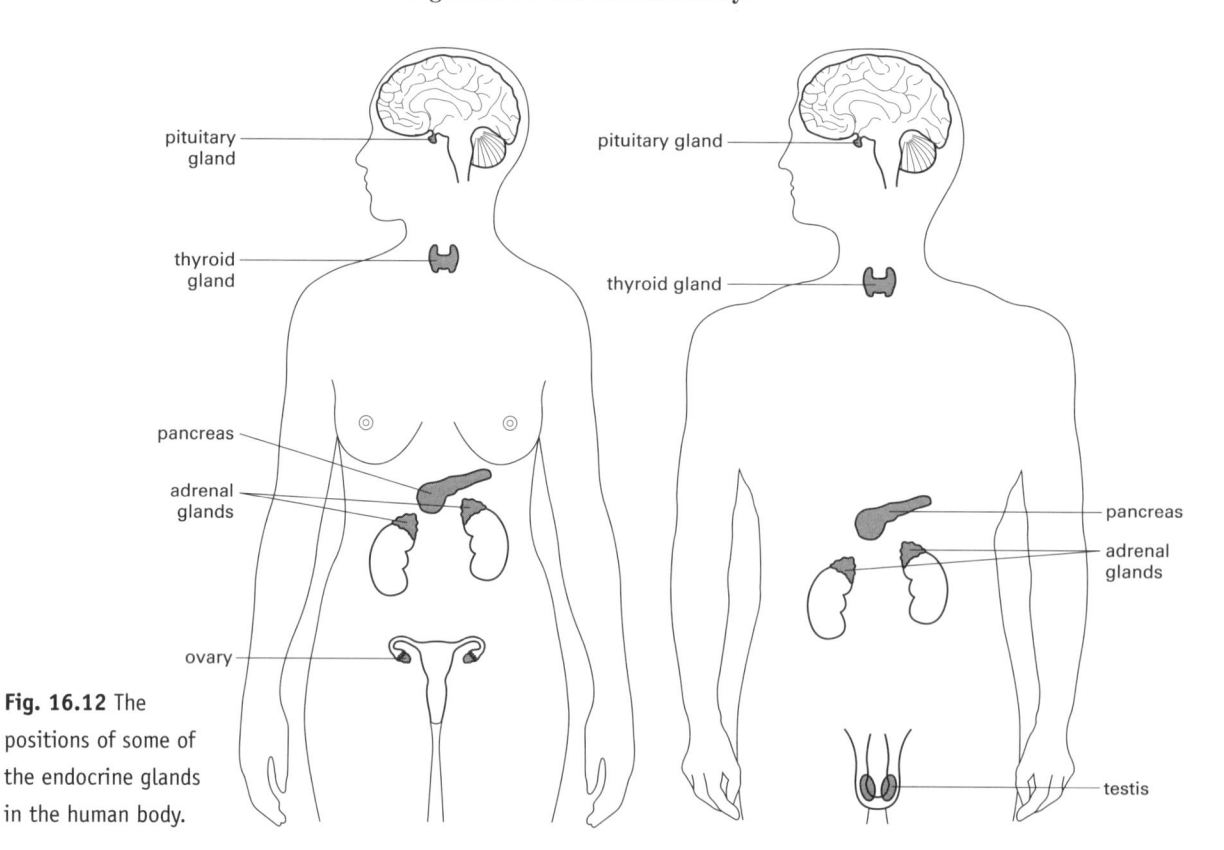

Fig. 16.12 The positions of some of the endocrine glands in the human body.

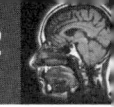

Many glands have a tube or duct to take the substances they make to the place where they are needed. For example, the sweat ducts in the skin carry sweat onto the surface of the skin. The endocrine glands are different. The hormones that are produced go straight into the blood that flows through them and are transported to areas of the body where they bring about changes.

There are two main characteristics shown by most hormones:
- Like the nervous system, the endocrine system carries messages, but the changes they bring about are not instant. They take place slowly over a long period of time.
- The changes can take place in many different parts of the body, not just in a single local area.

The pituitary gland

The **pituitary gland** is found in the brain. It is often called the 'master gland' because it controls the activities of other endocrine glands. It coordinates their activities so that they produce the correct amount of hormone. The pituitary gland also produces its own hormones. For example, it produces a hormone that causes the kidneys to take up more water when the body needs it. You also feel thirsty. This is called **antidiuretic hormone** (shortened to **ADH**). The pituitary gland also produces growth hormones.

If things go wrong: A diseased or damaged pituitary gland can affect the entire body in many different ways. For example, too much growth hormone can make a child grow too tall, too little can result in an underdeveloped child.

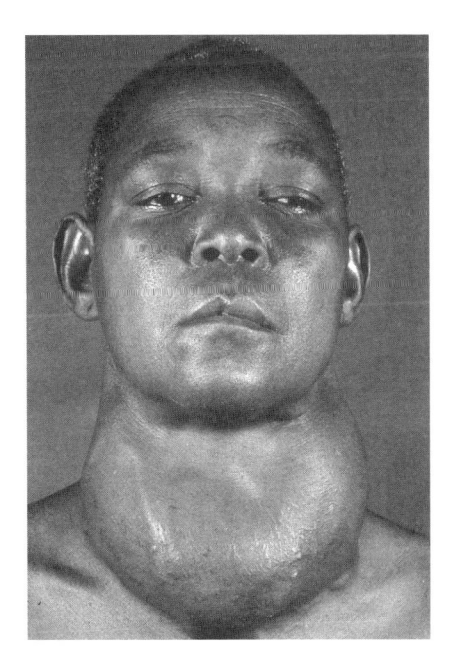

The thyroid gland

The **thyroid gland** is found near your voice box (larynx). It produces **thyroxine**, which controls the rate at which chemical reactions take place in the body cells.

If things go wrong: If too much thyroxine is produced, the person becomes thin and overactive, often with staring eyes. The chemical reactions in the cells are going too fast. If not enough thyroxine is produced, the person becomes tired and slow moving as the rates of chemical reactions are too slow. They may put on weight. Sometimes the thyroid gland swells up to form a swelling in the neck. This is called a **goitre** (Figure 16.13). Doctors can treat both conditions successfully.

Fig. 16.13 This person's thyroid gland has swollen up to form a goitre.

16.2 Systems in humans

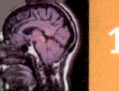

The adrenal glands

Have you ever felt frightened? Your heart beats faster, your stomach churns and you feel very tense. The pupils of your eyes get wider (dilate), to let more light into the eye. These changes are caused by the hormone **adrenaline**, produced by the **adrenal glands**, just above your kidneys. Unlike other hormones, it acts very quickly. It prepares your body for action. If you are frightened, you can run away. You may also feel like this before taking an exam at school, or before running a race. The churning in your stomach is caused by blood being diverted away from your alimentary canal and going to your muscles to supply them with as much energy as possible! How is this cricketer's adrenaline making him feel in Figure. 16.14?

Fig. 16.14 Waiting for the bowler to do his stuff!

→ Activity 'Adrenaline rush'

Write down all the times you can remember being frightened, or when you have felt very nervous. Here are some clues to help you to remember: watching a scary film on TV, crossing the road, being chased, doing exams, acting or singing in public, playing for your team, running in a race.

Discuss
Read out your experiences and listen to the experiences of your classmates. You need to say exactly what your body felt like.

The pancreas

You have already learned in Book 2, Topic 11.2 that the pancreas plays a part in digestion. It also produces the hormone **insulin**, which controls the amount of glucose sugar in the blood. Insulin stimulates the cells to take up glucose from the blood. It also makes the liver cells and muscle cells change excess sugar into **glycogen** for storage. Glycogen can then be changed back into sugar when it is needed.

What are hormones? 16.2

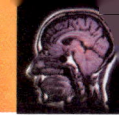

❓ Finding out

Diabetes

- People with diabetes can buy special foods to help them with their diet. Find out if any shops near you sell them and what sort of foods they are.
- Find out about the latest treatment for diabetes and any of the other conditions described in this topic. Use books and the internet to help you.

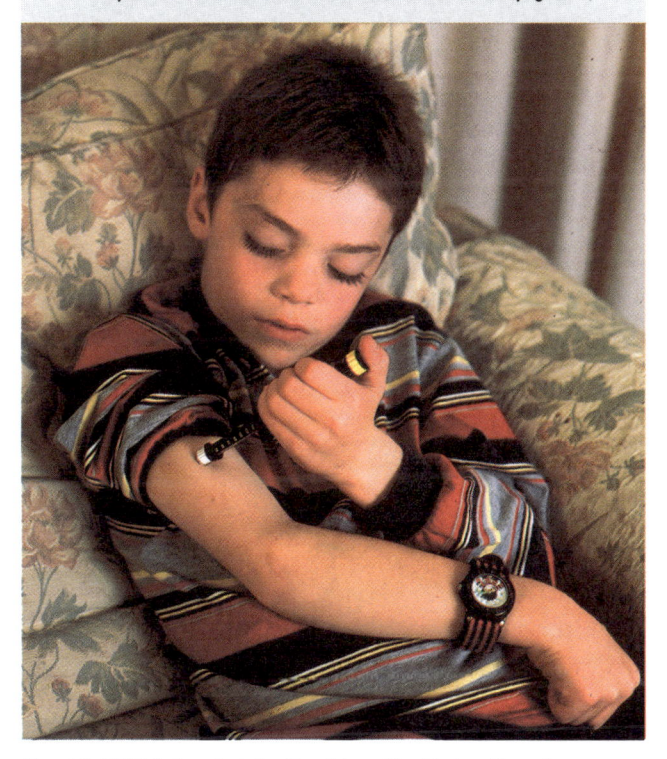

Fig. 16.15 This boy is injecting himself with insulin using a special injector 'pen'.

If things go wrong: Sometimes, a person doesn't produce enough insulin. This means that not enough sugar is stored as glycogen. The disease is called **diabetes**. People with diabetes have too much sugar in their blood. This makes them tired and irritable and they feel thirsty. The kidneys try to get rid of the extra sugar and it passes out of the body in the urine. Doctors test the urine for sugar if they suspect that a person has diabetes. If untreated, diabetes can lead to blindness, kidney failure and death. It cannot be cured, but is controlled by:

- having a special diet: people with diabetes avoid eating foods that produce excess sugar in the blood;
- taking tablets to lower blood sugar;
- injecting insulin so that blood sugar is changed into glycogen (Fig. 16.15).

Unfortunately, insulin is a protein. It cannot be given by mouth because it will be digested in the alimentary canal. This is why insulin has to be injected. Sometimes people with diabetes find it difficult to get the insulin dose they inject exactly right. They get to know the signs when they have injected too much insulin and usually eat some sugar lumps or glucose sweets.

▢ What you should know

- The endocrine system is another coordinating system in the body.
- Hormones are produced by endocrine glands.
- They pass directly into the blood and are carried to all parts of the body.
- The changes they produce often take place slowly over a long period of time.
- Important examples of endocrine glands include the sex organs, the pituitary gland, the thyroid gland, the adrenal glands and the pancreas.
- When things go wrong with the endocrine glands, the effects are experienced in many parts of the body.

16.2 Systems in humans

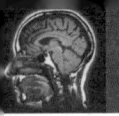

Questions

1. Describe the role of the following endocrine glands in the human body:
   a. adrenal glands;
   b. thyroid gland;
   c. pancreas.

2. Say which endocrine gland would probably be involved in these cases.
   a. Your friend is walking along the street, when a big dog starts to chase her. She screams and quickly runs away.
   b. A person is hyperactive, always on the go and has wide staring eyes.
   c. A person is on a special low-sugar diet and has to inject her/himself regularly with insulin.

3. Use a computer program that simulates how the body works to learn more about the endocrine system. You could start with http://www.heinemann.co.uk/hotlinks.

Systems in humans

16.3 Birth control

▶ Objectives

After studying this topic, you should be able to:
- explain why the population of a country may increase
- describe some different methods of birth control
- explain the importance of safe sex.

The number of people in a country is termed its **population**. The population of a country changes every day because babies are born and people die. If the number of babies born is greater than the number of people who die, the population increases (gets bigger). Governments record the number of people who are born and die every year. They record the **birth rate** and the **death rate**.

Because of improvements in health care, new methods of fighting disease, better food, clean water supplies and better education, the death rate has fallen in many countries of the world. The birth rate has, however, not fallen at the same rate, and sometimes it has risen, so that some countries have a large population that continues to grow.

There are problems when populations increase. For example, it can lead to food shortages, overcrowding and too few houses, unemployment, more pollution and so on. There are not enough resources (things people need). People worry about not earning enough money to feed, clothe and house their families. They also worry about the health and welfare of their children and other family members.

Sometimes an increase in the population can be seen as a good thing. For example, there are more people in work and paying taxes and more new jobs are created. In certain rural areas, for example, there might be a need to increase the population so that more people work on the land and produce more food. From a more personal point of view, some people

❓ Finding out

The population of my country

Find out about the size of the population in your country. Are there too many people, too few or does it seem just right? Are there food shortages, overcrowding, too few houses, and unemployment, or is there good health care and education, plenty of food and good supplies of clean water? Or does your country have some good things and some bad things? You can obtain information from your atlas, books, encyclopedias and the internet. You can also get information from older people in your family and local community.
If you think that the life of some or all of the people in your country could be improved, suggest how this could be done.

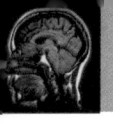

believe that having a large family means that there are more people in the family able to earn money. They may also believe that their children will look after them when they grow old. People may, of course, *choose* to have a large family because this is what makes them happy!

Whether population growth is a good thing or a bad thing depends on the country and the resources it has and the beliefs of the people.

What is birth control?

Before reading any further, take this opportunity to revise Topic 16.1 thoroughly. When people have sexual intercourse, it is always possible that pregnancy could be the result. People can use various methods to limit the number of children born in their family. This is called birth control. In many countries, the problems of an increase in the population have created the need for some form of birth control. For example, the government of China has passed laws that make parents limit the number of children that they have. In other countries, such as Caribbean nations, individuals make their own choices about birth control, depending on their values and beliefs.

The topic of birth control is a very controversial one in the Caribbean region. People often disagree with one another. The advances made in science have given many people the opportunity to control their reproductive lives, and a number of methods of birth control are available. Regardless of the choice of method used, the individual should take responsibility for him/herself, for others involved and for the unborn baby.

Birth control methods

Contraceptives are methods of birth control. They are the things people use to prevent pregnancy from occurring (Fig. 16.16). Birth control methods can:

- prevent ovulation (stop eggs being produced);
- prevent fertilization (stop the sperm reaching the egg);
- prevent implantation of the fertilized egg in the uterus (womb).

Prevention of ovulation: A common and reliable method of preventing the production of eggs (ovulation), is the use of the contraceptive pill. This is commonly referred to as 'the pill'. It is also known as oral contraception because women swallow the pills. (The word 'oral' means 'by mouth'.) The pills contain hormones and must be taken every day for 28 days. Then, the person starts again with a new pack of pills. Some people may experience some unpleasant side-effects when they take the pill. For example, they may feel sick or develop high blood pressure. For this reason, the pill should only be taken if prescribed by a doctor. Doctors and health workers can advise a woman about the most suitable type of pill for her to take. Contraceptive pills for men are being developed.

Birth control 16.3

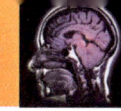

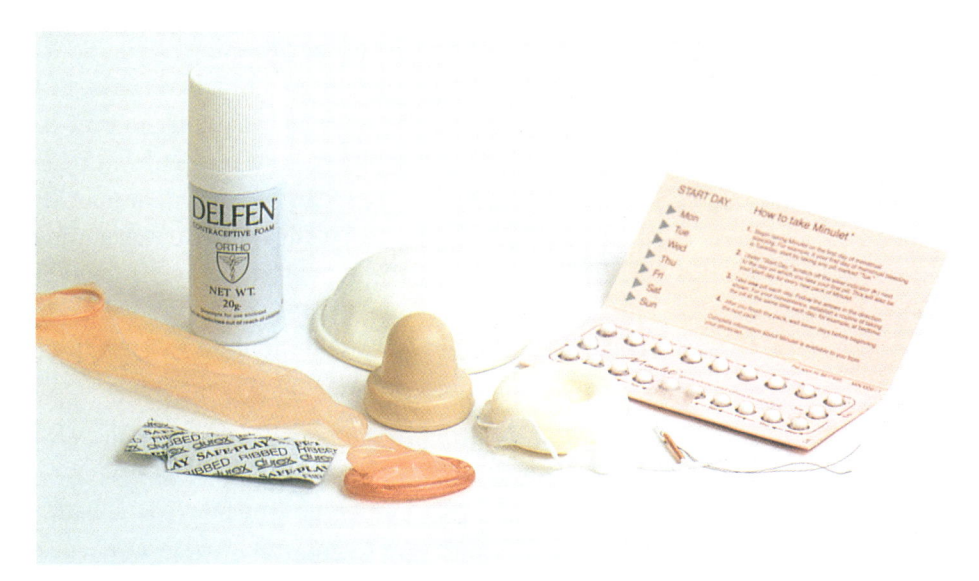

Fig. 16.16 There are many different types of contraceptives.

Prevention of fertilization: There are a number of methods men and women can use to prevent fertilization.

Natural methods of contraception can be used to prevent fertilization. The surest method is abstinence – not having sexual intercourse at all! Another method – the rhythm method – involves *not* having sexual intercourse when the woman is likely to be ovulating (producing eggs). Ovulation takes place in the middle of the month (between days 12 and 16) in a woman's menstrual (monthly) cycle. Another way of checking when ovulation is occurring is to take the body temperature with a clinical thermometer. The body temperature rises at ovulation from about 36.4 to about 36.8°C.

Chemical contraceptives may be used to prevent fertilization. They are known as **spermicides** because they kill sperm. They are creams, gels, foams or tablets that a woman places in the vagina before sexual intercourse. Any sperm coming into contact with these chemicals will die.

Another method of preventing fertilization is the use of barriers. Women may use diaphragms or caps that block the cervix, preventing the sperm from entering the uterus. The diaphragm should be first fitted by a trained professional, and the woman is taught how to use it correctly. The diaphragm or cap is also smeared with spermicidal gel or foam to help to kill the sperm.

Men may use a **condom** (also known as a sheath or 'rubber'). The condom is placed over the erect penis before sexual intercourse. Condoms are becoming increasingly popular as a means of preventing the spread of sexually transmitted diseases (STDs) and to help prevent the spread of AIDS. Condoms are thought to be the safest barrier against the viruses and bacteria that cause STDs.

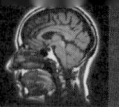

There are also methods of **sterilization** available for both men and women. Women can have an operation in hospital to tie off their oviducts. This stops the eggs from the ovaries reaching the uterus. Ovulation still takes place, but the ovum or egg cannot be fertilized by the sperm as the sperm cannot reach the egg. Men can also have an operation in which the sperm duct (which goes from the testis to the urethra and penis) is cut and tied off. This stops the sperms made in the testis from getting into the penis. The operation does not stop people having sexual intercourse. Sterilization is usually permanent and is difficult to reverse if a man or woman decides that they want children later on.

Prevention of implantation of the fertilized egg in the uterus: Intra-uterine devices (IUDs) are used to prevent the fertilized egg from implanting into the wall of the uterus. This principle is based on a very old tradition. It is said that women in ancient Greece inserted small pebbles into the uterus to prevent pregnancy. The nomads in the Sahara also used this method of contraception with their camels. The loop and the coil are the most popular IUDs used. They are made of plastic and copper. The loop or coil is put into place in the uterus by a trained health worker or a doctor, as if this is done incorrectly, it could damage the uterus. The advantage of this method is that the IUD can be left in place for a long time. IUDs may not be suitable for all women. They may cause bleeding, for example.

Are contraceptives always successful?

These methods of contraception can all fail for many reasons.

- Women may forget to take their contraceptive pills regularly.
- When using the rhythm method, it is difficult to guess when ovulation has occurred and when the 'safe period' to have sexual intercourse might be. Also, some women do not have a very regular cycle. This is often the case in your teens, when many body changes take place.
- If not enough spermicide is used it may not kill all the sperm.
- Condoms and diaphragms may not be used properly, or they may develop holes.
- IUDs may not be successfully placed in position.

➲ Activity Summarizing birth control

Read through the previous two sections and summarize what you have learned about methods of birth control by copying and filling in Table 16.1. The first row of the table has been filled in to help you.

16.3 Birth control

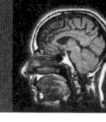

Table 16.1 Birth control methods, how they work and why they may not be completely successful.

Method of birth control	How it works (Does it prevent ovulation, fertilization or implantation?)	Why this method may not be successful
The contraceptive pill	It prevents ovulation	Women may forget to take their pills regularly
Abstinence (a natural method of contraception)		
The rhythm method (a natural method of contraception)		
Spermicides		
Diaphragm or cap (a barrier)		
Condom (a barrier)		
Female sterilization		
Male sterilization		
Intra-uterine devices (IUDs)		

The 'morning-after' pill

New methods of contraception continue to be developed. For example, the 'morning-after' pill can be used by women after intercourse (up to 48 hours). It prevents implantation of the fertilized egg. However, it makes the women feel very sick. It is usually only used if another method of contraception may have failed, for example if a condom has split.

Contraception is not always straightforward and there may be harmful side-effects. Some contraceptives may be obtained from a pharmacy or family-planning centre. Others can only be obtained from a doctor.

Activity More about birth control

1 Write a letter to your local family planning clinic, inviting someone to speak to the class about birth control. Before the talk, prepare the questions that you would like to ask.

2 Find out from the spiritual leader in your community what they advise on birth control, and why. Report your findings back to the class.

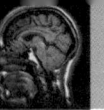

3 Ask your relatives and friends about any 'old wives' tales' they may know about birth control. Record them in a notebook. Discuss them with your class. Also discuss whether these tales are based on any scientific facts.

4 Hold a class debate on birth control.

Being responsible about sex

You have learned about STDs in Book 1, Topic 7.1 and in this topic about different methods of contraception. As individuals, you will need to make informed choices in the future. In other words, you must make decisions based on what you have learned from your family, at school and from your friends and other people in the community. One important thing to remember is that our behaviour usually affects other people. At some time in the future, you will begin to have sexual relations. Here are some things to help you to practise safe sex.

- Have a regular partner and avoid casual sex with people you do not know or have only just met.
- Use a condom, especially if you do not know the person very well. A condom helps to protect you against STDs.
- Using contraceptives helps to prevent unwanted pregnancy.

Activity The importance of practising safe sex

Discuss
1 Why is it important to practise safe sex?
2 What could happen if someone became pregnant while still at school?
3 What happens if someone catches an STD?

What you should know

- Advances in science have given many people the opportunity to control their reproductive lives.
- There are many different methods of birth control.
- Abstinence is the safest form of birth control.
- Birth control methods can be classified according to the function they perform: prevention of ovulation, prevention of fertilization or prevention of the implantation of the embryo.
- Birth control methods are not always successful.
- It is important to practise safe sex.

16.3 Birth control

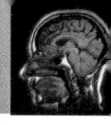

Questions

1. Write an essay on: 'Taking care of a baby is a serious responsibility'.

2. Describe the different forms of birth control methods that are available.

3. Draw a graph using the data in Table 16.2.

   Table 16.2 The number of teenage pregnancies during the period 1987–1997 for a Caribbean country

Year	Number of girls under 15 who became pregnant
1987	82
1988	75
1989	70
1990	85
1991	56
1992	60
1993	46
1994	33
1995	43
1996	36
1997	40

   a In which year is the lowest number of pregnancies?

   b In which year is the highest number of pregnancies?

   c If the total number of teen births (girls aged 13–19) was 3276 in 1991, what was the percentage number of births for girls aged under 15 for that year?

4. Teenage pregnancy is considered to be a problem in many Caribbean countries. Why do you think this is? List as many consequences of teenage pregnancy as you can, under the headings 'Disadvantages' and 'Advantages'. Do you agree that teenage pregnancy is a problem?

5. Defenders of large families may argue that 'with every mouth there comes a pair of hands'. What does this mean? How would you challenge this thinking?

Systems in humans

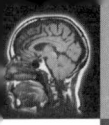

16.4 Coordination: the human nervous system

▶ Objectives

After studying this topic you should be able to:
- explain that the nervous system consists of the central nervous system (CNS) together with the nerves that branch out from it (the peripheral nervous system)
- explain that the CNS consists of the brain and spinal cord
- describe some examples of reflex actions
- explain the functions of the three most important parts of the brain
- describe some diseases of the nervous system.

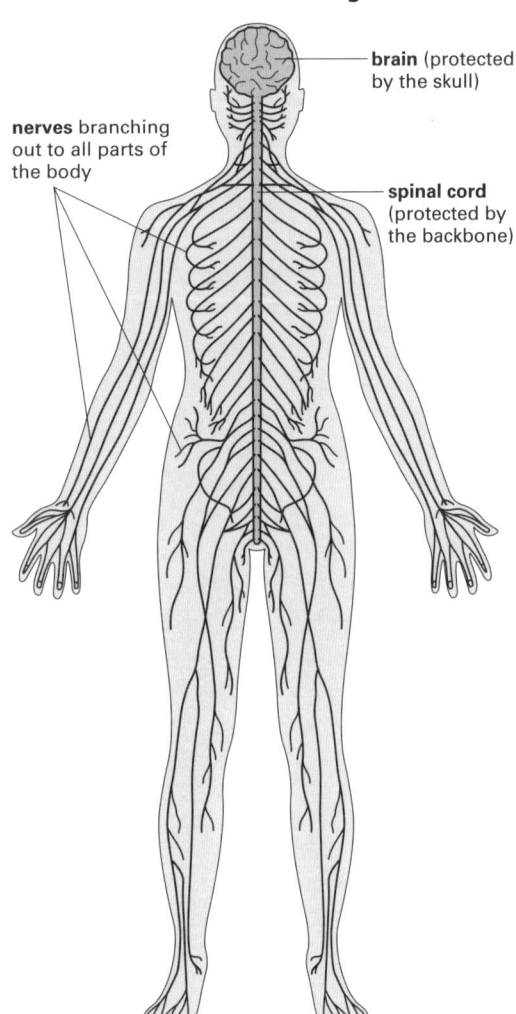

Fig. 16.17 The parts of the human nervous system.

In Book 1, Topic 1.5, you learned about the five senses: sight, hearing, touch, smell and taste. You have learned about the eye and ear in Topics 15.2 and 15.4. The eyes, ears, skin, nose and tongue are the sense organs. They have **receptor** cells that receive information from the environment. You now know that any change in the environment is a stimulus, and we react and respond to it.

What happens to the information we receive and how is it processed to enable us to respond? All the information goes to the **central nervous system** (shortened to **CNS**). This consists of the brain and spinal cord. The CNS is connected to various parts of the body through nerves. Some of the nerves come straight out of the brain itself. Others come out of the spinal cord and are called spinal nerves (Fig. 16.17). The nerves that are outside the CNS make up the peripheral nervous system.

Messages are carried by nerve cells

The brain, spinal cord and nerves contain nerve cells. The messages from the receptors are carried by nerve cells. You can compare a nerve cell to an electrical cable. The messages are like tiny pulses of electricity moving very quickly along a nerve cell. We call them impulses. The messages travel in one direction only along a nerve cell.

Coordination: the human nervous system 16.4

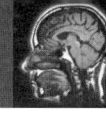

A reflex action

When you touch something hot, you react without thinking and pull your hand away. This is a **reflex action** (Fig. 16.18). But what happens? The heat is sensed by temperature receptors in your skin. The message travels along a nerve to the spinal cord, along connecting nerve cells in the spinal cord and out along another nerve to the muscle in your arm. The muscle is an **effector**, doing the action. The muscle contracts (shortens) causing you to pull your hand away from the hot object.

Fig. 16.18 Cross-section through the spinal cord showing its connection with a spinal nerve. Notice that the spinal nerve has two branches: the dorsal root and the ventral root. The arrows show the direction in which the message travels.

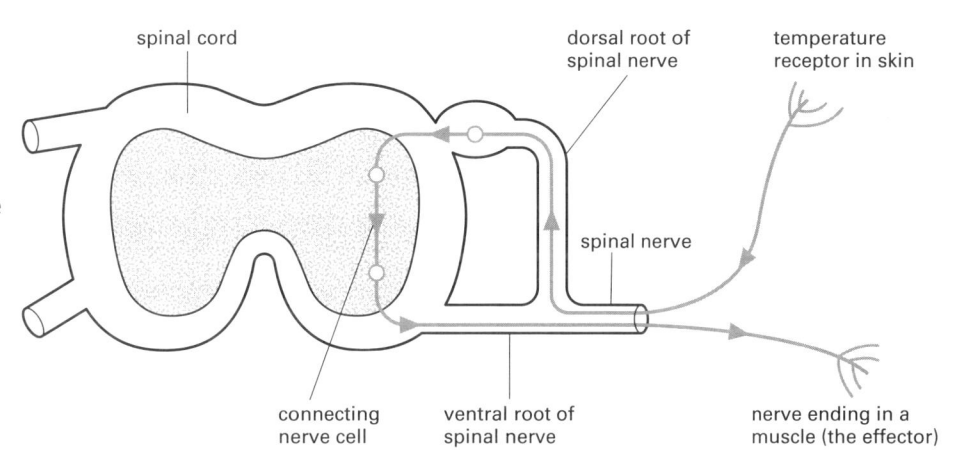

Reflex actions happen very fast. Messages whiz along nerve cells at a fraction of a second. For example, if something suddenly comes near your eyes you blink without thinking about it. The message from your eye passes straight to the brain through your optic nerves and back out through a nerve to the muscles of your eyelids.

⮕ Activity The knee jerk

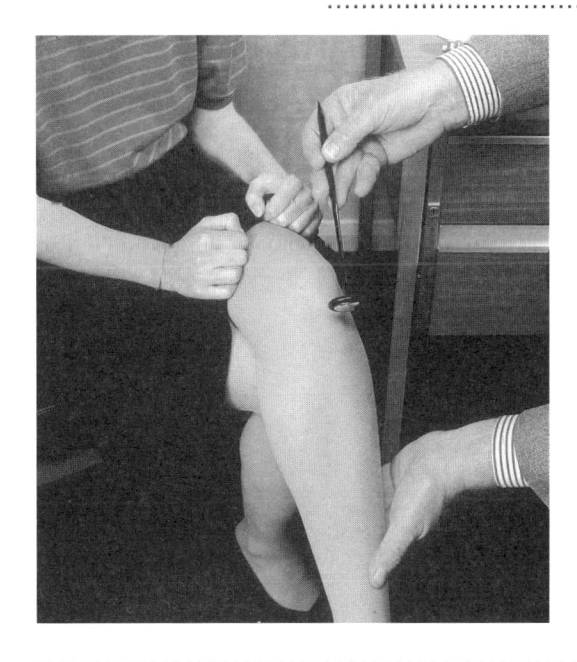

You will need
- yourself and a partner
- a stool

Method

1 Sit on the stool with one leg crossed over the other (Fig. 16.19).
2 Ask your partner to tap the knee of your crossed leg just below your kneecap where your knee curves in slightly. Your partner should use the outer side of his or her hand. Does your knee jerk up?
3 Ask your partner to tap your knee again, but this time try to stop your knee from jerking.

Fig. 16.19 The knee jerk. Doctors check reflex actions to find out if the nervous system is working properly.

16.4 Systems in humans

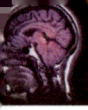

Discuss
What happened when you tried to stop your knee from jerking? Use a reaction timer to see how fast you can respond to stimuli. You can find one at http://www.heinemann.co.uk/hotlinks.

The brain

The brain is able to coordinate your activities so that your body systems work together (Fig. 16.20). If a part of the brain is damaged, for example, in an accident or if a person has a stroke, this can affect activities in the body. For example, if someone has a stroke, their speech might be affected and they may be paralysed down one side – their muscles stop working on that side.

Scientists continue to learn more and more about the brain, but many think that we will never unlock all its secrets. The brain has many different parts, and we now look more closely at three of them.

The cerebral hemispheres: This is the part of the brain where you think and control all your conscious actions. Your memory and intelligence are also located here. If, as you read these lines in this book you decide that you want to ask your teacher a question, the decision is made in your cerebral hemispheres.

The cerebellum: This part controls your balance. It also controls your very accurate movements, such as drawing, sewing, playing a musical instrument or playing football.

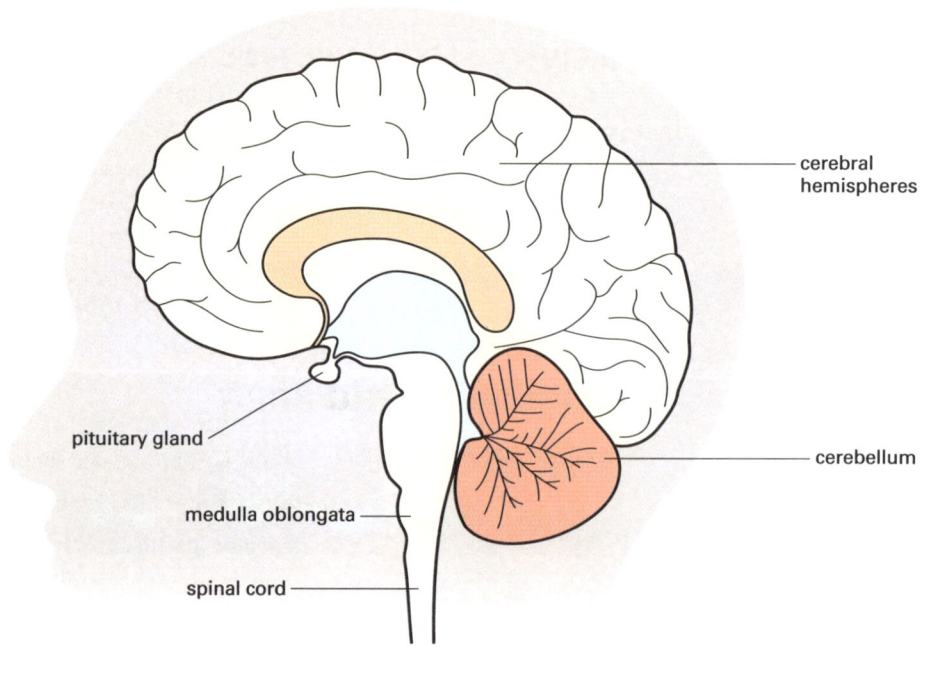

> **Did you know?**
> There are over 2000 million nerve cells in the human brain.

Fig. 16.20 The main parts of the human brain.

Coordination: the human nervous system   16.4

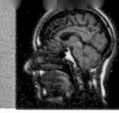

The medulla oblongata: This part of the brain controls all your unconscious actions – the ones that take place all the time without us thinking about them. These actions include digestion, breathing movements and the blood circulating around the body. Of course, you can control your breathing movements if you want to, by taking a deep breath if the doctor asks you to, or controlling your breath when singing. But most of the time you breathe in and out without noticing that you are doing it.

Activity Can you fool your brain?

You will need
- a marble (or any hard round object)

Method
1. Place the marble on a bench or table.
2. Cross your second finger over your index (first) finger.
3. Touch the marble with the tips of both fingers and roll it gently.

Suddenly, you will feel two marbles, not one! It gives you a bit of a shock. You know there is only one marble, but you were touching it with two separate fingertips. So two messages went to your brain at the same time. Your brain interpreted it as you touching two separate marbles!

Some diseases of the nervous system

Doctors check reflex actions to make sure that the nervous system is working properly, especially after an accident (Fig. 16.19).

Some diseases affect the nervous system. Sometimes the nerve cells going to the muscles become damaged. This is motor neurone disease and the person gradually becomes paralysed. Another disease is caused when the fatty outer coat of the nerve cells wears away. This is muscular sclerosis. Sometimes older people get Parkinson's disease. This affects their balance and causes the limbs to tremble so that it is difficult to hold things without dropping them. There is treatment, but doctors are not sure what causes Parkinson's disease.

What you should know

- The central nervous system (CNS) consists of the brain and spinal cord.
- Nerve cells inside nerves carry messages (electrical impulses) in fractions of a second, from receptors in the sense organs to the CNS.
- Nerve cells inside nerves carry messages from the CNS to effectors in the muscles and elsewhere.
- Reflex actions happen without thinking, for example, blinking.

16.4 Systems in humans

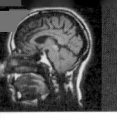

- The brain coordinates activities so that the body systems work together.
- Three important regions of the brain are the cerebral hemispheres (the site of conscious actions, thinking and memory), the cerebellum (which controls balance and accurate movements) and the medulla oblongata (which controls unconscious actions).
- Motor neurone disease, multiple sclerosis and Parkinson's disease are diseases of the nervous system.

Questions

1 Which of these is a reflex action?

   a Reading a book.

   b Blinking when a fly comes near your eye.

   c Drawing a picture.

2 Where are these activities controlled in your brain?

   a Remembering what you did yesterday.

   b Digesting your food.

   c Taking a deep breath before you start to sing.

   d Balancing on a plank of wood.

3 Research other parts of the brain and their functions.

4 Many people overcome illnesses and damage to the CNS. Research one problem and how it can be treated, controlled or overcome.

Forces

17.1 Understanding forces

> **Objectives**
>
> After studying this topic, you should be able to:
> - state that forces can change the way things move, and their shapes
> - use arrows to represent forces on diagrams
> - state that forces are measured in newtons (N)
> - understand the difference between mass and weight.

The idea of a **force** is a very important one in science. Forces can make things happen. Here are some examples of forces at work in an athletics competition.

- The sprinters are on their marks. They push back hard on their starting blocks so that they get off to a good start (Fig. 17.1).
- The hurdlers are racing down the track. They have to push down hard on the ground to make themselves rise up over each hurdle.
- The tug-of-war teams pull hard on the rope. Their feet are pushing hard on the ground (Fig. 17.2).
- The vaulting pole bends and then straightens, pushing the pole vaulter up and over the bar.

Fig. 17.1 The sprinters push their feet against the starting blocks to make a good start.

Fig. 17.2 The tug-of-war teams pull hard on the rope and push their feet against the ground.

A force is a push or a pull. (Look for the words push and pull in the sentences above.) Forces can:

- make things speed up or slow down;
- make things move in a different direction;
- make things change shape, by bending, stretching or twisting them.

17.1 Forces

Representing forces

You can't see a force, but you can learn to show forces on diagrams. You need to think about three things:

- How big is the force?
- In which direction is it pulling or pushing?
- What object is it pushing or pulling on?

We can show these things using labelled arrows, because an arrow can show direction. The size of a force is given in **newtons** (symbol **N**). This unit is named after Isaac Newton, an English scientist who studied forces and how they affect the way things move. Hold a single apple or orange in your hand. It is useful to remember that the weight of an apple or orange is roughly one newton (1 N).

The car's engine provides a forward force to start it moving

forward force due to engine starting

The pole vaulter and the pole are falling because the force of gravity is pulling them back down to the ground

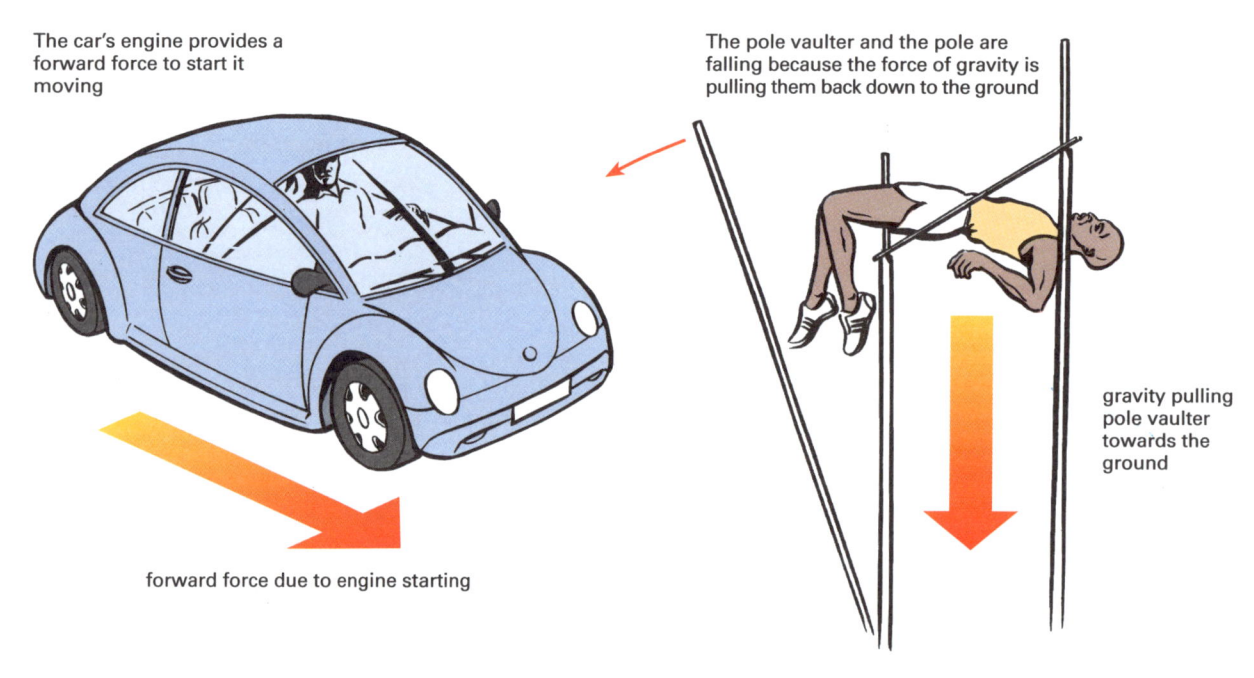

gravity pulling pole vaulter towards the ground

Fig. 17.3 Some examples of force diagrams.

In Figure 17.3, the car's engine is started and provides a forward force to start the car moving. The force of **gravity** is pulling the pole vaulter *and* the pole back down to the ground. The name for the force of gravity on an object is its **weight**.

➲ Activity Human forces

You will need
- bathroom scales

Understanding forces 17.1

Method

Your scales may show measurements in kilograms. To change to newtons, multiply by 10. So 10 kg means 100 N, 20 kg means 200 N, and so on.

1 What force do you produce by standing on the scales?
2 Push the scales against the wall. What force can you push with? Try one hand and then two (Fig. 17.4).
3 Can you produce a bigger force by pushing with your feet? Lie on your back with the scales against the wall.

Fig. 17.4 Finding out about human force using bathroom scales.

Record

Note down your measurements for each push in kilograms and newtons in a table.

Discuss

1 When you stand on the scales, are you pushing down with your feet? Are you recording your weight? Are you recording the force of gravity?
2 When you push the scales against the wall with one hand, is the force more, less or the same as pushing with two hands?
3 When you push the scales against the wall with your two feet, is the force more, less or the same as pushing with two hands?
4 Explain the differences in your results.

Fig. 17.5 This ornithologist has caught a bird and is weighing it using a forcemeter before setting it free.

Measuring forces

You have seen one way to measure forces – using bathroom scales. Another way is to use a **forcemeter** (a spring balance, also known as a **newtonmeter**) (Fig. 17.5). This has a scale in newtons. When you pull on the hook of the forcemeter, a spring inside is stretched. The pointer moves along the scale. The bigger the force, the more the spring stretches.

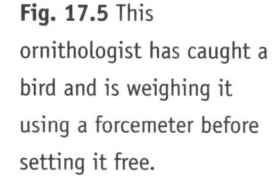

17.1 Forces

→ Activity Measuring some forces

You will need
- a forcemeter (spring balance)
- string
- brick, books, etc.
- roller skates

Method
1. Study Figure 17.6 carefully.
2. Tie some string around the brick. Tie the string to the hook of the forcemeter and pull the brick along the bench.
3. Use some string to hang the brick from the forcemeter to find its weight. Weigh some books in the same way.
4. Measure the force needed to pull a drawer open, and to open a door.
5. Measure the force needed to pull a friend on roller skates: attach one end of a piece of string to the hook of the forcemeter and ask your friend to hold the other end. Pull your friend gently along.

Record
Note down your results in newtons in a table.

Discuss
1. What force is needed to start the brick moving?
2. What did the brick weigh? What did the books weigh? Were they of different weights?
3. How much force was needed to open the drawer and the door?
4. Did everyone's friend need the same amount of force to pull them along on roller skates? If not, why?

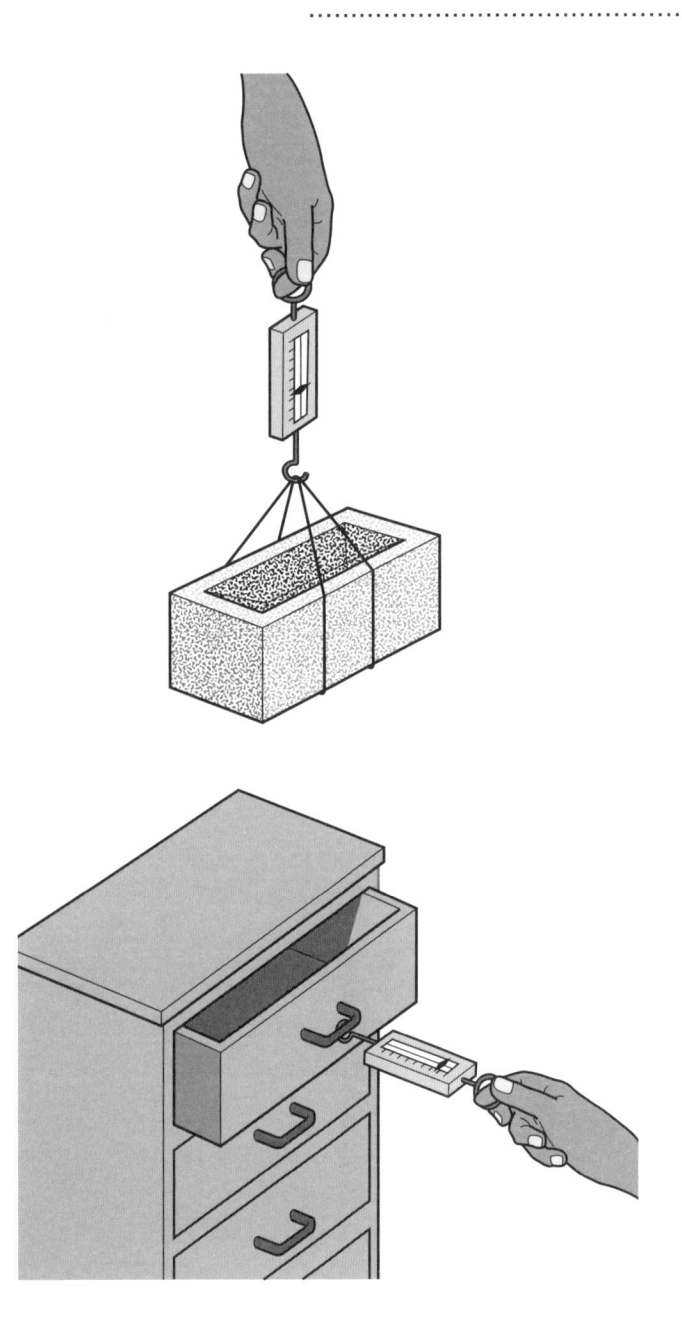

Fig. 17.6 Using a forcemeter to measure forces.

Understanding forces 17.1

The force of gravity

Gravity is an important force. The pull of the Earth's gravity gives us our weight. If you jump up in the air, your weight pulls you back down again. It is difficult to escape from gravity!

We live on a massive planet, the Earth. The pull of the Earth's gravity is quite strong. It pulls us towards the centre of the Earth. No matter where you stand on the Earth's surface, your weight pulls you towards the centre of the Earth (Fig. 17.7).

If you went to the Moon, you would discover that gravity is much weaker there. This is because the Moon is much smaller than the Earth. You would find it much easier to do the high jump on the Moon – if you didn't have to wear a heavy space suit! You weigh less on the Moon (see Fig. 17.8). When astronauts first visited the Moon, they took a golf club. They could hit a ball much farther than on Earth because the Moon's gravity did not pull it down so strongly.

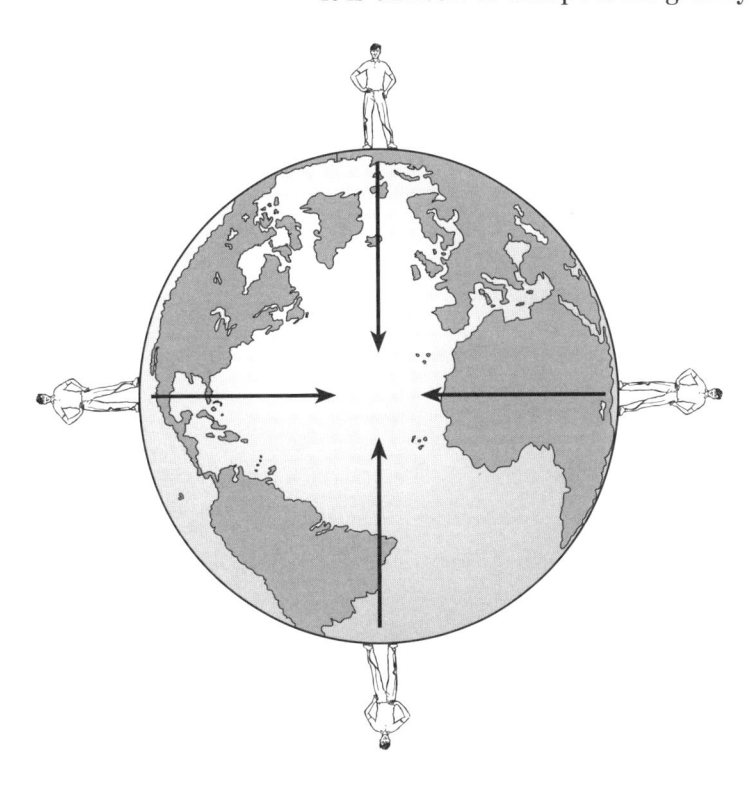

Fig. 17.7 Earth's gravity pulls us towards the centre of the Earth.

Fig. 17.8 The Slimmer's Club trip to the Moon.

17.1 Forces

Mass and weight

It is easy to get confused between mass and weight.

- Your mass is measured in kilograms. It tells you how much matter you are made of.

- Your weight is a force, so it is measured in newtons. It tells you how strong the pull of gravity is on you.

On the Moon, your weight is much less because gravity there is about one-sixth as strong as on Earth. However, your mass stays the same, because you are made of just as much matter (the same number of molecules) as on Earth. One day, astronauts may visit Mars. They will find that gravity is weaker there than on Earth, but stronger than on the Moon. Table 17.1 shows this.

Table 17.1 On Earth, gravity pulls with a force of about 10 N on every kilogram of mass. Gravity is weaker on the Moon and Mars.

Planet	Mass	Weight
Earth	50 kg	500 N
Moon	50 kg	80 N
Mars	50 kg	200 N

What you should know

- Forces are pushes and pulls.
- Forces can change an object's speed, direction or shape.
- Forces are measured in newtons (N).
- Weight is a force, caused by the pull of gravity.

Questions

1 Choose values from the list to match each quantity **a–d**:
   1 N   10 N   30 kg   300 N

   a The mass of a child.

   b The weight of a child.

   c The weight of an apple.

   d The pull of gravity on a 1 kg book.

2 Mass and weight are two important quantities in science.

   a What are the units of these two quantities?

   b Which of them is a force?

   c If you went to another planet, which of these two quantities would be unchanged? Explain why it remains unchanged.

3 Research how your weight would change if you stood on each of the planets in the solar system. (You can't actually stand on some because they are 'gas giants'!) Research weightlessness. Can you really be 'weightless'? Where and how?

Forces

17.2 Forces and motion

▶ Objectives

After studying this topic, you should be able to:
- describe the effects of friction, drag and air resistance on a moving object
- state that balanced forces leave an object moving at a steady speed in a straight line
- state that unbalanced forces cause an object to accelerate, decelerate or change direction.

The force of friction

The force of friction makes it difficult to move the teacher's car in Figure 17.9. You can feel friction when you rub your hands together, or when you come down a slide.

Friction tends to slow things down once they are moving but you need friction to start things moving in the first place (Fig. 17.10). Have you ever tried walking on ice, where there is little friction? It is difficult to start moving, and to stop moving but ice makes it easy for skaters to slide along. Smooth surfaces usually have less friction than rough surfaces.

Fig. 17.9 The teacher's car won't start. The pupils are helping him out by giving the car a push. It takes a big force to start a car moving.

Overcoming friction

There is friction if we try to move through the air. This is called air resistance or **drag**. There is drag also if we try to move through water. It is easier to keep moving if we can reduce friction. Oil is vital in a car engine to reduce friction so that the engine is more efficient. Reducing friction also helps to reduce wear and tear. The pictures in Figure 17.11 overleaf show other ways of reducing friction. You can probably think of many more.

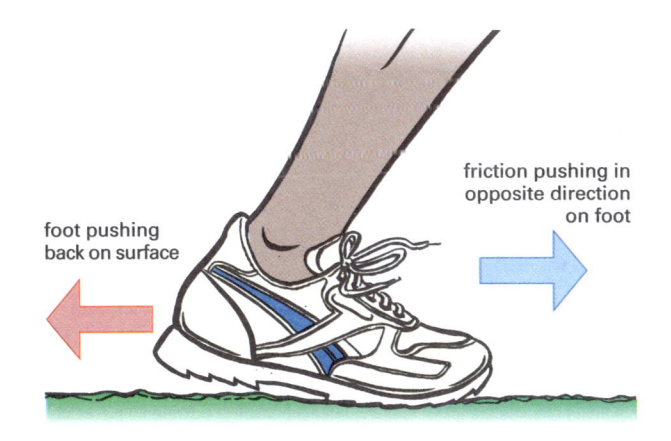

Fig. 17.10 We use the force of friction to start moving when we walk.

17.2 Forces

Fig. 17.11 Reducing friction. Left: grease is being applied to the axle to lubricate the moving parts; centre: a seacat rides up out of the water so that there is less friction; right: racing cyclists wear tight, smooth clothing to reduce air resistance.

Increasing friction

A wet road can be dangerous. A car's tyres can lose their grip, and the car can spin out of control. The tyres have a pattern of tread which gives good grip on a wet road. Bald tyres are a danger on a wet road because there is less friction.

If you ride a bicycle, you will know that friction is important for braking. The rubber pads press on the wheel rim and slow you down. On a rainy day, the wheel gets wet and there is less friction, so it is harder to stop.

Activity Investigating friction

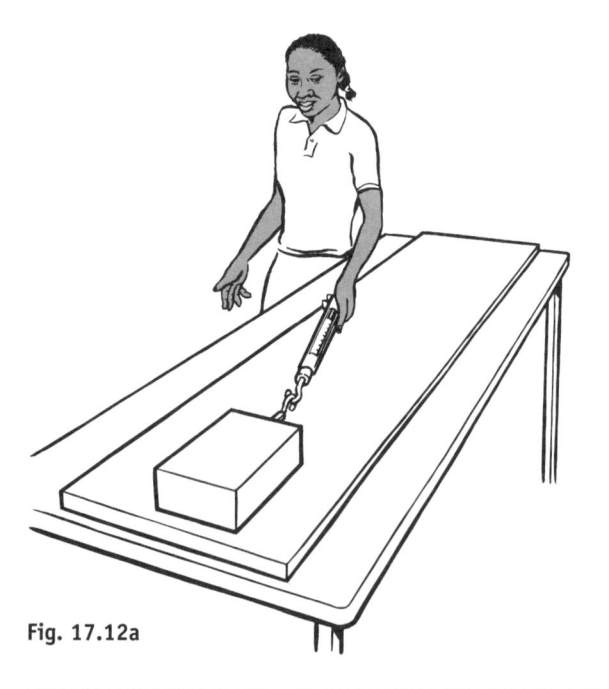

You will need
- a heavy wooden block or brick
- a forcemeter (spring balance)
- string
- a wooden board
- paper
- sandpaper
- cooking oil
- water

Method 1
1. Look carefully at Fig. 17.12a.
2. Lay the board on a bench.
3. Tie the string round the block.
4. Pull the block along the board using the forcemeter. Record the force used.

Fig. 17.12a

Forces and motion **17.2**

5 Change the surface of the block by fixing paper or sandpaper to it. Change the surface of the board by covering it with a thin layer of oil or water. In each case, find the force needed to make the block move. This tells you the force of friction between them.

Record
Record the force needed each time in a table.

Discuss
1 Which surfaces give most friction?
2 Which surfaces give least friction?

Method 2
1 Look carefully at Figure 17.12b.
2 Place the block on one end of the board.
3 Raise that end of the board slowly, until the block starts to slide.
4 Measure the angle of tilt, or the height of the end of the board.
5 Try different surfaces and find the ones with most and least friction.

Record
Record the height or angle of tilt each time in a table.

Discuss
Do you get the same answers as with Method 1? How does 'moving friction' differ from 'stationary friction'?

Fig. 17.12b

Pulling hard

The boy in Figure 17.13 is dragging a large suitcase along the ground. At first, he does not pull hard enough and the suitcase does not move. His

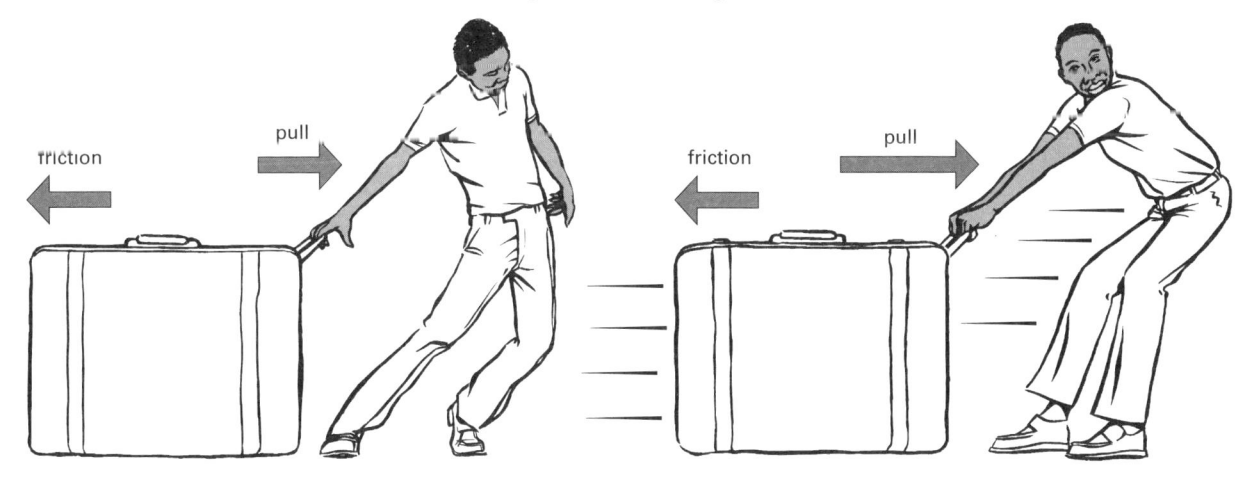

Fig. 17.13 Effort is needed to overcome the force of friction. The suitcase is stationary in the picture on the left. On the right, the boy is pulling hard enough to overcome friction and the suitcase is moving.

pulling force equals the force of friction. These forces are balanced. If the boy pulls with a force that is greater than the force of friction, the forces are unbalanced and the suitcase starts to move.

Speeding up

A car's engine provides the force needed to make the car go (Fig. 17.14). The driver can make the car speed up by pressing harder on the accelerator pedal. The force of the engine increases, and the car accelerates. To go at a steady speed, the driver must keep the accelerator pedal in exactly the same position. Then the forward force of the engine exactly balances the backward force of air resistance.

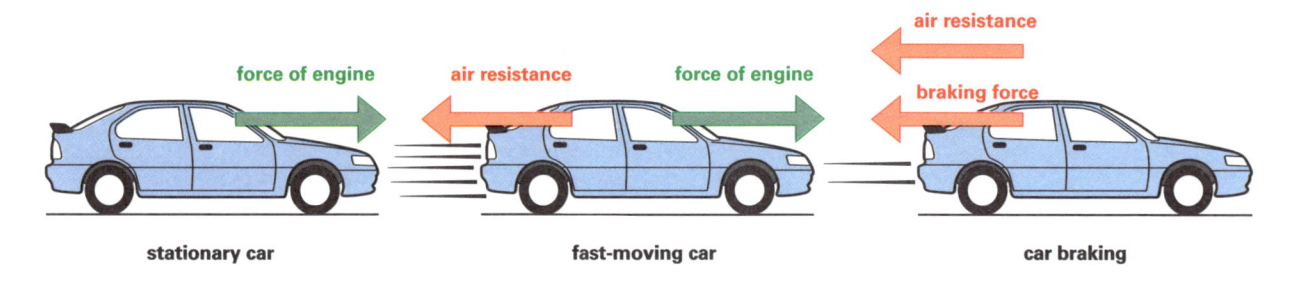

Fig. 17.14 A car's engine provides the force needed to start the car moving and overcome the force of air resistance.

To slow down, the driver presses on the brake pedal. Now the forces on the car are unbalanced again, and it slows down (decelerates).

- **Balanced forces:** speed remains constant.
- **Unbalanced forces:** speed changes (car accelerates or decelerates).

You will have found the same thing if you have ridden a bicycle. You have to keep pedalling at a steady rate to maintain a steady speed. Your force is balanced by the drag of air on you and your bike. You pedal harder to speed up and pedal less or apply the brakes to slow down. This idea is known as **Newton's first law of motion**:

> An object will stay at rest, or will continue to move at a steady speed in a straight line, unless it is acted on by an unbalanced force.

Understanding Newton's first law

Newton realized that you don't need a force to keep something moving. We are used to the idea that moving things soon come to a halt, for example, if you roll a ball or ride a bike. But this is because the ball and the bike are slowed down by the force of friction. Without friction, the ball and the bike would move for ever. Newton's first law tells us that, if an object is stationary or moving at a steady speed in a straight line, the forces on it must be balanced. The diagrams of the car in Figure. 17.15 show this.

Forces and motion 17.2

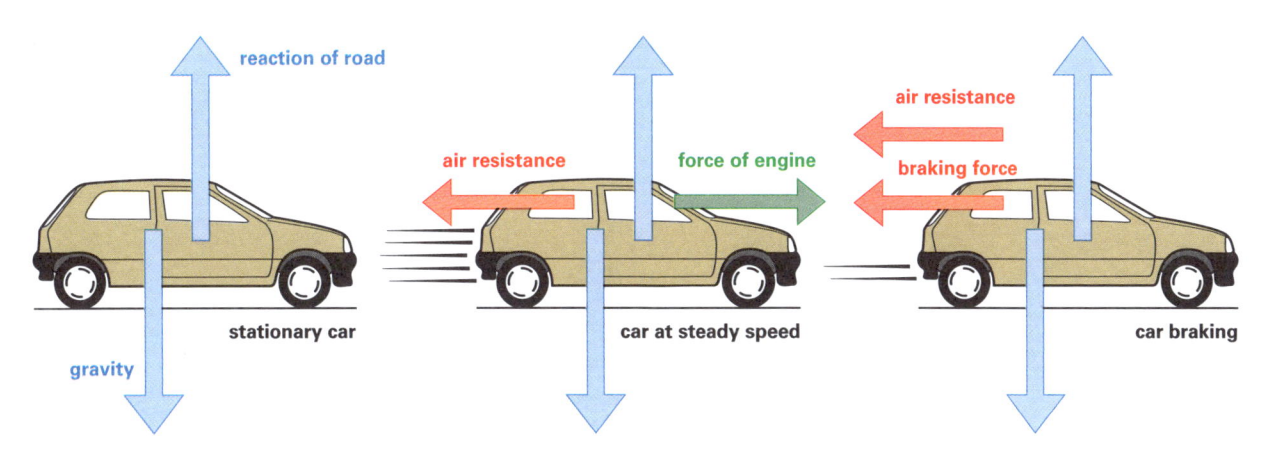

Fig. 17.15 If a car is stationary or moving at a steady speed in a straight line, the forces on it must be balanced.

When the car is stationary, two forces act on it:
- gravity pulls it downwards;
- the ground pushes back up with a force called the reaction of the ground.

These forces are balanced. Without the reaction of the ground, the car would disappear downwards.

When the car is moving at a steady speed, two more forces act on it:
- the engine pushes forwards, trying to make it go faster;
- air resistance pushes backwards, trying to slow it down.

These forces are also balanced, so the car maintains a steady speed. When the driver applies the brakes, there is an extra force:
- the backward force of the brakes.

Now the forces on the car are unbalanced, and it decelerates (slows down).

⬤ What you should know

- Friction, air resistance and drag are forces that tend to oppose motion.
- When the forces on an object are balanced, it will remain at rest or continue to move at a steady speed in a straight line.
- When the forces on an object are unbalanced, it will accelerate or decelerate.

17.2 Forces

Questions

1. The car in Figure 17.16 is crossing a bridge. Two forces acting on the car are shown.

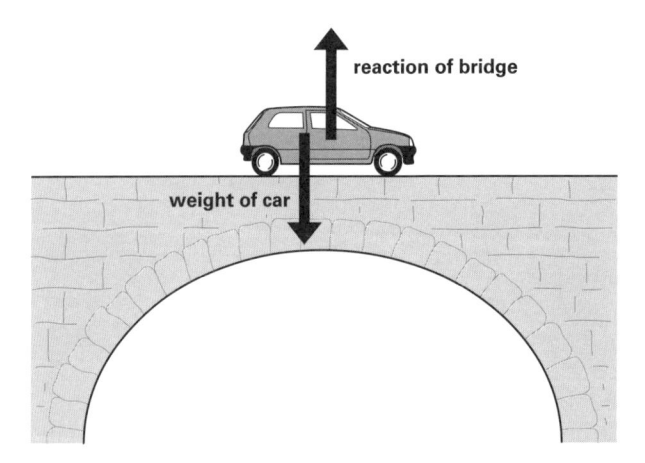

   Fig. 17.16

   a. Are the two forces shown balanced or unbalanced?
   b. What can you say about the sizes of the two forces and their directions?
   c. If the reaction of the bridge was less than the weight of the car, what would happen? Use the word 'accelerate' in your answer.

2. a. Copy out the sentence below. Choose words from the list below to fill the gaps.

   constant   remain   straight   unbalanced

   An object will ____ at rest, or will continue to move at a ____ speed in a ____ line, unless it is acted on by a force which is ____.

   b. What law is this a statement of?

3. friction   reaction   weight

   Choose words from the list which mean:

   a. the force of gravity on an object;
   b. the upward push of the ground on an object;
   c. the force caused by two surfaces rubbing together.

4. When oil has been spilled on the road, it is a good idea to pour sand on the oil. Why is this?

5. Research what happens when ice skaters are skating. What happens to the ice beneath the blade of the skate? What do you know about water and lubrication? Explain how ice skaters can skate so fast.

Forces

17.3 Machines – forces at work

> **Objectives**
>
> After studying this topic, you should be able to:
> - explain why machines are useful
> - state that the work done by a machine is equal to the amount of energy it transfers
> - calculate work done by a force when it moves
> - calculate power, in watts (W).

A machine is a device that helps us to do a job that we would otherwise find more difficult, or even impossible, to do. You will find a lot of simple, human-powered machines at home and at school: bottle openers, screwdrivers, pulleys and so on (Fig. 17.17). A bicycle is a complicated machine, made from several other simpler machines.

The idea of a machine is that it allows you to use a smaller force to do something. If you tried to crack a nut by hand, you would find it difficult to do. Nutcrackers can magnify (make larger) your force to make it big enough to crack the nut. For this reason, machines are sometimes known as force multipliers. We will look at several different types of machine in this section.

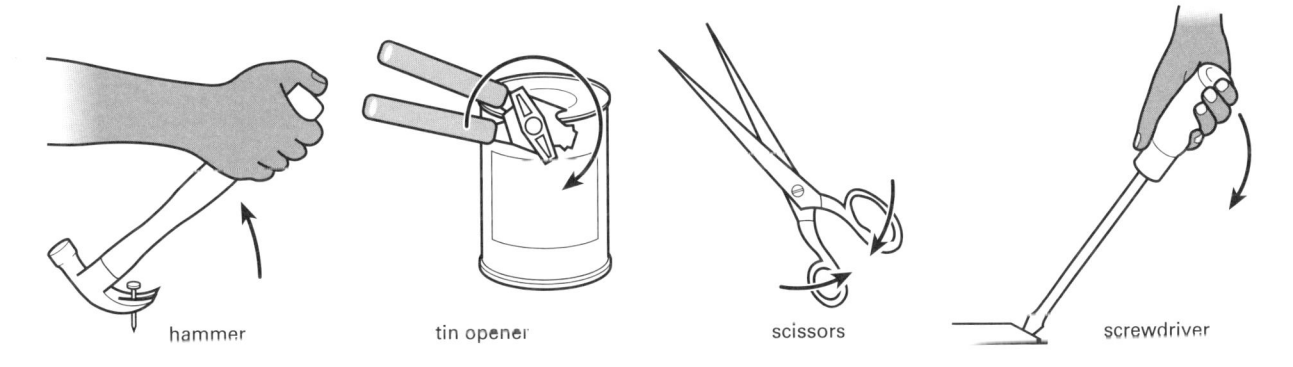

hammer   tin opener   scissors   screwdriver

Fig. 17.17 What tasks do these everyday machines help you with?

> **Activity** Up the slope
>
> **You will need**
> - heavy wooden block with hook
> - forcemeter (spring balance)
> - wooden board
> - pile of books

Method

1. Lift the wooden block with the forcemeter. What force is needed?
2. Use a pile of books to raise one end of the board (Fig. 17.18). Use the forcemeter to drag the block up the slope. What force is needed?
3. Slope the board at different angles, and measure the force needed to pull the block up it.

Fig. 17.18

Record
Note down the force needed in every case in the form of a table.

Discuss
1. How does the sloping board help you to raise the heavy block?
2. How does the force change as the angle of the slope changes?
3. Do you need less force or more force to pull the block up a steep slope?
4. Do you need less force or more force to pull the block up a shallow slope?
5. How are the angle of the board and the force needed to pull the block related?

Ramps

A sloping board like the one in the activity is an example of a machine called a ramp (or inclined plane). You need a smaller force to drag the block up the ramp than if you had to pull it straight upwards. Some public buildings have ramps at their entrances. This makes it easier for people, particularly people in wheelchairs or people who find climbing steps difficult, to reach the door. Builders often use a sloping plank as a ramp to push their wheelbarrows uphill.

Screws are used to join pieces of wood together. Take a close look at a screw. It can be described as a 'spiral ramp'. Work out why this is.

Block and tackle

Suppose you have to lift a heavy weight such as a packing case (Fig. 17.19). It is easier to do this if you use a **pulley** system. Attach a rope to the weight and pass it over a single pulley wheel. Now you can use your own weight to pull downwards on the rope and lift the object.

Better still, use a pulley system called a block and tackle. In Figure 17.19, a car engine is being lifted from under the bonnet (hood) of the car. You can see that the mechanic pulls downwards on one rope, but there are three ropes pulling upwards on the heavy engine. Each newton of the mechanic's pull is multiplied three times by the block and tackle.

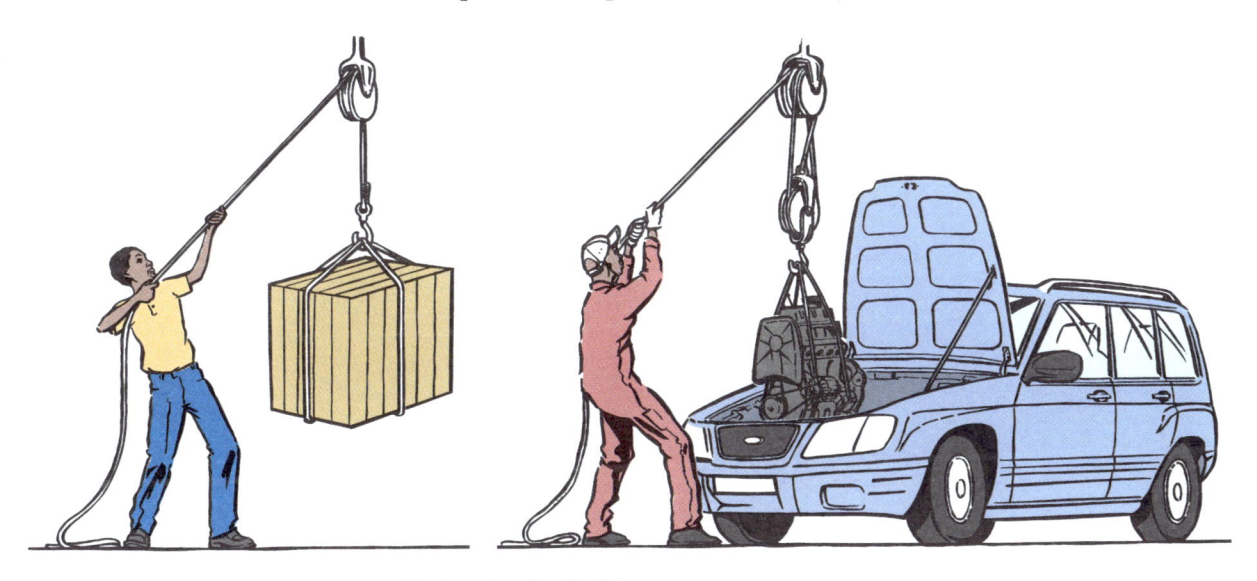

Fig. 17.19 A simple pulley (left) and a block and tackle (right).

Activity Balancing up

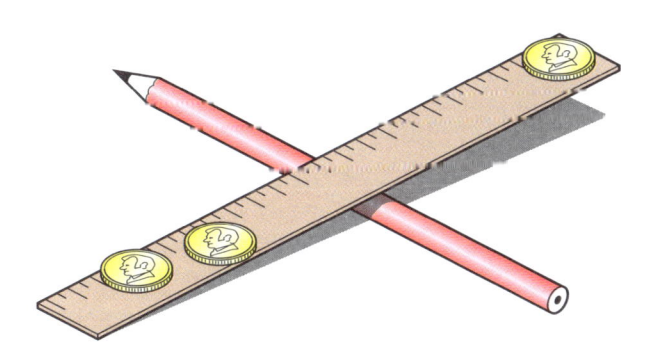

Fig. 17.20 Can one coin balance two coins?

You will need
- ruler
- pencil
- several identical coins (or similar weights)

Method
1 Look carefully at Figure 17.20 before you begin.
2 Check that the ruler will balance on the pencil. This can be tricky – it should balance with the pencil at the middle.
3 Put one coin on either end of the ruler. Will it balance?

17.3 Forces

4 Now put one coin at one end of the ruler, and two coins in a pile on the other end. The ruler will not balance. Where must you position the two coins to make it balance? You can probably guess the answer to this, but check it by doing the experiment.

The weight of the coins provides downward forces on either side of the **pivot** (the pencil). Your task is to find the connection between the number of coins and their distances from the pivot when the ruler is balanced. Remember to measure the distance from the pivot to the middle of the coins.

Record

Copy and complete Table 17.2 to show your calculations and results. Write a sentence to explain what you have found.

Table 17.2 Results of balancing experiment.

Number of coins on left	Distance from pivot	Calculation	Number of coins on right	Distance from pivot	Calculation

Discuss

1 When does the pivot balance in your experiment?
2 What is the connection between the number of coins and their distance from the pivot when the ruler is balanced?

The law of levers

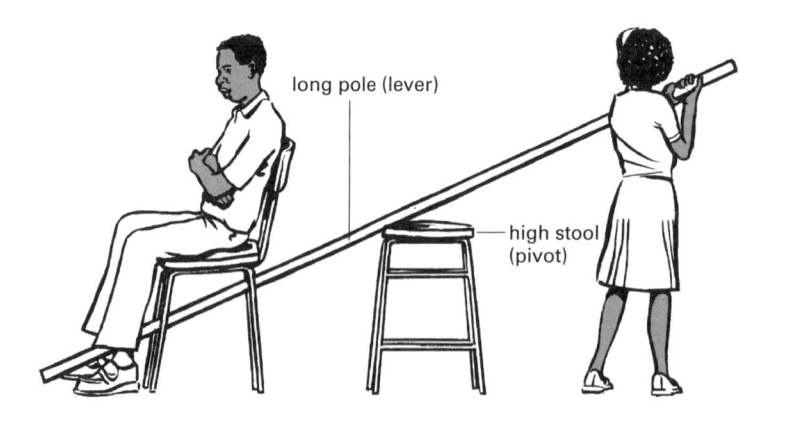

Fig. 17.21 A long lever is used to lift a heavy person.

A **lever** is a machine used for lifting heavy weights. Figure 17.21 shows how it is possible to lift a heavy person using a long lever. The lever in the figure is a long pole that tips about a point called the pivot (the high stool in Figure 17.21). The longer the lever, the easier it is to lift the **load** on the end. The girl can push down on the pole and lift the boy sitting on the chair.

Machines – forces at work 17.3

- The load is the weight of the object being lifted.
- The **effort** is the force used to do the lifting.

A see-saw is a kind of lever. If you have a playground with a see-saw in your local community, try to balance it in the same way you experimented with the ruler and coins in the activity you have just done. Use your friends instead of coins! Figure 17.22 shows how a lever works. People who weigh the same will balance if they sit at opposite ends. If one person weighs half as much as the other, they must sit twice as far from the pivot. This gives us the law of levers:

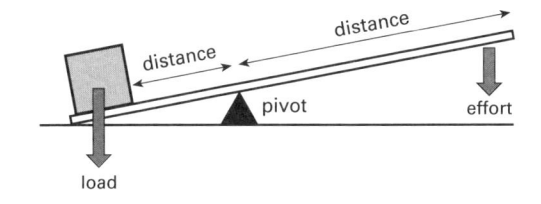

Fig. 17.22 How a lever works.

load × its distance from pivot = effort × its distance from pivot.

Classes of levers

By looking for the load, effort and pivot, we can identify three classes of lever.

Pivot at centre: examples: see-saw, laboratory balance, crowbar, scissors.

Load at centre: examples: wheelbarrow, nutcracker.

Effort at centre: examples: arm, fishing rod.

Figure 17.23 shows examples of these three kinds of lever. Read the caption carefully so that you can understand what each drawing shows.

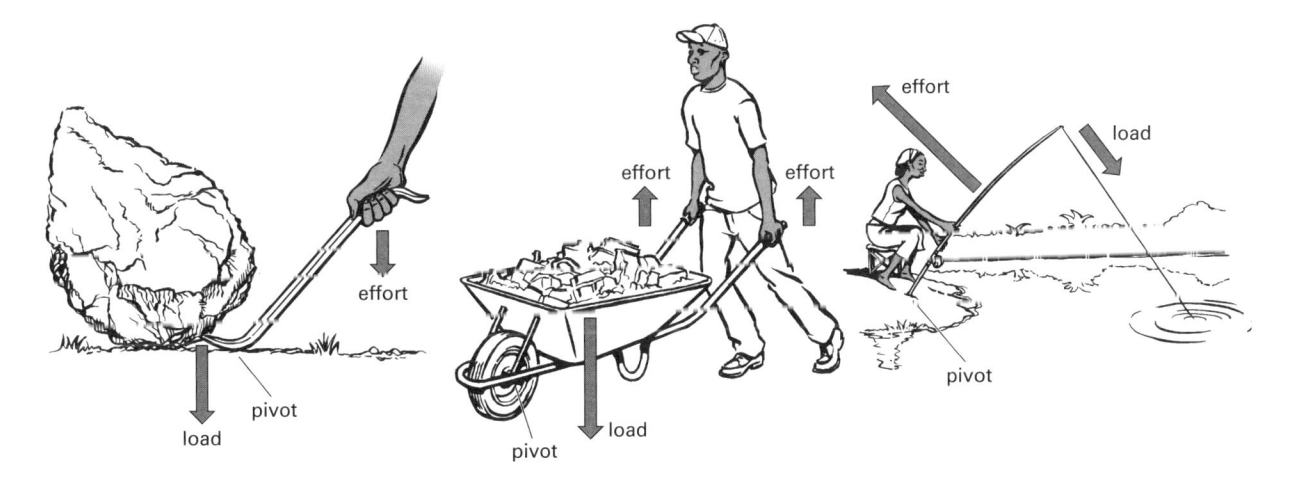

Fig. 17.23 Three kinds of lever. Left: A crowbar allows you to use a small force to lift a heavy object. The effort is further from the pivot than the load, so it is smaller. Centre: A wheelbarrow is pivoted at one end. Again, the load is closer to the pivot than the effort, so the load is greater than the effort. This is a force multiplier. Right: For the fishing rod, the effort is closer to the pivot than the load. This means that a large effort moves a smaller load, but the load moves farther than the effort. It is a distance multiplier.

17.3 Forces

Fig. 17.24 A steering wheel is an example of a wheel and axle.

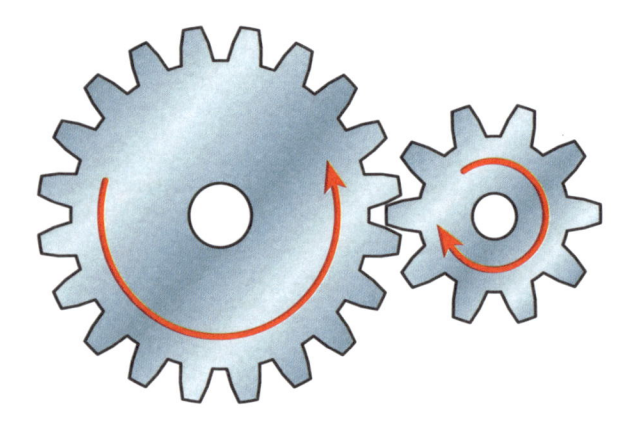

Fig. 17.25 Cog wheels turning. Note the directions in which they turn.

Fig. 17.26 The cog wheels of a bicycle.

Wheel and axle

A car's steering wheel is an example of a different type of machine, a wheel and axle (Fig. 17.24). The diameter is the width across the centre of a circle. A wheel is circular. The steering wheel has a large diameter, so it can be turned easily. The axle has a much smaller diameter, and magnifies (makes bigger) the driver's turning force to redirect the front wheels of the car.

A screwdriver is another example of a wheel and axle. The handle is fat. The end in contact with the screw is much smaller. To shift a stubborn screw, look for a screwdriver with a fat handle, not a long handle.

Gears

Cog wheels are at the heart of many machines. The wheels have little notches called teeth. One toothed wheel is made to turn, and this makes a second toothed wheel turn. In Figure 17.25, the first wheel has 20 teeth and the second has 10. When the first wheel turns once, the second turns twice (in the opposite direction).

A bicycle uses gears. The pedals cause the biggest toothed wheel to turn. The chain transfers this movement back to the smaller cogs (Fig. 17.26). Each time you rotate the pedals once, 60 teeth are turned. The smallest gear wheel at the back has only 20 teeth, so it rotates three times. This means that your feet only have to go round once to make the back wheel go round three times.

A bicycle makes use of several other machines. Look for the levers that operate the brakes and change the gears, and the handlebars, which work as a wheel and axle.

17.3 Machines – forces at work

Something for nothing?

Machines are useful because they allow us to produce much bigger forces than we would be able to do unaided. We can lift heavy loads, crack tough nuts and undo stiff screws. It almost seems as though we are getting something for nothing.

Fig. 17.27 Who is doing more work?

Look at Figure 17.27. The two children are transferring heavy boxes onto the school stage, which is 1 m high. The boy lifts a box weighing 200 N straight upwards. The girl pushes a similar box with a force of 100 N up a ramp that is 3 m long. Each child is said to be doing work. They are using up some of their **energy** (stored in their muscles), and transferring it to the box. The box ends up 1 m above its starting point, so it has gained gravitational **potential energy**. The amount of energy transferred by the child tells us how much work the child has done. Both work done and energy transferred are measured in joules (J).

work done = energy transferred

To calculate the amount of work done, we need to know two things:
- the size of the force – the bigger the force, the more work is done;
- how far the force moves – the further it moves, the more work is done.

Here is how we calculate work done:

work done = force × distance moved

For the boy, work done = 200 N × 1 m = 200 J (the boy lifted the box 1 m)

For the girl, work done = 100 N × 3 m = 300 J (the girl pushed the box 3 m)

So, although the girl uses a smaller force, she does more work than the boy, and uses up more of her energy.

⊙ Activity Calculating work done

You will need
- a heavy wooden block with hook
- a forcemeter (spring balance)
- a board
- a ruler
- a protractor for measuring angles

17.3 Forces

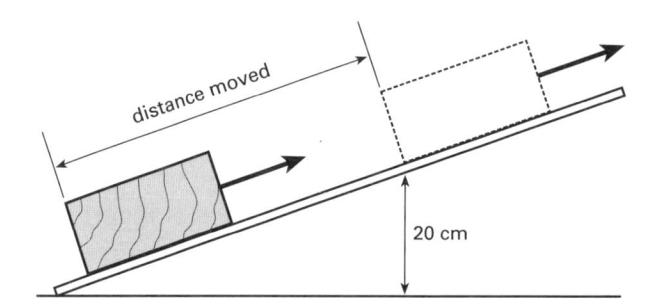

Fig. 17.28 Take care to measure from the back edge of the block.

Method

1. This is similar to the children lifting the boxes in Figure 17.27 described earlier. You have to raise the wooden block through 1 m vertically. You can lift it straight up, or pull it up a ramp, as shown in Figure 17.28.
2. For different angles of slope:
   - **a** Record the force needed to pull the block upwards.
   - **b** Measure and record the distance the block moves along the ramp as it moves 20 cm vertically.

Record

Table 17.3 Finding the amount of work done in moving the block with the ramp at different angles of slope.

Angle of ramp	Force needed (N)	Distance moved (m)	Work done (J)
90° (vertical)			
45°			

1. Copy and complete Table 17.3 to find the work done in moving the block.
2. Multiply force x distance to calculate work done.

Discuss

1. What angle of the ramp required the least work to raise the block?
2. What angle of the ramp required the most work to raise the block?

Power

Look back at the boy and the girl moving boxes onto the stage (Fig. 17.27, page 117). The boy can transfer boxes from floor to stage more quickly than the girl, because she has to move them a lot further. We say that he does work at a faster rate than the girl. His **power** is greater.

power = rate of doing work

$$\text{power} = \frac{\text{work done}}{\text{time taken}}$$

Power is measured in units called **watts** (**W**). Each time the boy lifts a box, he does 200 J of work. If he lifts one box every 10 s, his power is:

power = 200 J/10 s = 20 W

(Many electrical appliances are labelled with their power. A 60 W light bulb transfers 60 J of energy every second. A 2000 W heater transfers 2000 J every second.)

Activity Measuring your power

You will need
- a stopwatch
- a ruler
- bathroom scales (remember: 1 kg weighs 10 N)
- a staircase

Method

When you run up stairs, you are doing work. Your legs provide the force to raise your weight upwards. Your gravitational potential energy increases as you go up. How quickly can you transfer energy?

1. Use the bathroom scales to find your weight, in N.

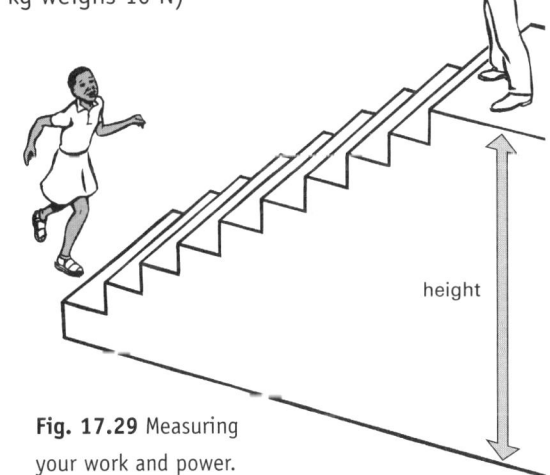

Fig. 17.29 Measuring your work and power.

2. Measure the vertical height of the stairs.
   (Measure the height of one step and multiply by the number of steps.)
3. Ask a friend to time how long it takes you to run to the top of the stairs.

Record

Record your results in a table. Calculate how much work you have done, and what your power is.

17.3 Forces

○ What you should know

- Machines are useful things (devices) that allow us to magnify the force we apply (the effort) to move a load.
- The work done by a machine is equal to the amount of energy it transfers.
- Energy transferred by a force = work done = force × distance moved.
- Power (calculated in watts, W) = work done/time taken.

◎ Questions

1. In what units are each of the following measured?
   a mass
   b force
   c work done
   d energy transferred
   e power

2. Jenny has been training in the gym. She finds that the most she can lift on her own is a load labelled 30 kg.
   a What is the weight of this load?
   b Explain how Jenny could use a lever to help her lift a load labelled 50 kg.

3. Figure 17.30 shows how to use a ruler pivoted on a pencil to compare the weights of two coins.

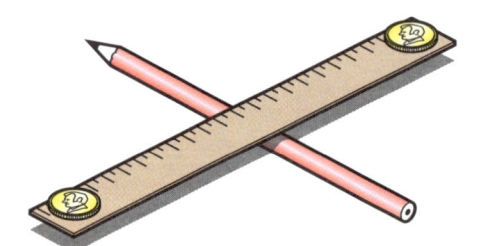

Fig. 17.30

   a Suppose you had three coins that looked alike, but you knew that one was a fake. It was heavier than the others. How could you use the ruler see-saw to find the fake?
   b If you had seven coins and one was the fake, how would you find it? You are only allowed two weighings!

4. Look at Table 17.3 on page 118. How would you use a computer spreadsheet program to help you work out the values in the final column? How could it show you the pattern relating the first and final columns?

The environment and its maintenance

18.1 What is ecology?

> **Objectives**
>
> After studying this topic you should be able to:
> - explain that ecology is the study of how living organisms interact with their environment
> - explain that an organism is adapted to live in its habitat
> - give some examples of communities and ecosystems
> - describe how an area is colonized and a climax community is established.

In Book 1, Topic 1.7, you learned that the environment is everything around us. It consists of the air, the land (rocks, minerals and soil), water (in the rain, ponds, streams, rivers, lakes, seas and oceans), the Sun's rays, the Moon and stars, all the plants and all the other animals. You also learned that all the living things, dead things or things made from living things are part of the biotic environment. Everything else makes up the abiotic environment (air, wind, rocks, soil, sun, etc.).

You have also learned about food webs and food chains (Book 2, Topic 10.3) and the nitrogen and carbon cycles (Book 2, Topic 10.4). You learned that all living things are interrelated and that they all interact with the abiotic environment. The study of living organisms and their interaction with the environment is called **ecology**. It comes from the Greek words '*oikos*' meaning 'home' or 'house', and '*logos*' meaning 'study of'. So, to put it simply, we are studying all living things in their homes!

Fig. 18.1 Can you see this cleverly camouflaged animal?

Living things can be found nearly everywhere on Earth. They can live in the soil, on rocks, in the sea, on trees, in grass and many other places. The place where an organism lives (its home) is described as its **habitat**. For example, the habitat of an earthworm is the soil. Organisms are suited to living in a particular habitat or environment. In other words, they are **adapted** to living in that environment. For example, fishes are adapted to live in water by having gills. They can't live on land because their gills would stick together and they wouldn't get enough oxygen.

Have you noticed that sometimes caterpillars are difficult to see on twigs, and frogs and toads are difficult to see in the undergrowth? These

18.1 The environment and its maintenance

animals either blend in with their surroundings because of their colour, or – like frogs and toads – can actually change their colour to suit their surroundings. This ability to hide or conceal themselves is called **camouflage** (Fig. 18.1). Being able to blend in with the surroundings protects many animals from predators. For example, a pale-coloured insect on a dark twig is more likely to be eaten by a bird than a darker or speckled one.

➲ Activity Looking for examples of adaptation

You can do this activity at home as well.

Method
Take a walk around the school area and look for any organisms living there – look around the base of trees, under stones, at the base of walls, on tree trunks and branches. Your teacher will help you to identify them. You only need to know the common names, such as beetle, caterpillar, ant, etc.

Record
Make a note of the organisms' names, where they were found and the various ways in which they were camouflaged.

If you study a pond, or a forest, you will find a number of different types (species) of animals and plants. Members of the same species make up a **population**. You might say, for example, that a pond has a large population of water snails. All the different types of plants, animals, algae, fungi and microorganisms (the living things) living in a particular place make up a **community**. The life of the community is affected by many things, such as the climate and the type of soil. We describe the community and its surroundings as an **ecosystem**. Ecosystems include forests (Fig. 18.2), grassland (Fig. 18.3), deserts (Fig. 18.4) and wetlands

Fig. 18.2 The rainforest is just one example of an ecosystem.

Fig. 18.3 Tropical grassland is also known as savanna.

18.1 What is ecology?

Fig. 18.4 A desert is very hot and dry but some organisms have adapted to living in this ecosystem.

Fig. 18.5 This wetland swamp supports a wide variety of plant and animal life.

(marshes, swamps or bogs) (Fig. 18.5). An ecosystem is a stable and balanced system that persists from year to year. The materials are constantly recycled (remember the carbon and nitrogen cycles). We will learn more about ecosystems in the Caribbean in the next topic.

The environment in any ecosystem is constantly changing. For example, there are changes in the weather, changes in temperature, day changing to night, changes in the seasons, and the movements of the tide on the seashore and in river estuaries.

Ecosystems can be damaged by extreme weather conditions such as flooding, forest fires, tropical storms, hurricanes, earthquakes, volcanic eruptions and climate change. They can also be damaged by the activities of people when forests are cut down, for example, and also by pollution. We will return to this in later topics.

Finding out

Hurricane Mitch

Hurricane Mitch developed on 26 October 1998 and into the early hours of 27 October. It moved slowly inland on 29 October and then began to weaken. As the winds weakened, the heavy rain caused thousands of people to be killed by flooding and mudslides in Central America. It then developed into a tropical storm in the Caribbean, causing even more damage, moved through Florida and finally left the land on 5 November. Find out about the effects of Hurricane Mitch on the lives of the people and on the ecosystems of the Caribbean. Use magazines and the internet to help you. If your country was affected, find out details from family, friends and the local community.

18.1 The environment and its maintenance

How do communities and ecosystems form?

When a community changes on a large scale because of natural catastrophes or because of human activities, the numbers in a population may fall or the population may even die out altogether. For example, on a small scale, a pond may dry out, or on a larger scale, a large area of forest may be chopped down. In the case of the pond, the plants and animals that are adapted to life in water will die. In the case of the forest, the shade-loving plants will die out and many animals that feed and shelter in the forest will also be seriously affected. Living things die if they are not adapted to live in the new environment.

But although the environment has changed, it will be suitable for other different types of animals and plants. New species will now start to live in those areas. This is known as **colonization**. When the plants grow, the animals will follow to feed on the plants.

In the case of the chopped-down forest, grasses will replace the shade-loving plants. If the area is left alone for a few years, bushes and then trees will begin to grow. This is called a succession. Eventually when the trees grow, the shade-loving species will return. The animals will also return and the forest will be established again, with large mature trees. This is called a climax community.

➲ Activity Investigating colonization

You will need to do this activity over a period of weeks or months. Your teacher will have prepared a small area of land near your school (minimum about two metres square). The soil will be completely bare. Your teacher (not you!) may have burned the patch of land to make sure that there are no roots left in the soil. The area should be closed off so that people don't walk over it by mistake.
Study the area every few days and observe and record the plants (and animals) that begin to colonize your bare (or burnt) patch. Your teacher will help you with the names. You may come up with some very interesting findings.

❓ Finding out

Has colonization of plants and animals occurred where there have been volcanic eruptions?

You may live in a country where a volcano has erupted in the past and is either dormant or extinct. Look again at Topic 14.1 and at your atlas to find out where there are volcanoes in the Caribbean. Find out from books and the internet and from your local area when and whether the land around particular volcanoes has been re-colonized. Your teacher will help you with your research. Remember that the ash from volcanoes is very fertile.

What is ecology? 18.1

◘ What you should know

- Ecology is the study of how living organisms interact with their environment.
- A habitat is where a plant or animal lives.
- Organisms are adapted to live in a particular habitat.
- Communities consist of populations of different plants and animals.
- Ecosystems are communities, together with their surrounding environment.
- Areas that have been altered by climate change or destroyed can be colonized by new species and a climax community can be established.

@ Questions

1. Explain the difference between the terms abiotic and biotic.

2. Fill in the gaps in the following sentences using these words:

    climax; surroundings; communities; population

    a. The members of the same species make up a _____.
    b. _____ are made up of different populations.
    c. An ecosystem is a community plus its _____.
    d. A forest with large mature trees is described as a _____ community.

3. Research the recovery of ecosystems after forest fires. Some plants have adapted to exploit the conditions after a fire. Find out about them.

The environment and its maintenance

18.2 Ecosystems in the Caribbean

▶ Objectives

After studying this topic, you should be able to:
- explain the importance of forests and the seashore
- list the benefits of forests and the seashore to human life
- describe the damaging effects of deforestation
- explain how sustainable development can help to reverse the damage
- explain how the ecosystems of the seashore are closely linked
- study an ecosystem by doing fieldwork.

Ecology of the Caribbean region

A large number of tourists visit the Caribbean countries throughout the year (Fig. 18.6). They are attracted by the climate, beautiful beaches and the exotic wildlife. In this section, you are going to study the ecology of your region to find out about the plants and animals that live alongside you.

The Caribbean islands were formed millions of years ago from two chains of mountains. The mountains gradually became submerged by the Atlantic Ocean and Caribbean Sea except for the mountain peaks, which today form the islands. One mountain chain runs west to east (the Greater Antilles). The other runs more or less from north to south (the Lesser Antilles). The Atlantic Ocean lies to the north and northeast of the Greater Antilles. To the south of these islands is the Caribbean Sea, which also washes the west coast of the Lesser Antilles. The Atlantic Ocean is to the north and east of these islands. The mountains of the islands of the Greater Antilles are surrounded by fertile coastal plains and all the islands are surrounded by submerged coral reefs. There are still active volcanoes on some islands of the Lesser Antilles. Some islands, such as Barbados and Antigua, have been formed by even older rocks than those of the mountain chains. Again, the original rocks have been worn away to leave an almost flat surface above the water.

Fig. 18.6 Tourists are attracted to the Caribbean by the climate and beautiful beaches. This is Pigeon Point, Tobago.

Ecosystems in the Caribbean 18.2

The vegetation that grows is affected by the type of rock (sedimentary rock such as limestone, igneous (volcanic) and metamorphic rock). The height of the land, the soil, the amount of rainfall and the humidity also affect plant growth. The limestone rocks have been eroded over time (Topic 14.5), causing the formation of features such as banana holes (sink holes), caves and cliffs.

Most islands have a wet season and a dry season. The annual rainfall ranges from about 800 to 2000 mm, but can be as much as 5000 mm on the highest peaks of the mountains. From December to April, the temperatures range between 24 and 27°C and between 29 and 32°C from May to November (the hurricane season). July and August are the hottest months, but the gentle trade winds may keep the temperature down to more comfortable levels below 32°C.

There is a wide variety of species of plants, animals and other organisms in the Caribbean. The variety of life forms within a particular country or region is called the **biodiversity**. For example, it is estimated that there are over 1300 plant species in St Lucia. In other words St Lucia has a high biodiversity of plants. By protecting our wild plants and animals we help to maintain biodiversity.

Biodiversity is important because it is an indicator of the health of natural communities. It also means that we have an interesting and varied environment in which to live. Furthermore, many wild species are known to be useful, for example for food or drugs, and there may be many more whose uses are still undiscovered.

Did you know?

The Amerindian people on mainland Guyana and Surinam and the Carib people in Dominica, Grenada and Trinidad are the original inhabitants of the Caribbean. They are described as **indigenous peoples**. Everyone else in the Caribbean has originated from other parts of the world such as Africa, Asia and Europe. Many plants and animals have also been here since ancient times when the islands were formed. These are described as **indigenous species** – for example, the tree ferns on the island of Dominica (Fig. 18.7). In contrast, certain plants and animals are not indigenous and have been transported here by humans. Cows, pigs and sheep came from Europe when the islands were colonized.

Fig. 18.7 The tree ferns on the island of Dominica are examples of native (indigenous) species.

18.2 The environment and its maintenance

Finding out

National emblems

Many countries have national flags or emblems with an animal or plant that is always associated with that country. They also have national dishes, for example, the national dish of Jamaica is akee. Find out about the national emblems of other countries in the Caribbean.

In the coastal regions, there are sandy beaches, some with coconut palms. Black and red mangrove trees form dense forests around lagoons and estuaries. Other plants include cacti and thorny shrubs. The most common land animals are mosquitoes and butterflies, frogs, lizards (especially iguanas), snakes and birds (especially ibises, hummingbirds, parrots and toucans). There are also bats (in caves along the rocky coasts and in the rainforests), the agouti (a large rodent) and manicou. The bird populations of the islands change considerably throughout the year. This is because the islands are on the migratory paths of birds flying south for the winter from the United States (and back to the north in the spring) (Fig. 18.8).

The coral reefs grow in abundance because of the clear warm waters and support an enormous variety of fish, shellfish and other animals. They include spiny lobsters, conch, manta rays, red snapper, flying fish, barracuda, sea turtles, manatees, dolphins and many more. Out at sea are the frigate birds and boobies and many other tropical birds, together with flying fish, tuna, kingfish and grouper.

The tropical rainforest

All Caribbean countries have forests of one type or another. Some islands like Jamaica and Trinidad and Tobago have wide expanses of mangrove forests. Countries like Guyana and Dominica have dense tropical rainforest that covers large areas. Small pockets of rainforest are found in Grenada, St Lucia, St Vincent, Barbados and St Kitts. The mangrove forests extend into mangrove swamps around the coastal fringe. Other types of forest in the Caribbean include Caribbean pine forests (in Cuba), semi-deciduous woodland (the Leeward Islands), montane forest in wet highlands and elfin woodland on exposed peaks of high mountains above the rainforest.

Fig. 18.8 Some examples of Caribbean wildlife. Do you recognize them?

Ecosystems in the Caribbean   18.2

Tropical rainforests are ecosystems that have developed over millions of years. They are found in countries north and south of the Equator, where it is hot and wet all the year round. There is a wide range of animals and plants in the rainforests. Their activities are all interrelated, forming complex food webs. The large trees in the rainforest represent the climax community. They can grow up to 40 metres high. The leaves of the trees grow out at angles from the branches to get the maximum amount of light for photosynthesis. They form a mosaic pattern. The leafy tops of the trees form a **canopy** over the other plants (Fig. 18.9). The canopy is so dense that only about 1% of the light gets through!

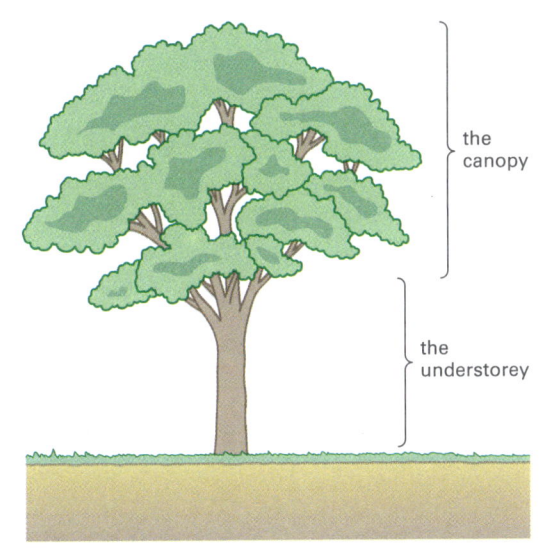

Fig. 18.9 The leaves form a close canopy above the understorey.

Beneath the canopy is the very dark **understorey**, where the lack of light prevents small herbaceous flowering plants from growing. Most of the soil beneath the trees consists of decomposing leaves. The organisms that can grow successfully are mosses on the bark of the trees, fungi, ferns and plants such as the heliconias. When the trees produce fruits and seeds, the young seedlings grow using the stored food reserves at first and then grow very slowly. They can only develop into new trees if the trees forming the canopy die or are damaged in some way by storms. Once gaps in the canopy develop, the light enables other plants to grow. These include herbaceous

Did you know?

Animals such as butterflies, moths, bees, beetles, hummingbirds (and even bats) help to pollinate the flowers that develop on the trees in the forest canopy (Fig. 18.10). The flowers are brightly coloured and have nectar and pollen to attract insects.

In tropical rainforests, different coloured flowers are pollinated by different types of animals.

- Most flowers that are pollinated by insects that are active in the day are orange and yellow.
- Most flowers that are pollinated by moths at night are white or pink.
- Most flowers that are pollinated by birds are red.

Fig. 18.10 Brightly coloured flowers with delicious nectar and pollen attract insects, beetles, birds and even bats to the rainforest canopy.

18.2 The environment and its maintenance

Did you know?

- Slower-growing trees in a rainforest can live for over 500 years and many others are 200 years old.
- The tropical rainforests have given us all these delicious foods: oranges, lemons, limes, mangoes, avocados, guavas, passion fruit, pawpaws, palm oils, cashew nuts, Brazil nuts, coffee beans and many more! Rubber is also a rainforest product that we use for making many things.

flowering plants, ferns and the young saplings. This is when long-dormant seeds start to germinate.

The trees need a constant supply of mineral nutrients, and so there are a large number of **decomposers** (Book 2, Topics 10.3–10.4), such as bacteria and fungi, which break down and recycle the dead material from the fallen leaves and branches. The nutrients are then washed into the soil for the roots to absorb.

There are many climbing plants such as vines growing in the rainforests. Lianas hook themselves on to the tree trunks and grow by winding their stems round and round the trunk up into the canopy towards the light. Epiphytes also grow abundantly. These plants have leaves where photosynthesis can take place, but they have long dangling aerial roots that have no contact with the soil. The roots get their nutrients from the rain washing over them! Many orchids are epiphytes (Fig. 18.11).

Other plants, for example, certain fig trees, are known as stranglers. They start off as epiphytes like the orchids. Their roots continue to grow downwards and into the soil, completely surrounding the tree trunk. They compete with the tree for light in the canopy and also with the roots for nutrients. Eventually the tree they live on dies and the strangler flourishes. It is almost as though it has strangled the tree to death!

Animals find shelter in the forests and feed on the fallen leaves, fruits and seeds. Some, like the termites, can even digest wood! All kinds of animals feed on the seeds and fruits growing on the trees and in this way also help to disperse them. The seedlings grow away from the parent plant, which helps to spread the species.

The rainforest has a range of land animals such as frogs, toads, lizards, snakes and rats. Some animals are not indigenous. For example, the mongoose (Fig. 18.12) was introduced throughout the Caribbean region in the eighteenth century to kill snakes in the sugar cane fields. After the snake populations declined, the mongoose

Fig. 18.11 Many orchids are epiphytes, with aerial roots.

Ecosystems in the Caribbean   18.2

Fig. 18.12 The mongoose is not an indigenous animal. It was introduced into the Caribbean from India.

preyed on chickens. Aquatic life, including interesting species of freshwater shrimps, is found in the many forest streams and rivers. These are kept supplied by the high levels of rainfall.

All forests, and especially the tropical rainforest, have a high rate of photosynthesis. As you know from Book 1, Topic 5.1, oxygen is produced and carbon dioxide is used up in photosynthesis and so the forests of the world contribute to the supply of oxygen and removal of carbon dioxide from the atmosphere. The roots of forests help to stabilize the soil and prevent soil erosion, which you will learn about in Topic 18.3.

Forest trees also play an important role in the water cycle (Book 1, Topic 3.2) as they give out water from their leaves by transpiration and take up water from the soil through their roots. These factors, together with the products for human use that the rainforest provides show how important this ecosystem is for human beings.

In past times, the Caribbean region was covered with ancient forests; however, many trees were cut down by the owners of sugar plantations to provide firewood for their sugar refineries. In many countries, there has also been a policy of slash and burn to clear land for agriculture (for growing cash crops and for cattle ranching) and for building and industry. The destruction of forests is called **deforestation**. It has occurred all over the world, not only in the Caribbean. The rainforest has been plundered for many reasons. It provides firewood, timber, hardwood (teak, ebony and mahogany, for example), minerals and other valuable products. Many important drugs for treating diseases have been discovered in certain rainforest species.

It is only in recent years that the effects of deforestation have become obvious to scientists. It has had major effects on the climate as well as on animal and plant populations.

- Deforestation has resulted in the destruction of habitats of many animals and plants. Some species are in danger of dying out altogether. These species are listed by scientists and are described as endangered species.
- Because the rainforests play an important role in the water cycle, their destruction results in the climate becoming drier with far less rainfall. Also, there are no roots to bind the soil together and so the rain that does fall is not retained and the underground water supply in the rocks diminishes.

? Finding out

Drugs from the wild

Many drugs are derived from plants. Find out the names of two West Indians who have made eye drops for glaucoma from the cannabis plant.

Many local people make medicines from plants. How do they decide on the amounts to put in their medicines; the doses to give; and which plants to use?

131

18.2 The environment and its maintenance

? Finding out

Endangered species in the Caribbean

Find out about some of the endangered species in the Caribbean and what is being done to protect them. Your teacher will help you to obtain information from conservation associations in your country, such as the Caribbean Forest Conservation Association. You can also obtain information from the World Wide Fund for Nature (WWF), from books, encyclopedias and the internet. Here are some examples of endangered species in the Caribbean to start you off with your research: the West Indian whistling duck (Fig. 18.13), the red-neck Amazonian parrot and the Nassau grouper.

Fig. 18.13 The West Indian whistling duck is an endangered species on many Caribbean islands.

Did you know?

- About 140 million people are forest dwellers (Fig. 18.14).
- About 2 billion people all over the world use wood in their homes for heating and cooking.

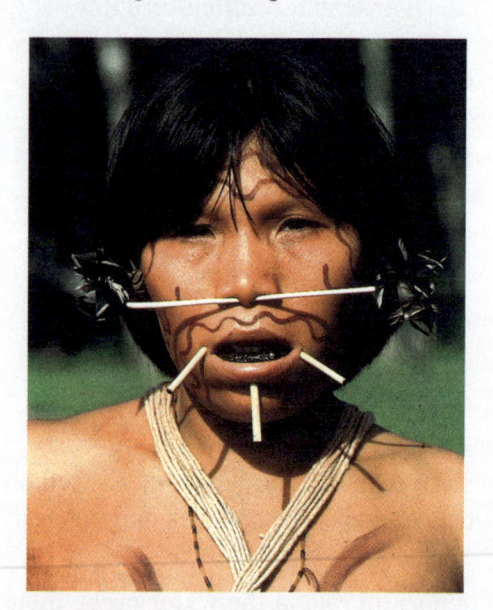

Fig. 18.14 This Yanomani Indian lives in the Amazonian rainforest. If this part of the rainforest were to be destroyed, he would lose his home and livelihood.

- Livelihoods and homes of entire populations of people have also been destroyed. Many people live in forests and rely on them completely for food and shelter – for example, the people of the Amazonian rainforest.

Many countries, including many Caribbean countries, have now passed laws to protect the forests. Of course, no-one is suggesting that wood should be no longer used for fuel or for timber, furniture and other products. But what has been suggested is that we use the environment wisely. This is called **sustainable development** and in the case of forests includes planting new trees to replace what we have used (reforestation, sometimes called afforestation). For example, trees planted for fuel should be fast growing and, if possible, should also put nitrogen back into the soil. The Mexican ipil ipil (*Leucaena*) and the acacia are good examples. Reforestation is practised in Jamaica, and Trinidad and Tobago. In these countries, new trees are planted at the same rate as trees are felled. Designing more efficient wood-burning stoves is another way of helping to solve the problem.

Ecosystems in the Caribbean 18.2

Did you know?

The Caribbean National Forest is on the island of Puerto Rico. It is the smallest rainforest in the Caribbean and is known by the local people as El Yunque (Fig. 18.15). It is named after the Taino Indian spirit 'Yuquiyti', who, according to the legend, lived at the top of the mountain and protected the Puerto Rican people. The forest has over 200 indigenous species of trees and 50 indigenous species of orchids. The water flowing through the forest is used for domestic and industrial purposes and many dams and hydroelectric power stations have been built.

Fig. 18.15 El Yunque on Puerto Rico.

Activity Rainforests in the Caribbean

You will need
- your atlas
- books for reference

Method
1 Look at a map of the Caribbean region.
2 Use your atlas and books to list the Caribbean countries that have rainforest.

Discuss
1 Find out some examples of countries that have lost most of their rainforest. Choose one and try to find out why this may have happened.

2 Find out some examples of countries that are preserving their rainforest. Choose one and try to find out how this is being done.

3 What can individual people do in their communities to help save the rainforests?

4 Find out if there are examples of sustainable development in your country. What can you do to help?

The coastal ecosystem

All around our beautiful islands, and along the rivers of Guyana are beautiful sandy beaches and rocky shores. There are also mangrove wetlands, seagrass beds and coral reefs. Coastlines are very variable and it is sometimes difficult to find definite boundaries, but roughly speaking,

18.2 The environment and its maintenance

Did you know?

Some people try to make a living by sand mining – taking sand from beaches to sell, to builders for example. Usually the sand miners are not intentionally harming the environment. However, they do not realize that their actions cause damage because it can take a long time for the effects to be seen. But by then it is too late.

Sand mining is a serious problem for many Caribbean governments, who are trying to keep their people happy *and* protect the environment.

we can divide the coastal region into the sea, the shore and the land behind the shore.

- The sea extends outwards from the lowest tide line. This offshore region consists of shallow water with seagrass beds and coral reefs teeming with marine life. (The word 'marine' means 'associated with the sea'.)
- The shore stretches from the low tide line inland to a cliff or the sand dunes. It may be a sandy or rocky shore.
- The coastal area behind the shore includes sand dunes or lagoons or mangrove swamps. It may be very narrow if the land rises steeply.

We can consider the shore, the seagrass beds, the coral reefs, the mangrove swamps, the lagoons and the muddy bottoms of river estuaries as separate ecosystems making up the coastal zone. We can also think of each one as a habitat. All are very closely linked and depend on one another for development and survival.

Shores: Shores are made of sand, pebbles, corals and rocks. They are constantly changing because of the tides, storms, hurricanes and changes in sea level. People also cause major changes, especially in the Caribbean, where the sandy beaches attract many tourists. Vegetation has been cleared, sea walls have been built and some of the sand has been removed for the building industry. Reptiles, birds and other animals breed and nest on the shores. For example, sea turtles dig their nests and lay their eggs on sandy beaches (Fig. 18.16). They hide the nests by covering them with sand. Crabs, clams and other animals make their burrows in the sand.

Although there is not a great distance between high and low tide lines in most of the Caribbean, at some point when the tide goes out animals and seaweed are exposed to the air. In stormy weather the waves are higher and stronger and the sea moves much further up the beach than in calm weather. Many animals have adapted to tidal movements by attaching themselves to rocks, for example, sea anemones, limpets, winkles and barnacles. At low tide, there are often rock pools, and these contain a wide variety of animals, including rockfish, crabs, sea urchins, brittle stars, starfish and sea cucumbers. Figure 18.17 shows marine organisms. See how many you can identify in a rock pool. The different types of seaweed are algae. The drink 'seamoss' is made from red seaweed found growing on rocks

Fig. 18.16 Turtles move out of the sea to lay their eggs in the sand.

Ecosystems in the Caribbean 18.2

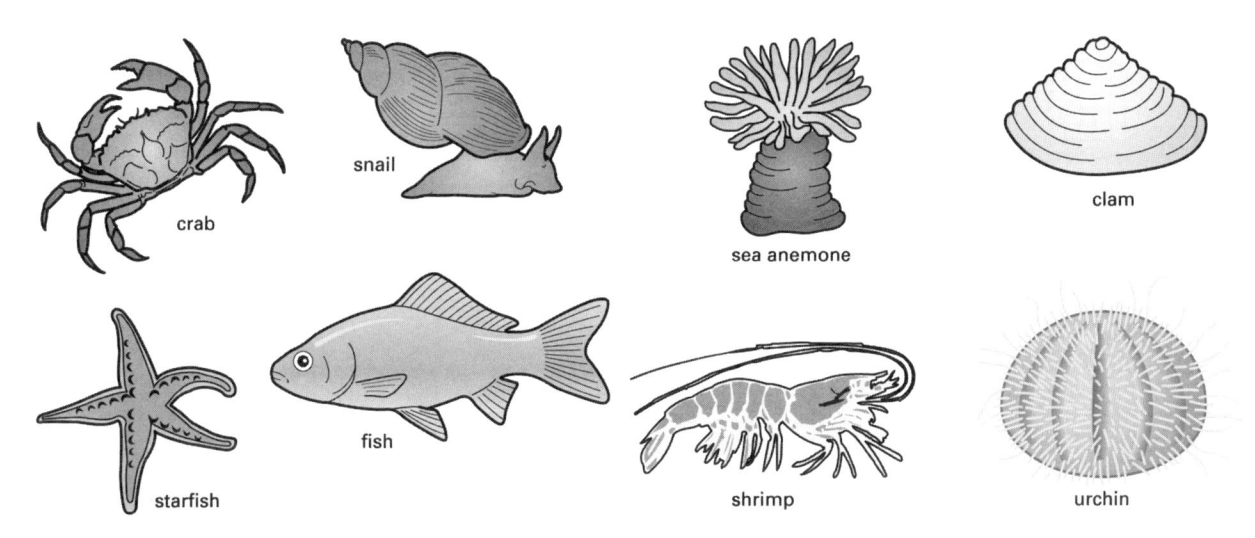

Fig. 18.17 Some of the marine life you might find in a rock pool.

Fig. 18.18 Seagrass provides food for many animals.

near to the shore. Some types of dried seaweed are highly nutritious and are used for feeding livestock.

Sea grasses: Sea grasses are flowering plants! You wouldn't really expect them to live in this type of environment, but they do. They have male and female flowers, for sexual reproduction, but usually reproduce asexually by means of underground stems called **rhizomes**. The main species are turtle grass (*Thalassia testudinum*) and manatee grass (*Syringodium filiforme*). Seagrass meadows are found between the reefs and the shore (Fig. 18.18). Turtles, sea urchins and many different fishes graze on the blades of grass, and algae and small invertebrates attach themselves to the leaves. The roots and rhizomes of these grasses help to trap the bottom sediment and stop it being washed away by the currents. In this way they help to keep the waters of the coral reefs clean and clear and provide a barrier between the sea water and the land. Many commercial fishermen use seagrass beds as nurseries to rear young fish.

Coral reefs: Coral reefs (Fig. 18.19) grow well in the warm and clear shallow waters. They are often described as 'the tropical rainforests of the ocean'! Corals are tiny animals (polyps) resembling sea anemones. They have tentacles that they use to feed on the tiny marine organisms floating in the sea (**plankton**). Corals live in colonies. Each animal produces a skeleton of calcium carbonate. When the animal dies, the soft parts decay but the skeleton remains. This is how coral reefs are built up. The reefs

18.2 The environment and its maintenance

Did you know?

Microscopic algae live inside some of the cells of the coral polyps. They can photosynthesize and give the polyp cells extra oxygen for respiration. In return, the algae get carbon dioxide (for photosynthesis) from the polyp cells when respiration takes place. In other words, they swap carbon dioxide and oxygen. This relationship for mutual benefit is called **symbiosis**. The pigments of the algae (which trap the Sun's energy) cause the corals to have beautiful colours. Without the algae, the corals would be white.

Fig. 18.19 A coral reef.

start as fringing reefs, extending out to sea. They can also develop into barrier reefs separated from the shore by a lagoon (the Great Barrier Reef along the north Australian coast is the best-known example). Sometimes the reef grows into a circle around a lagoon and either the sea level rises or the coral sinks and forms an atoll. Corals provide food and shelter for fish and other marine animals such as shrimps and lobsters. They also form a barrier or breakwater from the open sea and protect the coastal areas from erosion and the effects of storms. Tiny bits of coral on the beaches make the sand white.

Mangroves: Mangrove forests and swamps grow along many parts of the coastline. Mangroves are unusual plants because their roots are adapted to being submerged in salt water. They have buttress roots for extra support so that they can withstand high winds (Fig. 18.20). Mangroves also act as a barrier. They trap and filter sediments (particles) being washed down from the land, and prevent them from being carried into the sea. Like the sea grasses, mangroves help to keep the sea water around the coral reefs clean and clear. They can act as windbreaks and also take the force of storm waves and tidal currents. This helps to protect the land behind the forests from both wind and sea erosion.

Fig. 18.20 The buttress roots of mangroves provide a habitat for many marine animals.

Ecosystems in the Caribbean 18.2

Many small fishes, crabs and other invertebrates live amongst the roots and, like the sea grasses, many people use the mangrove swamps as areas for raising young fish for commercial purposes.

Estuaries, lagoons and other wetlands: These are also very fertile ecosystems with large amounts of nutrients for many organisms. Many worms make their burrows in the muddy bottom. These areas also provide nurseries for young fish, nesting sites for many birds and trap sediments washed down from the land. The heaviest particles sink to the bottom. Salinas are shallow ponds or lakes full of salty water. They also trap sediments and help to keep the coral reefs clean. When allowed to dry out, they are valuable sources of common salt (sodium chloride).

The seashore is therefore a very complex series of ecosystems, all depending and interacting with one another. When one part is disturbed or damaged, this has consequences for the others. If coral reefs become polluted or damaged for any reason, this affects all the animals that live in the ecosystem. If large areas of mangroves are removed, this affects not only the animals that feed on them, but also the amount of sediment getting onto the beaches and into the sea. Also, the land behind the coast is exposed to erosion from the effects of the wind and sea.

> **Did you know?**
>
> The Mankote mangrove in St Lucia is an example of successful management of the environment. Here a group of charcoal producers have been working with various government and non-government bodies to preserve the mangrove forest while continuing to harvest it to make charcoal.

➔ Activity A field trip

Many of you will live near a beach and this is probably where your teacher will take you (Fig. 18.21). If this is not possible, then a trip to the nearest woodland or forest will be just as enjoyable and rewarding.

Remember:
- Stay in groups while you work and never wander off on your own.
- The beach and the forest can be dangerous places if you do not know the area or you misbehave.
- If you are near water, take care not to fall in.
- Only collect animals and plants for observation when the teacher gives you permission.
- Always handle animals carefully and gently, and always put them back after you have observed them.
- As you are in a hot climate, drink water often to prevent getting dehydrated.
- Have fun learning about your environment!

You will need
- food and plenty of water and drinks
- suitable clothing, including a hat to protect your head from the Sun

18.2 The environment and its maintenance

Fig. 18.21 A field trip is a wonderful opportunity to learn about the environment and ecosystems.

- suitable shoes
- suncream to protect your skin
- sunglasses if necessary
- insect repellent to ward off midges and mosquitoes in the forests and sand flies at the beach
- a notebook or a clipboard with sheets of paper (a clipboard makes it easier to write when you are out of doors)
- a pencil
- a large plastic bucket
- several transparent plastic containers
- some transparent plastic bags
- a measuring tape
- a ball of string
- some tall sticks or bamboo canes
- a metre square made from wire coated with plastic, or from wood
- fishing nets
- a hand lens
- books to help you to identify the organisms you see
- transport to the study site if necessary

Method

1 When you arrive, look carefully around and draw a sketch of the area.

2 Write down important features, for example, whether the beach has a cliff or is bordered by mangroves, or the type of land or other features at the edge of the forest. Is the beach sandy or rocky? What are the rocks or sand like? Are there streams or rivers in the forest? This will enable you to describe your study area.

3 Your teacher will then select a smaller area for you to study. Start off by observing the plants and animals you see and identify them. Use the books to help you. You could also collect shells and feathers and identify what animals they belong to.

4 If you are investigating organisms in a shallow stream or a rock pool, you could half-fill the plastic bucket with water from the sea or stream and then carefully collect some of the animals and seaweed or water plants in the plastic containers and then pour them gently into the bucket. You may be able to place some animals in the bucket using the fishing net. You can then take your time and not rush your observations.

5 You might be able to find out what the animal feeds on as you are observing it. Write down your observations.

Ecosystems in the Caribbean   18.2

6 If plants of certain species (or seaweed on the beach) are very plentiful, you could pick one or two stems to identify and draw them. Otherwise, leave them alone. Your teacher will advise you. You can store them in the plastic bags with labels. In a forest, you can collect fallen leaves and fruits to draw later.

7 When you have learned to identify the organisms, take your metre square, place it on the ground and work out the percentages (roughly) of certain organisms in the square. Draw the square and mark in the areas the organisms covered. The metre square is called a quadrat. Choose a flat area on a rocky shore.

8 Measure a line across the area with the string (20–30 metres) and then place your quadrat at say, 5-m intervals to see if the numbers of species varied along the line. This is a line transect.

9 If you are doing a transect along the beach, go from an area of high tide to low tide. You might find that the species you come across change as you move towards the sea. If you are working in a forest or woodland, take your line from the shade into the Sun.

10 At the end, collect up all your equipment carefully and check there is no litter.

Record

1 When you get back to school, write a report of your trip. Include your sketch map of the area, and your observations.

2 Make a collage of your collections of shells and feathers.

Discuss

1 Were the organisms higher up the beach different from those living nearer the sea? For example, was the seaweed higher up the beach mainly a different colour from the seaweed lower down the beach? Why?

2 Were the plants growing in shady areas in the forest different from those in sunny areas?

⇨ Activity Would you like to be a twin?

You now know a great deal about your country and the Caribbean in general. Write a letter to an imaginary person of your own age in another country in the Caribbean. First, describe yourself, your hobbies and your school. Then describe your country and the things you love best about it. Ask your teacher if your class could be 'twinned' with a class of the same age in another country. Your teacher may have contacts in another country, or may be able to find out the name of a school and ask if they would like to 'twin' with your school! If this is possible, you could start by drawing the faces of your entire class on a big sheet of paper with your names, or your teacher could take a photograph and send it to them. Later, you could exchange information about your scientific studies, especially in ecology!

18.2 The environment and its maintenance

What about the future?

We damage the ecosystems at our peril. We should always think about the effects that our activities could have in the future. The harmful effects of human activities on the environment (soil, air and water) and ways of preventing further damage are covered in the topics that follow.

What you should know

- The Caribbean islands are formed from volcanic rock and sedimentary rock such as limestone and are surrounded by submerged coral reefs.
- The wide variety of exotic wildlife is possible because of the tropical climate.
- Rainforests and the ecosystems of the coastal areas support a large number of species.
- Rainforests and the coastal ecosystems benefit people in many ways.
- Deforestation has had a damaging effect on humans and the environment.
- Sustainable development can help to reverse the damage.
- The ecosystems of the seashore are closely linked and must be managed carefully to avoid damaging the delicate balance of interrelationships between organisms.

Questions

1 Name three examples of animals that pollinate the brightly coloured flowers of the rainforest.

2 What is an endangered species?

3 What is meant by sustainable development?

4 How do seagrasses and mangrove forests help to keep the sea water clear for corals to grow?

5 Describe an area near you – its ecology and ecosystems – and any environmental threats to it. How can it be sustained and protected?

18.3 Soil erosion and conservation

Objectives

After studying this topic, you should be able to:
- explain the importance of soil conservation
- explain how soil erosion takes place
- describe farming methods that can be used to prevent soil erosion
- describe methods of improving soil fertility.

The importance of soil conservation

You have already learned that soil is an important natural resource because all living things in one way or another depend on it (Book 2, Topic 10.5). It is the natural habitat for many animals and plants. Plants obtain water and nutrients from the soil, and animals (including humans) depend on plants for food, either directly or indirectly. People cultivate the soil to grow food, and good soil provides good-quality grass for grazing animals. For these reasons it is important to conserve the soil and protect it from damage.

Soil erosion

Soil particles can be removed naturally from the surface of the soil by the action of both wind and water. This is called **soil erosion**. The loose particles of the topsoil are removed very easily. In heavy rain, especially when there are tropical storms in the wet season, the running water can wash the soil away rapidly, causing mudslides (Fig. 18.22). In the dry season, the soil dries out and the surface looks very dusty (Fig. 18.23).

Fig. 18.22 Torrential rain during a storm has caused this mudslide. Loose soil has been washed down the slope.

Fig. 18.23 This bare soil has dried out and is cracked and dusty. Particles of topsoil can easily be blown away.

18.3 The environment and its maintenance

Fig. 18.24 Cutting down large areas of trees exposes the soil to the effects of erosion by wind and rain. This barren landscape is in Haiti.

Wind can then blow away the very fine particles. Erosion will occur faster on sloping land, and light soils are eroded more quickly than heavy soils.

Human activities can also damage the soil. Deforestation (Fig. 18.24), mining, farming and building involve removing trees and other plants from large areas of land. The plant roots bind the soil particles together and so if there are no roots to do this, the soil is more likely to be eroded by wind and rain. Trees also act as windbreaks, and so any flat land next to these areas will also be more exposed to the wind.

Did you know?

It takes hundreds of years for a layer of topsoil 1 cm deep to develop. Soil erosion can remove this layer in a few months.

Another effect of soil erosion is the removal of the topsoil. This is the most fertile soil layer, containing the most nutrients. The result is that the plants will not grow well if the fertility of the soil is reduced. Instead, they will become stunted and weak. When the topsoil is washed away into streams, rivers, lakes and estuaries, it causes these water bodies to silt up and chokes the aquatic plants growing there, so having a damaging effect on these ecosystems.

Erosion can affect the soil surface in different ways. Sheet erosion occurs when rain loosens small particles of the soil and they fill the pores between the larger soil particles. The surface of the soil becomes smoother and flatter like a sheet. Rain water then runs over the surface of the soil rather than soaking down between the particles.

Sheet erosion can lead to rill erosion, where small channels form in the soil, allowing the water to run off quickly. In some islands such as St Lucia, rill erosion can develop into mudflows down the mountain slopes.

Even deeper channels can form leading to gully erosion. Gully erosion is a common feature of the landscape in Grenada, St Kitts and Nevis, and also in Tobago.

Activity Investigating soil erosion (1)

Hygiene: make sure you wash your hands thoroughly after handling soil.

You will need
- some very dry soil
- a spoon
- a Petri dish
- a dropping pipette
- some water

Method
1. Place a spoonful of the dry soil on the Petri dish and blow across the surface.
2. Add enough water to the soil, a few drops at a time, to make it solid and sticky.
3. Now blow across the surface again.

Discuss
1. Which type of soil erosion does blowing over the dry soil represent?
2. What component of soil helps prevent it from drying out?
3. Are there any examples of soil erosion in your local area?
4. How can we combat soil erosion?

● Activity Investigating soil erosion (2)

Hygiene: make sure you wash your hands thoroughly after handling soil.

You will need
- a bucket of very dry soil
- a trowel or large spoon
- a large plastic pan
- a jug
- some water

Method
1. Place a large heap of dry soil at one end of the pan to represent a hill.
2. Pour some water gently over the top of the hill to represent light rain.
3. Repeat the experiment with more dry soil in a dry pan, but this time pour the water over the hill very quickly to represent heavy rain.

Discuss
1. What happened to the soil in the pan in 'light rain'?
2. What happened to the soil in the pan in 'heavy rain'?
3. How can soil on mountains be protected from the effects of heavy rain?
4. Are there places near you where this happens? How are mudslides prevented?

Controlling soil erosion and practising soil conservation

Responsible farming methods help to prevent soil erosion and also can enable damaged soil to recover.

Contour ploughing: This is practised in hilly areas, where soil erosion is more likely to occur. In this method, ploughing follows the natural contours of the land. The furrows run around the hills at roughly the same heights rather than going up and down the slope. This means that less soil is washed down the hillside by the rain, often reducing soil erosion by up

18.3 The environment and its maintenance

Fig. 18.25 This hillside in Malaysia has been terraced to reduce soil erosion.

Fig. 18.26 Strip cropping in Colombia. The banana plants provide shade for the coffee plants beneath and the two crops together give dense soil cover to prevent erosion.

to 80%. Contour ploughing is practised on some hilly slopes in Trinidad and Montserrat.

Terracing: When a hillside is terraced, it is cut and shaped into rows of flat level strips of land, rather like the steps of a giant stairway (Fig. 18.25). The flat strips of land are supported by stone walls. The terraces reduce soil erosion and also help retain water. Terracing is practised on St Lucia. In many Mediterranean countries farmers have used this method for centuries to grow grapes for wine making.

Strip cropping: In this method, ground-cover plants such as grass or alfalfa are planted between the rows of crops to reduce erosion of the surface soil. This method is practised in many places, for example Barbados and Colombia (Fig. 18.26). Sometimes instead of planting a ground-cover plant, the soil between the rows of crops is covered with dead leaves, grass or straw. This is called **mulching**. Mulching also reduces soil erosion by covering the surface and has the extra benefit of adding nutrients to the soil. Sometimes strip cropping and contour ploughing are combined.

As you have already learned in Topic 18.2, planting new fast-growing trees at the same rate that trees are felled (reforestation) prevents large areas of soil from being exposed to erosion by wind and rain.

Improving the soil

Dead plants decay and replace the nutrients in the soil for the living plants to use. If crops are planted and then harvested, the plant parts are removed and not returned to the soil as they would be in natural conditions. This interferes with the natural cycle of nutrients and the soil becomes less fertile. If you grow plants year after year in the same soil, the soil deteriorates.

Farmers overcome this problem by **crop rotation**. They plant different crops in a field every year. This is even better if the farmer grows peas or beans, because these are legumes. They have root nodules containing

Soil erosion and conservation 18.3

Fig. 18.27 Farmers put manure on their fields after harvesting to replace lost nutrients.

nitrogen-fixing bacteria and so they contain plenty of nitrates (see the nitrogen cycle, Book 2, Topic 10.4). If the roots are ploughed back into the soil after the peas and beans are harvested, this enriches the soil with nitrates. The soil is more fertile for next year's crops.

Manure and compost are natural fertilizers and can be added to the soil (Fig. 18.27). Artificial fertilizers can also be used, but only with great care as they can be washed into the soil water and have harmful effects, as you will learn in Topic 18.4.

What you should know

- Soil conservation is important because soil is a natural resource.
- Wind and water cause soil erosion.
- Human activities can contribute to soil erosion, including deforestation, mining, farming and building.
- Responsible farming methods help to prevent soil erosion and can also enable damaged soil to recover.
- Good farming practices include contour ploughing, terracing and strip cropping.
- Crop rotation, adding natural fertilizers and responsible use of artificial fertilizers help to improve soil fertility.

Questions

1 Which of the following is a soil conservation practice?
   a contour ploughing
   b deforestation
   c slash-and burn agriculture
   d weathering

2 Name three farming methods that can help prevent soil erosion.

3 Why does crop rotation benefit farmers?

4 Topsoil is often removed when new buildings are erected. Discuss the advantages and drawbacks of this practice.

5 Visitors to nature reserves can affect the soil on and near pathways with their trampling feet. Write a pamphlet explaining to visitors how over-visiting can affect the environment.

The environment and its maintenance

18.4 Water pollution and its control

> **Objectives**

After studying this topic, you should be able to:

- explain that clean water courses are being destroyed by pollution in all Caribbean islands
- explain that drinking water and water in the environment can be contaminated through the activities of people
- describe the most common types of pollutants in water
- explain that serious health problems are caused by water pollution
- explain that polluted water results in the death of many living organisms
- explain how water pollution can be reduced and avoided
- become a strong campaigner against water pollution.

You have already learned that water is an important resource (Book 2, Topics 10.1–10.3). It is essential to the well-being of all living things. Most of the Earth is covered by water, yet countries such as Trinidad and Tobago are running out of a drinkable (potable) groundwater supply.

Water pollution is the result of human activities in which chemical waste and sewage (human waste) get into the water sources and water-storage areas. The waste materials are often described as toxic wastes or **pollutants**. Many of these products are poisonous and the water becomes unfit to drink. Pollution affects plants and animals too.

The seas and oceans are also badly affected by pollution. If the sea is contaminated (contains poisonous substances), this affects organisms that live in the sea. For example, fish may take harmful substances into their bodies. If we then eat the fish, the harmful substances get into our bodies. This means that the food chain is affected.

In many Caribbean countries it is now considered unwise to drink water straight from the streams and rivers – a practice that was very common in the past in all the islands. The source of the water supply determines the type of pollution that could occur in the water.

Agricultural chemicals

Agricultural chemicals such as fertilizers and pesticides pollute the waters of all Caribbean islands.

Farmers use fertilizers (rich in nitrates and phosphates) to grow healthy crops. You learned in Book 2 (Topic 10.4) that some of these fertilizers are washed into the soil by the rain. They get into the groundwater that flows into streams and rivers. An increase in nitrates in a pond or river causes too many algae to grow, and the pond or river turns green! This is called **eutrophication** (Book 2, Topic 10.4). This affects the food chain. The algae die and decay. The bacteria that feed on the dead algae (decomposers) multiply so fast that they use up all the oxygen. This results in the death of the fish and other organisms – they suffocate. Nitrates in drinking water can also affect young babies.

Pesticides are used to kill organisms that cause crop diseases. They include the **insecticides** used to kill insects that damage our crops in many ways. These chemicals can also harm living organisms. They can get into the food chain in the same way as fertilizers. Farmers need to use these chemicals sparingly and responsibly.

Sewage

Another source of water pollution is the discharge of untreated sewage into the groundwater, streams, rivers, lakes and sea (see Fig. 18.28). Sewage is the waste people produce when they go to the lavatory and includes dirty water from homes and all types of buildings. Sewage carried in pipes to a sewage works is treated and made safe. Some areas have a poor sanitation system. There are open sewage pits or open drains and people pass urine and faeces and throw dirty water into rivers or on streets, which can be very dangerous for health. Water contaminated by sewage carries many microorganisms that can cause serious diseases such as dysentery, typhoid and cholera. It also carries harmful chemicals (such as bleach) that we use for cleaning our homes and buildings.

In the Caribbean, this problem has been made worse by building on land in watershed areas (land between two rivers) and building large hotels on beach fronts (often without planning permission). Some hotels discharge their untreated waste directly into the sea, therefore contaminating the coastal waters.

Areas of some islands are often flooded during periods of heavy rain and in the hurricane season. Untreated sewage can be carried from open sewage pits and poorly managed sanitary systems into the groundwater, streams and rivers, causing pollution.

Fig. 18.28 Discharge of untreated sewage into the water is a major cause of pollution.

18.4 The environment and its maintenance

18.29 Gustavia, St Barthélemy, is one of many busy Caribbean ports.

Fig. 18.30 Oil has spilled out of this tanker, polluting the sea.

The shipping industry and boat owners also contribute to coastal water pollution, as many visiting and local boats discharge their waste directly into the sea (Fig. 18.29). Tourist ships with thousands of visitors that sail on the waters of the Caribbean sometimes leave behind trails of untreated sewage that pollute the sea.

Oil

Oil from boat engines pollutes seas, lakes and rivers. You may have heard of disasters that have occurred when huge oil tankers have been involved in serious accidents at sea. The large oil spills (known as oil slicks) have killed many fish, sea birds and other organisms in the sea (Fig. 18.30). When the oil has washed up onto the shore, it has damaged beaches for local people and tourists, and harmed

Water pollution and its control 18.4

Fig. 18.31 The oil sticks to the bird's feathers, preventing it from flying. People can wash the oil off with detergent.

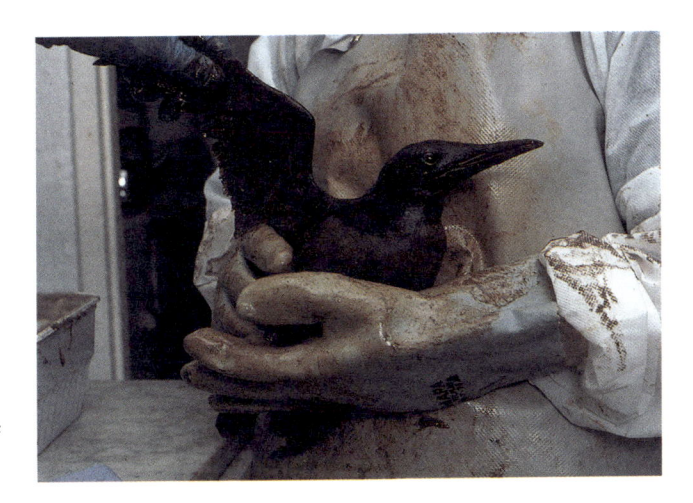

and killed birds and other wildlife (Fig. 18.31). Large oil slicks can be broken up by spraying them from the air with detergents, but the detergents themselves are harmful to wildlife!

Industrial waste

Industrial pollutants such as lead and mercury can contaminate water both on land and in the seas and oceans. Within recent times, high levels of mercury from industrial activities have found their way into the sea and into the food chain. The World Health Organization (WHO) advises that the amount of mercury in drinking water should not be greater than 50 parts per million, but higher levels than this have been found in many areas.

Factories making detergents sometimes pump their waste into nearby rivers, killing the wildlife (Fig. 18.32).

Household waste

People who dump household waste along cliffs at the sea front, and in rivers and streams also pollute the waters in these areas (Fig. 18.33). This illegal dumping of waste not only spoils the beauty of the environment, but also leads to the build-up of non-biodegradable waste. Some waste can be broken down naturally by the activities of bacteria, for example food waste such as potato peelings. This is biodegradable waste. Other waste, such as things made of plastic, glass bottles and tin cans, remains where it is dumped. Such waste is non-biodegradable. Household

Fig. 18.32 Soap suds from a detergent factory are polluting this river in the UK.

18.4 The environment and its maintenance

Fig. 18.33 This household waste has been dumped near a river in Scarborough, Tobago.

waste not disposed of properly also acts as a breeding place for vermin (rats and mice) and many bacteria that cause diseases.

Thermal pollution

Many industries use large amounts of water to cool machinery. If the hot water then flows directly into a river, for example, thermal pollution occurs. Living things can survive only within a certain temperature range. If the water is too hot, they die. Many fish have been killed in this way.

How can we solve the problem of water pollution?

We will never be able to get completely safe drinking water and unpolluted lakes, rivers, streams and seas everywhere for everyone. The world population has risen sharply over the last century and continues to rise. This means that there are more people and more activities, more industry, more demand for food and other things people need, more people using water for drinking and for recreation (swimming, water sports and sailing).

- Waste water can be re-used if the pollutants are taken out.
- Governments can encourage people to channel the runoff water from agricultural land away from rivers and streams.
- Governments can pass laws to limit the amount of pollutants that industries produce and put into the water.
- Sewage can be treated in sewage works.
- People should be discouraged from dumping household waste near water. People should get rid of their waste safely.
- People all over the world are now more aware of damage to the environment. In many countries there has been a demand for 'green' products. These are products that cause less or no damage to the environment. People who feel strongly about protecting the environment have persuaded governments and industry to clean up the environment. This is known as 'The Green Movement'. Some governments have introduced 'The Polluter Pays' policies, which means that if an industry pollutes the environment, it must pay to clean it up. Some manufacturers are beginning to use recyclable materials to package food, water and soft drinks.

Water pollution and its control   18.4

➔ Activity Local water sources and sewage

Method
1. Find out how your home and area gets water for drinking and washing.
2. What kinds of toilets are there at home, at school and in your local area? For example, the waste from your home may be carried by pipes to a sewage works, or the sewage may be buried in large pits.

Ask your family and local people for information. Find out if the systems could be improved in your area. Are there any problems with the water and sewage systems? Your teacher can help you to get information, for example from your local water and sewage authority.

Record
Write a report about what you have found, and organize a class discussion.

Discuss
1. Is there any pollution of the water supply in your area?
2. Is the system of sewage disposal good or poor in your area?
3. If there are problems, how can these systems be improved?

➔ Activity Community action on water pollution

Find information in local newspapers and magazines. Your teacher could take you for a walk around your area. Here are some suggestions to help.

- Find out if household waste is dumped in your community near rivers and streams or on the beach. Observe the waste, but do not touch it.
- Look for signs of pollution in the water, for example, dead fish, a film of oil on the water, dirty or murky water or the unpleasant smell of sewage. Take great care when you are near riverbanks or harbours not to fall in the water.
- Look for factories or oil refineries near rivers that may be producing waste.
- Find out if fertilizers and pesticides are used on the farms in your area.

Discuss
1. As a class, discuss your findings and suggest ways of solving any problems. For example, we could persuade people to get rid of household waste safely.
2. Make a poster to show your friends and family how harmful water pollution can be to living things and what we can do to help stop it.

18.4 The environment and its maintenance

What you should know

- Clean water courses are being destroyed by pollution in all of the Caribbean islands.
- Drinking water and the water in the environment can be contaminated through the activities of people.
- The most common forms of pollutants are: chemicals from domestic use, chemicals from industry, sewage, oil, household refuse (garbage) and hot water from industrial processes.
- Serious health problems can result from drinking polluted water.
- Pollutants can get into the food chain.
- Governments, industry, farmers and individual people can reduce and avoid water pollution if they know about its harmful effects on the environment and are willing to do something about it.

Questions

1. Name two types of chemicals used in agriculture that can contaminate soil water.
2. What happens if people drink water contaminated with sewage?
3. Name two harmful metals produced by industry that can pollute water.
4. Name two examples of biodegradable things and two examples of non-biodegradable things and explain what the terms mean.

The environment and its maintenance

18.5 Air pollution

> **Objectives**
>
> After studying this topic, you should be able to:
> - list the main substances that cause air pollution
> - explain that pollutants can be produced by natural events as well as by human activities
> - describe the main effects of air pollution on human health, plants and animals, and the environment
> - explain how air pollution can be controlled and avoided
> - describe the effects of smog, acid rain, the greenhouse effect, global warming and development of holes in the ozone layer
> - explain how countries can cooperate to combat global warming and the damage caused to the ozone layer.

In our modern society, many of our activities lead to pollution of the air we breathe. Smoke from industries and the exhausts of motor vehicles fill the air with substances that can harm our health (Fig. 18.34). Air pollution has now become a global problem because most countries now have industry of one sort or another. The problems have become so great that the control of pollution requires not only local solutions, but also international cooperation to solve these problems.

Fig. 18.34 The smoke from this sugarcane factory pollutes the air over a wide area.

Types of pollutants

- Some air pollutants are gases, like carbon dioxide, that are found naturally in the air, but are produced in such large quantities that they cannot be used up by the natural processes such as photosynthesis.
- Other pollutants are synthetic chemicals, not natural ones. They are not poisons by themselves, but harm the environment by combining with other substances in the air. An example is the damage done to the **ozone layer** by CFCs, which we will return to later.

Some common pollutants

The main air pollutants produced by human activities are gases from power stations, domestic heating boilers, factories, road traffic vehicles, aircraft and incinerators. But there are natural sources of air pollution, too. For example, toxic gases and ash are produced when volcanoes erupt. Ruminant herbivores such as cattle produce methane gas as a result of their digestive processes. Methane gas is also produced by rice growing in paddy fields.

The most common substances that cause air pollution are: sulphur dioxide, nitrogen dioxide, carbon dioxide, carbon monoxide, fine dust and soot, and lead compounds from petroleum. You have already learned that carbon dioxide is produced mainly by burning fossil fuels such as coal, oil and natural gas (Book 1, Topic 4.1).

The effects of air pollution

Air pollution has very serious effects on all living things and on the environment in general.

- It damages our health. It causes many respiratory diseases such as asthma and bronchitis.
- It causes acid rain, killing trees and other plants.
- It produces smog over large cities.
- Stone and brick buildings are damaged by acid gases eating away at them, especially buildings made of limestone.
- It causes the greenhouse effect, and is thought to be leading to global warming that could cause climate change.
- It has damaged the ozone layer.

How can we control air pollution?

The best way of controlling air pollution is to reduce the amount of pollutants that industry produces. For example, coal, oil and natural gas are commonly used to produce electrical energy in power stations. Alternative methods could be used to avoid burning these fossil fuels. These include using hydroelectric power and wind power (see Book 1, Topic 4.2). There are also nuclear power stations, but many people are very uneasy about building more of these because of the difficulties in disposing of the nuclear waste and because of the risk of nuclear accidents. If an accident occurs, radiation released has catastrophic effects on all living things and the environment.

There is also another problem that you are already familiar with (Book 1, Topic 4.1). Fossil fuels are non-renewable energy sources. What will

Air pollution 18.5

> **Did you know?**
>
> In 1986, there was a serious accident at a nuclear power station at Chernobyl in the former Soviet Union. Thirty-one people were killed, and later 10 people died from thyroid cancer. The radiation continued to spread from the plant for 10 days and clouds of radioactive dust spread into the air over northern Europe. Scientists continue to study the after-effects of the accident on the people most affected and people in other European countries. Radiation causes cancer and leukaemia, which may not develop until years later.

happen in the future when the coal, oil and natural gas run out?

It will take a long time to persuade governments to change over to other methods of generating electricity for our daily needs and to use renewable energy sources. But we can all help as individuals by conserving energy and not being wasteful. Simple measures like remembering to turn off lights can help!

Many factories have already helped to reduce pollution by using 'scrubbers' to filter out soot and dust and to remove gases such as carbon dioxide and sulphur dioxide from the smoke they produce.

Many of these pollutants are carried by the wind to other places and to a certain extent are diluted by the enormous quantities of air in the atmosphere. But many of the gases combine with water vapour and come back down in rain and snow to pollute the land and the water. Some collect high in the atmosphere and affect the ozone layer.

Smog

Smog is a kind of smoky fog. The word has come about by combining parts of the words '*sm*oke' and '*f*og'. Smog often settles over large cities and large industrial developments (Fig. 18.35). But small towns can develop into large cities and small industrial complexes can develop into large ones. So these are problems that affect us all now or could affect us in the future. Smog is a mixture of smoke, soot, dust and harmful chemicals and can stay for days or weeks. It damages health – children and older people are particularly at risk.

Fig. 18.35 The dense layer of smog over the city of Los Angeles in California is the result of vehicle exhaust fumes from traffic. It can last for days or even weeks.

Ozone (chemical formula O_3) is a colourless gas. Ozone smog is produced when vehicle exhaust gases combine with nitrogen oxides. Although naturally occurring ozone gas high in the atmosphere protects us, its effects down at ground level are very nasty. It causes coughs, eye irritation, breathing difficulties and headaches.

18.5 The environment and its maintenance

Carbon monoxide in smog is also produced by vehicle exhausts. It is more efficient at combining with haemoglobin in the blood than is oxygen and so it makes us short of oxygen. This is especially harmful for people with heart disease, whose circulation is not very efficient anyway.

Nitrogen oxides in smog also harm the lungs, and hydrocarbons from vehicle exhausts (especially diesel exhausts) are thought to cause lung cancer. Lead is added to petrol (gasoline) to improve the efficiency of engines in vehicles. But lead accumulates in the body and causes lead poisoning, which affects mental development and coordination in children.

We can do something about this, especially as motor vehicles are major sources of these pollutants.

- We can reduce traffic in cities by encouraging people to use public transport more often.
- We can walk or ride a bike for short journeys.
- Many countries have passed laws that require the car industry to produce vehicles that use lead-free petrol (gasoline).
- Many modern vehicles are fitted with a **catalytic converter**, which changes many of the harmful gases into water and carbon dioxide.
- Vehicles have been developed to run on less polluting fuels instead of petrol (gasoline) – for example, battery-powered cars.

> **? Finding out**
>
> **Acid rain causes forest death**
>
> Find out from encyclopedias, books and the internet how acid rain has affected countries such as Sweden in Scandinavia.

Acid rain

Sulphur dioxide and nitrogen oxides, mainly from power stations and vehicle exhausts, combine with water vapour in the atmosphere to form droplets of acid. This means that rain falls as **acid rain**. The droplets may be carried far away from their place of origin, even to other countries. Erupting volcanoes also produce sulphur dioxide, which can also cause acid rain.

Many scientists believe that acid rain has caused the death of trees and wiped out huge areas of forest, especially in Europe and North America (Fig. 18.36). Acid rain can directly damage leaves and can also get into the soil and leach out essential plant nutrients. The soil becomes more acid, as does the water draining through the soil. It percolates through to rivers and lakes. The acid conditions make certain metals such as aluminium more soluble. Fishes and other wildlife die from aluminium poisoning, not from the acid itself. Their gills are destroyed and the fish cannot breathe.

Fig. 18.36 Acid rain is thought to have caused enormous damage to trees and forests.

The greenhouse effect and global warming

As you know, the Earth is surrounded by an atmosphere. Certain gases in the atmosphere, especially water vapour and carbon dioxide, act rather like the glass in a greenhouse. They allow light and other radiation from the Sun to pass through and warm the Earth's surface. However, the infrared radiation (heat) from the heated Earth's surface is trapped by these so-called **greenhouse gases**. This **greenhouse effect** maintains the atmosphere at a temperature about 35°C higher than it otherwise would be – an effect that is vital for the continued existence of life.

Carbon dioxide is produced naturally by the respiration of plants, animals and other living organisms. Further amounts are given off as a waste gas by the burning of coal, oil and other fossil fuels. It is also produced by burning wood, for example after trees are cut down when clearing forests. Most of the carbon dioxide released by these processes is 'recaptured' from the air by plants, algae and other organisms that perform photosynthesis. This is the basis of the carbon cycle (see Book 2, Topic 10.4), which maintains a steady concentration of atmospheric carbon dioxide over time. However, since the Industrial Revolution in the eighteenth and nineteenth centuries, there have been large increases in carbon dioxide emissions from factories, power stations and vehicles. There has also been large-scale deforestation. Trees, which are among our planet's most effective absorbers of carbon dioxide, have been felled for construction, fuel or to create new agricultural land.

> **? Finding out**
>
> **Working together to combat climate change**
>
> In 1992 the United Nations set up the **United Nations Framework Convention on Climate Change**. Leaders and government representatives from countries all over the world meet together at certain times to agree on a course of action to tackle the challenge of climate change.
>
> Find out more about the aims of this convention and what has been achieved so far. You can get information from encyclopedias, science magazines and the internet.

The increased global output of carbon dioxide resulting from human activities is causing the level of atmospheric carbon dioxide to rise. This rise is adding to the greenhouse effect, and gradually increasing the overall temperature on the Earth's surface – an effect called **global warming**. Scientists now think that this will have two major effects.

- The polar ice caps could melt and sea levels could rise all over the world. This will cause many islands to become submerged and many low-lying areas around the coastlines will be flooded.

- There could be **climate change**. Patterns of rainfall could change all over the world. Deserts might get bigger as it gets hotter. Colder drier areas could get warmer and wetter. Farming would be disrupted. Many animals and plants could find themselves living in climates that are unsuitable for them and some species could die out. Life in the sea would also be badly affected. Weather conditions might become more extreme, and storms and hurricanes could become more severe.

However, a word of caution.

- At present these are theories about climate change and it is extremely difficult to forecast long-term changes in climate, especially as they might affect the entire world.
- Also, remember that the Earth's climate has changed ever since time began. The changes that are being recorded may be naturally occurring shifts in climate.
- Accurate measurements of atmospheric gases and weather are only comparatively recent considering the age of the Earth itself. So scientists can only put forward theories based on recent statistics.

The ozone layer

The **ozone layer** is 10–50 km above the Earth's surface. It shields us from 99% of the harmful ultraviolet (UV) rays from the Sun. UV radiation can damage the eyes, causing cataracts and blindness, and can also cause skin cancer. High UV levels also slow down the rate of photosynthesis in plants and as UV rays can penetrate sea water up to depths of 20 metres, they can affect marine life too.

Damage has been caused to the ozone layer by compounds called **chlorofluorocarbons** (**CFCs**). They react with the UV rays and produce active chlorine atoms, which destroy the ozone gas, but are not themselves used up or destroyed by the reaction. The frightening thing is that once these active chlorine atoms are formed, they stay around and destroy more and more of the ozone.

CFCs don't usually react with anything else and have been used for years in aerosol sprays, and in refrigerators and air conditioners. Solvents such as carbon tetrachloride – once widely used in the dry-cleaning industry – and compounds known as halons, used in fire extinguishers, are also culprits in destroying the ozone layer. Nobody predicted that these chemicals – originally regarded as harmless and used in so many everyday things – would eventually be responsible for causing serious damage to the upper atmosphere.

Alarm bells were ringing as far back as 1974 and the worst fears were confirmed in 1982 by the British scientist Joe Farman and his colleagues

Did you know?

In 1991, the hole in the ozone layer was 13 times bigger than it was in 1981, and now extends north as far as Chile in South America. In the northern hemisphere, the ozone layer thinned by about 6% between 1980 and 1990.

Find out what the position is at present. You can get information from science magazines and the internet.

Air pollution 18.5

working in Antarctica. In 1983 they noticed a 40% loss of ozone over Antarctica. Today, the hole in the ozone layer is much bigger (Fig. 18.37).

In 1987, The United Nations Environment Programme (UNEP) arranged for representatives of all the world's leading industrial nations to sign the Montreal Protocol. They promised to cut down on CFC emissions. But in 1989, new evidence showed that things were getting worse and so 80 nations promised to ban CFC emissions completely by the year 2000, although this has not yet been accomplished.

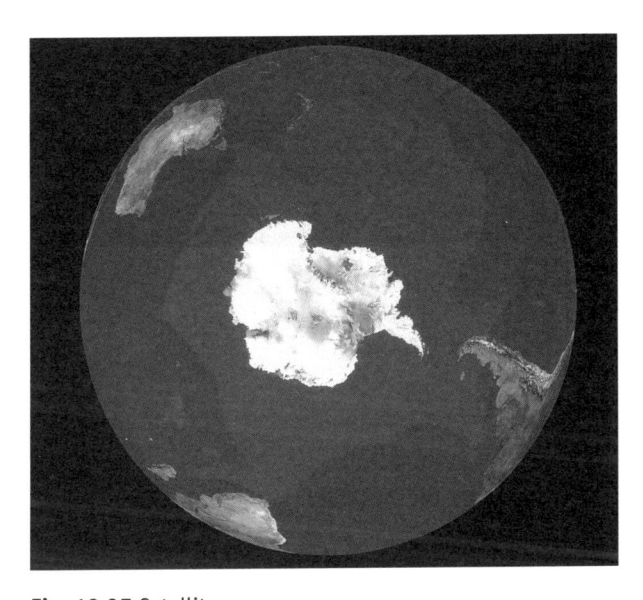

Fig. 18.37 Satellite picture showing the hole in the ozone layer over Antarctica.

Activity How can I help to prevent air pollution?

1 Discuss how you as an individual can help to combat air pollution. Think about these points: energy efficiency, cars, using renewable resources, using environmentally friendly products.

2 Design a poster to inform people about the harmful effects of air pollution.

3 Your teacher will help you to find out what your government is doing to tackle air pollution and climate change.

In these last topics you have learned about the harmful effects of pollution and how it can affect countries far away from the source, and even the world's climate. But now we also know that we can help prevent further damage and even restore parts of our environment to their normal state; we can use this knowledge for our benefit and learn from past mistakes. Promoting the idea of sustainable development and being aware that our actions have consequences can help us to look after our beautiful planet. We are the caretakers for future generations of people.

Finding out

During the months of February to May, giant dust clouds blow across the Atlantic Ocean from the Sahara region of Africa. These dust clouds bring pollutants such as the poisonous elements arsenic and mercury from the open pit mines in Africa, as well as viruses, and spores of bacteria and fungi. These all affect the lives of animals and plants in the Caribbean region, and it is thought that they may have contributed to the increase in asthma in the region.

Find out more about Saharan dust clouds. You can get information from your science and geography teachers, science and geographical magazines and the internet. You can get more information at http://www.heinemann.co.uk/hotlinks.

18.5 The environment and its maintenance

What you should know

- The main substances that cause air pollution are sulphur dioxide, nitrogen oxides, carbon dioxide, carbon monoxide, methane, fine dust and soot, and lead compounds from petroleum.
- Pollutants are produced by natural events as well as by human activities.
- Air pollution can have serious effects on human health, plants and animals, and the environment.
- Air pollution can be controlled and avoided.
- Smog, acid rain, global warming and holes in the ozone layer are all produced by air pollution.
- Many countries are cooperating to combat global warming and the damage caused to the ozone layer.

Questions

1. Name two air pollutants that are produced by natural processes.
2. List three ways of generating electricity in power stations apart from using fossil fuels.
3. Which two things can people do to reduce pollutants in car exhaust fumes?
4. What are the two main effects of global warming?

Questions

Unit 14: The Earth

Multiple choice

1. Which of the following is NOT part of the structure of the Earth?
   A mantle
   B core
   C skin
   D crust

2. A sealed metal box contains air. Which of the following would reduce the pressure of the air in the box?
   A forcing more air into the box
   B carrying it up a mountain
   C heating the box
   D cooling the box

3. The rock cycle describes:
   A a music band
   B soil formation
   C rock formation
   D soil and rock formation

4. Marble is formed from:
   A limestone
   B mudstone
   C sand
   D slate

5. The largest mass of the Earth's crust is the element:
   A aluminium
   B calcium
   C silicon
   D oxygen

6. Which of the following is NOT a property of metals?
   A They are soft
   B They conduct electricity
   C They conduct heat
   D They can be shaped

7. Lava is:
   A hot molten rock inside a volcano
   B the crust of the Earth around a volcano
   C steam from the Earth
   D the cracked surface of the Earth

Short answers

1. Name two metals found in the Earth's core.

2. Volcanoes attract tourists. Suggest two other ways in which a volcano can be useful to the local economy.

3. Name the scale used to measure the magnitude of an earthquake.

4. What instrument is used to record earthquakes?

5. Describe briefly how you could show that air can be compressed.

6. Name the two most common elements in the Earth's crust.

7. Winds are caused by differences in atmospheric pressure.
   a What instrument is used to measure atmospheric pressure?
   b If there are big differences in pressure, what will the winds be like?
   c What force gives rise to waves as the wind blows across the sea?
   d If the wind produces big waves, what will happen to the strength of the wind?

8. Pure metals are rarely found in nature.
   a Why is this?
   b Haematite is an ore of iron. What is an ore?
   c Iron is extracted from iron oxide by heating it with carbon. What gas is produced?
   d What is the name for this process?

   Aluminum cannot be extracted in this way.
   e From what ore is aluminium obtained?
   f What process is used to extract aluminium?
   g What other substance must be added to make this possible?

Essays

1 Describe some ways in which minerals are used for construction purposes in Caribbean countries.
2 Explain what we mean by the rock cycle. Illustrate your answer with a diagram.

Unit 15: Light and sound

Multiple choice

1 Beams of light that spread out from a source are described as:
   A bright
   B convergent
   C divergent
   D parallel

2 A shadow forms when:
   A light travels around corners
   B a solid object prevents light from reaching a surface
   C light passes through a transparent object
   D light bounces off a transparent object

3 The speed of light is:
   A 300 000 000 metres per second
   B 3 000 000 metres per hour
   C 3 000 000 kilometres per second
   D 3 000 000 metres per hour

4 Eyesight deteriorates as a person gets older because:
   A the brain is tired
   B the eye lens does not change shape properly
   C the pupil remains fixed in shape
   D the person does not produce as many tears

5 Sounds travel by:
   A vibrations in a vacuum
   B vibrations of the air
   C light waves
   D fast-moving air molecules

6 What is the normal range of human hearing?
   A 20–20 000 hertz
   B 20–20 000 decibels
   C 20 000–100 000 hertz
   D 20 000–100 000 decibels

Short answers

1 Do concave or convex lens magnify objects?
2 Fill in the blank spaces in the following sentences.

   A pinhole camera give an image that is _____ and _____ . A large pinhole gives a _____ but _____ image. A _____ pinhole gives a _____ but _____ image. The _____ in a pinhole camera can be photographed. This is referred to as a _____ image.

3 What is refraction?
4 Name three optical instruments that use lenses.
5 What does the term 'binocular vision' mean?
6 Explain the term 'accommodation' as it refers to sight.
7 Give three uses of ultrasound.
8 What is the difference between sound and noise?

Essays

1 Draw a diagram of the ear, labelling all the parts that you know. Give the functions of the parts labelled.
2 Describe how we hear sounds, starting from a vibrating object and ending with the message that is transmitted from the ear to the brain.
3 When you look in a mirror the image is inverted laterally. Draw a diagram to show how this happens.
4 When you watch a film, you are actually seeing a sequence of still pictures. Explain why you apparently see smooth-running action.
5 Often we can hear sounds, but we cannot see the source. Explain how this happens.
6 Describe what happens when we hear an echo.

Unit 16: Systems in humans

Multiple choice

1. The joining up of the sex cells is called:
   A ejaculation
   B fertilization
   C menstruation
   D reproduction

2. Which of the following is NOT a hormone?
   A glucose
   B insulin
   C testosterone
   D thyroxine

3. Oral contraceptives are taken through the:
   A blood vessels
   B ears
   C mouth
   D vagina

4. Which of the following DOES NOT contain receptors?
   A ear
   B eye
   C muscle
   D nails

Short answers

1. Say which gland would be mainly responsible for reactions in the following cases:
   a Your friend is jogging along the street, when a big dog rushes at him/her. He/she screams and runs at a fast pace.
   b Your grandmother's body can no longer regulate its blood sugar level.
   c An individual is hyperactive and sweats a lot.
   d A child is very much taller than the other children in its class.

2. Why does the scrotum lie outside of the male's body?

3. Is the fallopian tube connected to the ovary?

4. How is the fetus connected to the mother's uterus?

5. Describe how fraternal twins are formed.

6. How does an embryo obtain its food?

Essays

1. Describe the different forms of birth-control methods that are available to adult persons.

2. Write an essay describing how to take care of a baby.

3. Draw and label a diagram of the female reproductive system.

4. Explain what happens in diabetes, and how it is treated.

Unit 17: Forces

Multiple choice

1. Which of the following is NOT a force?
   A weight
   B mass
   C air resistance
   D friction

2. Which of the following can be used to measure a force?
   A a barometer
   B a thermometer
   C a newtonmeter
   D a lever

3. Gravity is stronger on Jupiter than on the Earth. Which row in the table might correctly show measurements of the mass and weight of an object on these two planets?

	Mass on Earth	Weight on Earth	Mass on Jupiter	Weight on Jupiter
A	10 kg	100 N	25 kg	250 N
B	10 kg	10 N	10 kg	25 N
C	10 kg	100 N	10 kg	250 N
D	10 kg	100 N	10 kg	100 N

4. Which of the following is the unit of energy?
   A newton
   B metre per second
   C joule
   D watt

5 Which of the following is NOT a force that tends to slow things down?
 A air resistance
 B drag
 C friction
 D atmospheric pressure

6–9 Choose from the list A–D quantities which might match those listed.
 A 0.1 kg   B 40 kg   C 5 N   D 20 000 N

6 The mass of a child
7 The weight of an elephant
8 The pull of gravity on a bag of fruit
9 The mass of an apple
10 Which of the following is NOT a machine?
 A a lever
 B a newtonmeter
 C a ramp
 D a block and tackle

Short answers

1 After which famous scientist is the unit of force named?
2 What three things might change when an unbalanced force acts on an object?
3 State Newton's first law of motion.
4 What is the weight of a rock of mass 20 kg on the surface of the Earth?
5 Give two examples of levers in everyday use.
6 A baggage carrier transfers 120 000 J of energy in 10 minutes. Calculate his power.
7 A car is moving along the road. Its engine provides a forward force of 500 N. There is a force of 400 N which tends to slow it down.
 a Draw a diagram to show these forces.
 b Are the forces on the car balanced?
 c How will the speed of the car change as a result of these forces?
 d The driver now applies the brakes. Explain what happens.

8 When you sit on a chair, two forces act on you: your weight, and the contact force of the chair.
 a Draw a diagram to show these forces.
 b What other name is given to the upward force of the chair?
 c If you are sitting still, what can you say about the sizes of these forces?
 d Are the forces balanced or unbalanced?

9 In the diagram, a lever is being used to lift a heavy weight.

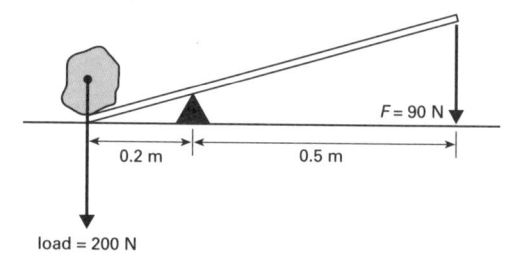

$F = 90$ N
0.2 m   0.5 m
load = 200 N

 a Is this force big enough to lift the load? Show how you worked out the answer.
 b Could you lift a 25 kg rock with this lever? Again, show how you worked out your answer.

Essays

1 Friction can be a problem, but it can also be very useful. Describe two situations in which friction can be a problem. For each, describe how its effects can be reduced. Describe two situations in which friction is useful.
2 Dylan is carrying a box of mass 20 kg upstairs.
 a What is the weight of the box?
 b Dylan raises the box 5 m. How much work does he do on the box?
 c By how much does the box's energy increase?

Unit 18: The environment and its maintenance

Multiple choice

1 Which of the following is a soil conservation practice?
 A contour ploughing
 B deforestation
 C slash-and-burn agriculture
 D weathering

2 Acid rain falling onto the soil will:
   i   make aluminium in the soil more soluble
   ii cause forest death
   iii contaminate the ground water
   A i only
   B ii only
   C iii only
   D i, ii and iii

3 Which of the following activities does not contribute to the greenhouse effect:
   A burning fossil fuel
   B waste gases from industry
   C oxygen produced during photosynthesis
   D burning large areas of forests

4 Global warming refers to:
   A the heating of the Earth's atmosphere
   B the heating of the South Pole
   C the increase in temperature of the Caribbean Sea
   D the hot weather during the dry season

5 Which of the following practices could lead to soil erosion?
   A the planting of young trees
   B the wise use of herbicides
   C cutting down trees for firewood
   D terracing of the hill slopes

6 Every year, the Ministry of Agriculture advises against the setting of bush fires because:
   A soil erosion could result
   B unauthorized gardens could be established
   C the amount of oxygen in the atmosphere needs to be controlled
   D the amount of carbon dioxide being removed from the atmosphere needs to be controlled

Short answers

1 Name three local animals that are considered endangered.

2 Name two groups of chemicals used in agriculture that can contaminate soil water.

3 How do some hotels and tourist ships contribute to the contamination of the sea water?

4 Why should sewage-contaminated water not be ingested?

5 Name two metals that may become water pollutants if disposed of carelessly by factories.

6 What does the term 'biodegradable' mean?

7 Of what value are reforestation programmes to the environment?

Essays

1 Write a letter to your pen friend, telling him/her why some animals have become endangered, and what you could do to help to protect these animals.

2 Slash-and-burn is an old agricultural practice in the Caribbean islands. Say why you support or do not support this method of agriculture.

3 Draw a diagram to show the vertical distribution of trees in a rainforest.

4 Discuss the term 'sustainable development'. Give examples to illustrate your points.

5 What steps should Caricom take to prevent the misuse of the rainforests of the region?

6 Some countries get rid of their toxic waste by dumping it in the oceans. Discuss whether this is a good system of disposal.

7 Discuss whether other countries such as France should be allowed to ship nuclear waste through the Caribbean Sea en route to Japan.

Science words

Here is a list of some important science words you have read in this book.

accommodation the adjustment of the eye that allows it to focus on objects at different distances
acid rain rain that has acidic gases dissolved in it
adaptations characteristics of an organism that make it possible for the animal to live in a particular environment
adrenal glands endocrine glands that lie just above the kidneys and produce adrenaline
adrenaline a hormone produced by the adrenal glands which prepares the body for action
altimeter an instrument for measuring height above sea level (altitude)
amplifier a device that makes sounds louder
amplitude the greatest distance a vibrating object moves from its rest position
androgens male sex hormones
angle of incidence the angle between an incident ray and an imaginary line at right angles to the surface of the mirror
angle of reflection the angle between a reflected ray and an imaginary line at right angles to the surface of the mirror
anode the positive electrode in an electrical cell
antidiuretic hormone (ADH) the hormone produced by the pituitary gland that makes the kidneys take more water back into the body
anvil one of the bones in the middle ear
atmosphere the layer of air surrounding the Earth
atmospheric pressure the force the atmosphere exerts on the surface of the Earth
auditory nerve the nerve that carries messages from the ear to the brain

barometer an instrument for measuring the pressure of the air
beam a number of rays of light

binocular vision seeing with two eyes, which allows us to see in three dimensions
biodiversity the variety of life forms within a particular region
birth rate the number of people who are born in a country each year

camouflage the ability of an organism to blend in with its surroundings so that it cannot be seen
canopy the top leafy layer of a forest, which shades the rest of the plants
catalytic converter a device fitted to vehicle exhausts to change certain harmful gases into water and carbon dioxide
cathode the negative electrode in an electrical cell
central nervous system (CNS) the brain and the spinal cord
cerebellum the part of the brain that controls balance and accurate movements
cerebral hemispheres the part of the brain where we think
cervix the narrow opening at the bottom of the uterus
chlorofluorocarbons (CFCs) chemicals that damage the ozone layer
ciliary muscles muscles in the eye that adjust the size of the lens
climate change a long-term shift in the pattern of weather around the world
clone an exact copy of a particular individual, whether produced by asexual reproduction or by genetic engineering
colonization the spread of organisms to new areas
community a group of living organisms that live in the same place
concave lens a lens that is thinner in the middle than at the edges; a diverging lens
condom a rubber sheath placed over the erect penis before sexual intercourse, to prevent pregnancy and avoid spreading or catching sexually transmitted diseases

convergent beam a beam of light that becomes narrower as it travels
convex lens a lens that is thicker in the middle than at the edges; a converging lens
cornea the curved clear layer at the front of the eye
crop rotation planting different crops in a field each year
crust (of Earth) the layer of solid rock at the surface of the Earth
cryolite a mineral that is added to alumina to lower its melting point in the extraction of aluminium by electrolysis

death rate the number of people who die in a country each year
decibel (dB) the unit of loudness of sound
decomposer an organism that breaks down dead matter
deforestation cutting down trees
diabetes a disease caused by lack of insulin
diffuse reflection when light bounces off a rough surface in many directions
diffusion (in physics) the scattering of light in different directions
divergent beam a beam of light that spreads out from its source
drag resistance to movement caused by air or water

echolocation a means of navigating by detecting high-pitched sounds reflected from objects; used by bats
echo sounding a method of measuring the depth of water
ecology the study of living organisms and their interaction with their environment
ecosystem a community of living organisms and its surroundings, e.g. a forest or a lake
effector a muscle that carries out an action
effort the force used to produce an effect on a load, for example when lifting an object

Science words

electrode a terminal that allows electricity to pass in or out of a substance that conducts
electrolysis breaking down substances when molten or in solution, by passing an electric current through them
endocrine gland a structure that produces one or more hormones
energy the ability to do work
epicentre the point on the ground directly above the focus of an earthquake
erection the swollen and stiffened state of the penis during sexual arousal
eutrophication the excessive growth of algae in a pond, caused by leaching of fertilizers into the water

fallopian tube see *oviduct*
fertilization the joining of a male sex cell with a female sex cell
focus (of an earthquake) the centre of an earthquake, usually deep underground, from which the shock waves spread
focus (of light) a point at which light rays meet or appear to meet
force a push or pull
forcemeter a spring balance (also called a newtonmeter) used for measuring forces
frequency the number of times an object vibrates per second, measured in hertz (Hz)
fundamental frequency the main frequency of a musical note

global warming an overall increase in the average temperature of the Earth
glycogen the form in which excess sugar (glucose) is stored in the body
goitre a swelling of the thyroid gland
gravity the force of attraction between an object and the Earth
greenhouse effect the result of gases such as carbon dioxide building up in the upper atmosphere and trapping the Sun's rays so that the Earth warms up. Such gases are called greenhouse gases

habitat the natural home of a plant or animal
hammer one of the bones in the middle ear
harmonics additional, fainter frequencies that make up a musical note (also called overtones)
hormone a chemical produced by a gland; it is carried in the bloodstream to other parts of the body, where it regulates biological processes
hurricane a storm with violent wind

igneous rocks rocks formed when hot magma is pushed up from below the surface of the Earth and solidifies
image a likeness of something (the object) produced by rays of light passing through a lens or being reflected off a mirror
incident ray the light ray that comes from a source and strikes a mirror or lens
indigenous describing the human inhabitants or wild organisms that originated in the region or country where they live
insecticide a chemical that kills insects
insulin a hormone produced by the pancreas; it controls the amount of sugar in the blood
isobars lines on a map that join places with the same air pressure
IUD intra-uterine device, used to prevent pregnancy

larynx the voice box; a chamber in the throat containing the vocal cords
lava molten rock that flows out of volcanoes
lens a piece of glass or other transparent material shaped so that it will make a parallel beam of light either converge or diverge
lever a machine that tips about a point (the pivot) in order to lift a heavy load
load the force produced by the weight of something, such as an object being lifted
luminous source an object that gives out light

magma molten material below the Earth's crust; it may flow to the Earth's surface during volcanic activity
medulla oblongata the part of the brain that controls unconscious actions such as breathing
metamorphic rocks sedimentary or igneous rocks that have been changed by heat and pressure into new forms
meteorologist someone who studies and forecasts the weather
minerals the substances of which rocks are made
mulching covering soil with dead leaves or grass to prevent erosion

newtonmeter see *forcemeter*
newtons (symbol N) the unit used to measure size of a force

octave the difference between two musical notes when the frequency of one is twice that of the other
oestrogens female sex hormones
opaque material a material that light cannot pass through
optic nerve the nerve that carries electrical impulses from the retina to the brain
ore a mineral that is a source of a useful metal
oviduct the tube that connects the ovary to the womb (also called fallopian tube)
ovum (plural **ova**) a female sex cell or egg
ozone layer a layer of the Earth's upper atmosphere which contains ozone; ozone shields the Earth from most of the harmful ultraviolet radiation from the Sun

parallel beam a beam of light that stays the same width – all the rays are parallel
penis the male organ through which urine and sperm leave the body
penumbra a partial shadow, where some light falls
pesticide any chemical that is used to kill weeds, insects or other pests of crops

Science words

pituitary gland a gland located underneath the brain that produces various hormones (including antidiuretic hormone) and controls a wide range of body functions

placenta the part of the uterus wall where an embryo is connected to its mother's blood supply

plane mirror a flat mirror

plankton very small animals and plants floating in the sea

pollutants waste materials such as chemicals, sewage and smoke that make the air, water or soil dirty or poisonous

population the number of people in a country; all the members of a species in an ecosystem

potential energy energy stored in a body

power the rate of doing work, measured in watts (W)

pressure gauge an instrument used to measure air pressure

puberty the stage of human development when the person becomes sexually mature

pulley a wheel with deep rims over which you pass a rope to change the direction of a force

pupil the hole at the front of the eye that allows light to enter

quality (of sound) the particular mix of fundamental frequency and overtones that make up a sound

receptor part of the nervous system adapted to detecting stimuli

reflected ray the light ray that bounces off a mirror

reflex action an automatic action that happens in response to a stimulus, without you having to think about it

regular reflection when light bounces off a very smooth surface in a regular way, so that it forms an image

retina a layer of light-sensitive cells at the back of the eye

reverberation sound bouncing off hard surfaces

rhizome an underground stem

Richter scale a scale used to measure the magnitude of an earthquake

rock cycle the process by which old rocks are weathered away to sediments, which eventually form new sedimentary and metamorphic rocks

secondary sexual characteristics bodily features such as breasts and facial hair that develop at puberty according to whether you are a girl or boy

sediment tiny solid particles that settle out of a liquid

sedimentary rocks rocks formed when particles of sediment deposited from sea water are squeezed together by the pressure of sediment and water above them

seismogram a chart produced by a seismograph

seismograph an instrument that records vibrations in the Earth

semicircular canals three liquid-filled tubes in the inner ear that help us to keep our balance

sense organ a group of receptors in the body that respond to a particular stimulus, e.g. the eye

sex cell a special type of cell involved in reproduction

smelting extracting a metal from its ore by heating it with coal or coke (carbon)

soil erosion the removal of soil by wind or water

sperm duct the tube leading from the testis to the urethra

sperm a male sex cell

spermicide a chemical that kills sperms

sterilization surgery that makes someone unable to have children

stirrup one of the bones in the middle ear

sustainable development using the environment wisely, to make sure that we replace what we use

symbiosis a close association between two different types of organism that benefits each partner

testis (plural **testes**) the male sex organ that produces sperm

thyroid gland a gland in the neck which produces thyroxine

thyroxine a hormone that controls metabolism (the rate at which chemical reactions take place in the body)

translucent used to describe a material that lets some light through but which you cannot see through clearly

transparent used to describe a material (e.g. clear glass) that lets light through and through which you can see clearly

ultrasonic waves sound waves with frequencies too high for humans to hear

ultrasound high-frequency sound that the human ear cannot detect

umbilical cord a cord that joins a fetus to the placenta, through which the fetus gets food and oxygen from its mother

umbra a full shadow, where no light falls

understorey the dark lower part of a forest

urethra the tube leading from the bladder to the outside of the body

uterus the female organ in which the fetus develops (also called the womb)

vagina the passage from the cervix to the outside of the body

vocal cords two tough membranes in the voice box (larynx) which vibrate when air is forced through them and allow us to make sounds

watt (symbol **W**) the unit of power

weathering the breakdown of the rocks by exposure to the atmosphere

weight the force of gravity on an object

womb see *uterus*

zygote the cell that results when a male sex cell joins with a female sex cell

Index

abiotic environments 121
accommodation 53, 166
acid rain 154, 156, 160, 166
adaptation 121, 122, 124, 125
adrenal glands 82, 84, 85, 166
adrenaline 84, 166
AIDS 89
air
   pollution 154–160
   pressure 12–13, 17, 19
   resistance (drag) 105, 109, 166
altimeter 15, 166
aluminium 24, 156
amplification 61, 166
amplitude 64, 166
androgens 79, 82, 166
angles of incidence and reflection 166
anode 29–30, 166
antidiuretic hormone (ADH) 83, 166
anvil bone (inner ear) 69, 166
asexual reproduction 78
atmosphere 12, 157–158, 166
atmospheric pressure 12–14, 15, 19, 166
atoll 135
auditory nerve 69, 166

balancing objects 113–114
barometer 15, 16–17, 166
bauxite 24, 26, 27
beams of light 38–39, 166
binocular vision 54, 166
biodiversity 127–128, 166
biotic environments 121
birth 75–77, 80
   control 87–92
   rate 87, 166
Bourdon gauge 15–16
brain 96–97

camouflage 122, 166
canopy (in forests) 129, 130, 166
carbon dioxide 153, 157, 160
care of children 75, 76, 77, 80
catalytic converters 166
cathode 29–30, 166
cement and concrete 33, 35
central nervous system (CNS) 94–97, 166
   diseases of 97, 98
cerebellum 96, 98, 166
cerebral hemispheres 96, 98, 166
cervix 73, 80, 166
children, care of 75, 76, 77, 80
chlorofluorocarbons (CFCs) 153, 158–159, 166
ciliary muscles 52, 53, 166
climate change 157–158, 166
climax communities 124, 125
clones 78, 166
coastal ecosystems 133–136
cochlea 69
colonization 124, 125, 166
colour blindness 56

colours 56
communities 122, 125, 166
   climax 124, 125
concave lenses 166
condoms 89, 92, 166
conservation of soil 141, 143–144, 145
contour ploughing 143, 145
contraception methods 88–91
convergent beams 166
convex lenses 166
coordination 94, 98, 156
coral 23
   reefs 135–136, 137
cornea 52, 166
corrosion of metals 26
crop rotation 145, 166
crust of the Earth 1, 4, 24, 166
cryolite 30–31, 166

deafness 70
death rate 87, 166
decibels (dBs) 63, 166
decomposers 129, 147, 166
deforestation 31, 131, 140, 142, 145, 157, 166
diabetes 85, 166
diffuse reflection 166
diffusion (scattering) of light 39, 43, 166
diseases of the central nervous system (CNS) 97, 98
divergent beams of light 38, 166
drag (air resistance) 105, 109, 166
drugs 131

ears 58–59, 69–70
Earth
   core of 2, 4
   crust of 1, 4, 24, 166
   elements in 24
   mantle of 2, 4
   structure of 1–2, 4
earthquakes 1, 6
   detection of 9–10
   epicentres 9, 166
   safety rules for 7
   world distribution of 8–9
echo sounding 64, 166
echoes 64–65, 68
echolocation 65, 166
eclipses 41
ecology 121, 125, 166
   of the Caribbean region 126–136
ecosystems 122–123, 124, 140, 166
   coastal 133–136, 140
effectors 95, 97, 166
effort 114–115, 119, 166
eggs *see* ova
electrodes 29–30, 167
electrolysis 26, 28–30, 32, 167
elements 24
embryos 74, 80
endangered species 132
endocrine glands 82, 85, 167

energy 117, 120, 167
   potential 117, 168
environments 121
erection 73, 166
erosion 20–21, 25, 131, 141–144
eutrophication 147, 167
external fertilization 78
extraction by of metals by electrolysis 26, 28–30, 32, 167
eyes 52, 54, 57

fallopian tubes (oviducts) 72, 74, 80, 167
fertilization 72, 74, 80, 167
   external 78
fertilizers 145, 146–147
fetuses 74, 80
focus of an earthquake 167
forcemeter (newtonmeter) 101–102, 167
forces 99–103, 104, 105–106, 108–109, 112, 167
   and motion 105–109
fossil fuels 155
frequency (measured in Hz) 68, 167
   fundamental 167
friction 105–107, 109

gears 116
German measles (rubella) 75
glass manufacture 34
global warming 157–158, 160, 167
glycogen, 84–85, 167
goitres 83, 167
gravity 100, 103–104, 167
greenhouse effect 154, 157–158, 167

habitats 121, 125, 167
hammer bone (inner ear) 69, 167
harmonics (overtones) 63, 167
hearing aids 70
hormones 79, 82–83, 85, 167
household waste 149, 151
hurricanes 12, 17–18, 167

igneous rocks 23, 25, 167
images 43–44, 49–50, 167
implantation 75
incident rays 43, 167
indigenous peoples and species 127, 167
industrial pollutants 149
insecticides 147, 167
insulin 84–85, 167
intra-uterine devices (IUDs) 90, 167
isobars 17, 167

joules (J) 117

larynx (voice box) 66, 68, 167
lava 2, 167
lenses 47–49, 50, 52, 167
levers 114–115, 116, 167

Index

light 36–40
  beams 38–39, 166
  diffusion (scattering) of 39, 43
  luminous sources of 36, 167
  path of 37–38, 50
  reflection of 36–37, 43–44
  refraction of 46–48, 50
loads 114–115, 119, 167
loudness (amplitude) of sounds 62–63, 68
luminous sources of light 36, 167

machines 111, 120
magma 2, 167
mangroves 136–137
mass 104
medulla oblongata 96–97, 98, 167
menstruation 79
metals 26–29, 32
  corrosion of 26
  extraction by electrolysis 26, 28–30, 32, 167
  smelting of 26–28, 32, 168
metamorphic rocks 22, 23, 25, 167
meteorologists 17, 167
microscopes 56
minerals 24–25, 167
  used in construction 33–35
mirrors 43–46, 167
molecules in air 14, 19
mulching 144
musical sounds 61–62, 63

nerve cells 94–97
Newton's first law of motion 108–109
newtonmeter (forcemeter) 101–102, 167
newtons (symbol N) 13, 99–100, 101, 104, 167

octaves 63, 167
oestrogens 79, 82, 167
oil spillage (slicks) 148–149, 151
opaque materials 40, 50, 167
optic nerve 52, 95, 167
optical instruments 50
ores 26, 27, 167
ova (singular ovum) 73, 167
ovaries 72, 80
oviducts (fallopian tubes) 72, 74, 80, 167
ozone 155
  layer 153, 158–159, 160, 167

pancreas 82, 84–85
parallel beams of light 167
parental care 76, 80
penis 73, 167
penumbra 41, 167
periscope 45
persistence of vision 55–56, 57
pesticides 147, 167
photosynthesis 131, 153, 157
pinhole camera 42
pitch (frequency) 59–61, 64
pituitary gland 82, 83, 85, 168
pivots 114, 115
placenta 75, 80, 168
plankton 135, 168

pollutants 146, 149, 151, 153–154, 160
pollution 31, 123, 168
  of air 154–160
  control of 151, 154–155, 156, 159
  of water 146–152
populations 87, 122, 168
post-natal care 76
potential energy 117, 168
pottery 33–34
power 118–119, 120, 168
pre-natal care 75
pregnancy 75, 80
pressure
  air 12–13, 14, 15–18, 19
  atmospheric 1, 13–14, 19
  gauges 15–16, 19, 168
puberty 79, 80, 168
pulleys 113, 168
pupils (of eyes) 52, 168

quadrats 139
quality of sound 168

radiation 155
ramps (inclined planes) 112
receptors 94, 95, 168
reflection of light 43–44, 50, 168
reflex actions 95–96, 98, 168
reforestation (afforestation) 132, 144
refraction of light 46–48, 50, 52–53
retina 52, 168
reverberation 64, 168
rhizomes 168
Richter scale 10, 168
rock cycle 23–24, 168
rocks 20–21
  igneous 23, 25, 167
  metamorphic 22, 23, 25, 167
  sedimentary 20, 22, 23, 25, 168
  underground movement of 8–9
  weathering of 20–21

safe sex 92
salinas 137
scrotum 73
sea grasses 135
secondary sexual characteristics 79, 168
sediment 168
sedimentary, rocks 20, 22, 23, 25, 168
seismographs 9–11, 168
semicircular canals 70, 168
sense organs 94, 168
sewage 147–148, 151
sex
  cells 168
  safe 92
sexual reproduction 72–73
sexually transmitted diseases (STDs) 89, 92
shadows 40–41
shores 134–135, 137
sight, extension of 56
smelting of metals 26–28, 32, 168
smog 155–156, 160
soil
  conservation 141, 143–144
  erosion 141–144, 145

SONAR 65
Soufrière Hills volcano (Montserrat) 1, 2–4
sound insulators 59
sound 58–59, 68
  loudness (amplitude) 62–63
  musical 63
spermicides 89, 168
sperm 72, 168
sterilization 90, 168
stirrup bone (inner ear) 69, 168
stone and bricks 33
strip cropping 144, 145
structure of the Earth 1–2
sustainable development 132, 140, 168
symbiosis 136, 168

telescopes 57
terracing 144, 145
testes (singular testis) 72, 73, 80, 168
thermal pollution 150
thyroid gland 82, 83, 85, 168
thyroxine 83, 168
tourists 126, 134
transects 139
translucent materials 39–40, 50, 168
transparent materials 39–40, 50, 168
transpiration 131
tropical rainforests 128–133, 140
tuning fork 58

ultaviolet (UV) rays 158
ultrasonic waves 168
ultrasound 65–66, 68, 168
umbilical cord 75, 168
umbra 41, 168
underground movement of rocks 8–9, 11
understoreys (in forests) 129, 168
urethra 73, 168
uterus (womb) 72, 168

vagina 73, 80, 168
vibration (oscillation) 58, 61
vision, persistence of 55–56, 57
vocal cords (larynx) 66, 68, 168
voice 66, 68
  range of 67–68
volcanoes 1, 2, 4, 124
  benefits of 4, 5
  distribution of 3
  scientific monitoring 4

water
  cycle 131
  pollution 146–152
watt (symbol W) 168
waves 17, 19
weathering of rocks 20–21, 168
weight 104, 168
wetlands 137
wheels and axles 116
wind instruments 62
womb (uterus) 72, 168
work 117–118, 119–120

zygote 72, 168